ARLINGTON NATIONAL CEMETERY
Shrine to America's Heroes

James Edward Peters

WOODBINE HOUSE · 1986

Some of the biographies in this book contain information obtained from the book
*Milestones into Headstones: Mini Biographies of Fifty Fascinating Americans Buried in
Washington, D.C.* by Peter Exton and Dorsey Kleitz (EMP Publications, Inc.,
1003 Turkey Run Road, McLean, Virginia 22101, ISBN 0-914440-84-5, ($9.95).
Copyright 1985 Peter Exton and Dorsey Kleitz. All rights reserved.

ISBN: 0-933149-04-2

Cover Design and Illustration: Gary A. Mohrmann
Book Design & Typesetting: Wordscape, Inc., Washington, D.C.
Photos: Library of Congress, United States Archives, and James Edward Peters

Manufactured in the United States of America

The Library of Congress has cataloged the first printing of this title as follows:

Peters, James Edward.
   Arlington National Cemetery, shrine to America's heroes/James Edward Peters. —
Kensington, MD : Woodbine House, 1986.

   viii, 313 p., [1] folded leaf of plates : ill. ; 22 cm.

   Includes index.
   ISBN 0-933149-04-2 (pbk.) : $9.95

   1. Arlington National Cemetery (Va.)   2. Heroes — United States — Biography.   I. Title.

F234.A7P47 1986 973'.09'92 — dc19 86-50284
            [B]   AACR 2   MARC

Library of Congress

Paperback Edition (ISBN 0-933149-04-2)
1st Printing, November 1986
2nd Printing, April 1987
3rd Printing, October 1987

Hardcover Edition (ISBN 0-933149-23-9)
1st Printing, October 1987

3 4 5 6 7 8 9 0

DEDICATION

In loving memory of my sister, Judy,
and of her children, Dawn and Darren,
I dedicate this book.
It seems the good, they die young;
I just looked around and they were gone.

TABLE OF CONTENTS

AUTHOR'S NOTES

As I was growing up in Quincy, Illinois, there were two cemeteries near my family's home. The larger of the cemeteries, Woodland, provided my brothers and sisters and me with hours of adventure, exploring the cemetery's rolling hills along the bluffs overlooking the Mississippi River. Here, family burial plots became army fortresses and tombstones provided excellent hiding places for grand-scale games of hide-and-seek, as long as we could avoid detection by the caretaker. Throughout this period, however, I paid little attention to the unfamiliar names on the endless rows of headstones.

Then one day, as I was using the cemetery as an unauthorized route between the municipal swimming pool and our home, I spotted a name on a headstone that was familiar to me, John Wood. I had recently learned in school that John Wood had been the first settler in Quincy, later becoming Governor of Illinois. Of course, **Wood**land Cemetery! I stopped and stared at the headstone, struck by the thought that right in front of me was the grave of someone important, someone I knew something about. Suddenly it occurred to me that all of those names on all of those headstones were real people with real pasts. And I found myself reading each stone, searching for clues among the names and dates, trying to solve the mysteries of who these people were. If a book is born at the instant one discovers a genuine interest in the subject matter, then this book on Arlington National Cemetery was born that day in Quincy's Woodland Cemetery because I have never stopped looking at headstones nor searching for clues.

I was an elementary school student in November 1963 when I first became aware of Arlington National Cemetery. Like millions of other Americans that weekend in November, I watched the televised burial services for President John Kennedy. A few years later, as a delegate to the American Legion's Boys' Nation in Washington, D.C., I paid my first visit to Arlington National Cemetery. There I saw the eternal flame and read the simple inscription on the stone tablet above John Kennedy's grave, remembering the story of his life and death. Looking over my shoulder as we climbed back on the bus that day, I realized that the endless rows of headstones which dot the hillsides of Arlington Cemetery represent thousands of men and women whose stories were left untold.

My interest in cemeteries is simply an extension of my interest in history. To me, reading headstones is not some morbid obsession with the dead. Rather, it is a celebration of the memories of people who lived in another time. And, at Arlington, one discovers the names of hundreds of people whose memories deserve celebration. Even now, when I visit the graves of famous Americans at Arlington, I feel as though I am face-to-face with these legendary figures, and I am awestruck by the memory of their achievements.

When I moved to Washington in 1985, I made several expeditions to Arlington, each time discovering new and more interesting facts about the people buried here. The ornate headstones of Civil War era veterans revealed plenty of clues about the persons whose names they bear. Even the thousands of simple, white regulation headstones divulged some small part of the lives of the men and women they name. But there was so much more to know.

I looked for publications which would answer my many questions about the cemetery. What was the history of the land? How had it become the home of Robert E. Lee? What were the circumstances that allowed formation of a cemetery here on Lee's estate? Who was eligible to be buried here? And what about the numerous monuments and memorials? I rummaged through bookstores and scoured library shelves, but was unable to find any current definitive guide to this great national shrine. Finally, a search at the Library of Congress revealed that there simply was no current book on Arlington National Cemetery that would answer the questions of a visitor like myself.

It was then that I began the research and the writing that has resulted in this book. Throughout its preparation, however, I have relied heavily upon the contributions of other persons. And if I am successful in my goal to better inform the American people about our greatest national cemetery, then literally dozens of people must share in that success.

During my numerous visits to Arlington Cemetery, the Library of Congress, and the National Archives, I was always greeted by friendly faces and was offered invaluable assistance. To all of those friendly (albeit nameless) faces, I am grateful. A source of unending encouragement came from two extraordinary people—my parents—Richard and Kathleen Peters. Gary Mohrmann's constant encouragement and advice were invaluable. The high quality of his contributions is evidenced by his masterful illustration which dignifies this book's cover. I am also extremely grateful for the steadfast support offered by my very dear friends, Ron Lefrancois and Maria Sharer Lefrancois. Peter Porosky, whose professional direction guided this book through its infancy, merits my sincere thanks. And special recognition must also be extended to Congresswoman Nancy Johnson of Connecticut. Her good offices provided frequent assistance and expert guidance.

To Superintendent Raymond J. Costanzo and the staff at Arlington National Cemetery, I owe an extraordinary debt of thanks, especially to Vicki Tanner for her assistance in obtaining technical information about the cemetery. Truly, two of the most important resources for this book have been Arlington Cemetery historians Kerri Childress and Tom Sherlock. Their generous contributions of time and information are greatly appreciated and to them I am forever grateful. Courtenay Welton of the Military District of Washington provided information and guidance without which I would have been unable to witness many important Arlington ceremonies. Cemetery architect Julius Smith volunteered both his technical advice and his fascinating personal insights concerning Arlington which are built upon a twenty-five-year association with the cemetery. And my dozens of requests for information concerning burial sites and dates always received a conscientious and quick response from Delores Peterson, Linda Proctor, and their co-workers at the Arlington Cemetery Visitors Center.

During the course of this writing, I made many visits to Arlington House, the Robert E. Lee Memorial, and received the expert counsel of Curator Agnes Mullins. Her extensive knowledge of Arlington House and its history greatly inspired my work. To Mrs. Mullins, the National Park Service, and to the many volunteers at Arlington House—who were often unaware of my particular reason for requesting information but were always willing to answer my many questions—I am deeply appreciative. To historian Dr. Francis A. Lord, whose keen eye and love of country gave me confidence and inspiration, I say thank you.

Finally, my special thanks are reserved for Woodbine House. Their collective commitment to this book never wavered. Terry Rosenberg's insightful initial interest and her editorial prowess deserve recognition. Also, my warmest regards are extended to Marshall Levin whose patient and thoughtful editorial supervision of this manuscript contributed immeasurably to its timely and accurate completion. And for her careful and professional preparation of this text, I am eternally grateful to Betty Hunt.

I would like to express my deep appreciation to Peter Exton and Dorsey Kleitz for providing useful information for the biography section of this book, and for specific facts in selected biographies in this book. I recommend their fine book, *Milestones into Headstones: Mini Biographies of Fifty Fascinating Americans Buried in Washington, D.C.* (EPM Publications, Inc. 1985.)

Cemeteries can be like libraries; they can perpetuate knowledge. And if this book advances the public's knowledge of Arlington National Cemetery and spurs greater interest in this shrine to America's heroes, then all of us have achieved our goal.

INTRODUCTION

"Let us here highly resolve that these honored dead shall not have died in vain."

Abraham Lincoln
The Gettysburg Address

President Lincoln spoke those words on November 19, 1863 at the dedication of the National Cemetery on the Civil War battleground at Gettysburg, Pennsylvania. In 1920 that sentiment was reaffirmed when his words were permanently engraved in the new Memorial Amphitheatre at Arlington National Cemetery. Lincoln's words remind all who visit here that for more than two hundred years, thousands of men and women have given their lives in defense of this great nation, and that their contributions to our liberty must not be forgotten.

Arlington National Cemetery is dedicated to the memories of those gallant men and women. This cemetery is more than just a military burial ground; it is one of the most important national shrines in America and, as such, is visited by millions of people every year. Yet, whether the reader actually visits Arlington or not, this book presents a vivid picture of the cemetery and serves both as an on-site guide to present-day Arlington as well as an historical text.

Unlike the White House, the Capitol, or any of the other great monuments which grace the Washington D.C. area, the creation of Arlington National Cemetery did not result from years of careful planning. It was not the product of a commission specially appointed to review prospective plans and to select the most appropriate site before unveiling the shrine in a blaze of patriotic glory. Rather, it was born of tragic necessity.

During the Civil War, thousands of soldiers and civilians lost their lives in the unrelenting battles in and around Washington.

As a grim testament to the human costs of that war there was a shortage of space in which to bury the dead. Therefore, on an afternoon in June 1864, without public fanfare or formal ceremonies, and with only the simple affixing of his signature, the Secretary of War designated the estate of Robert E. Lee's wife as a military burial ground. Thus Arlington began, and unlike the great buildings of government across the Potomac, the marble stones at Arlington were not used to create large public structures; instead, they were placed side by side in seemingly endless rows, adorned simply with names and dates.

At that time in America's history, it was no honor to be buried at Arlington. Only those who died unknown or whose families could not afford the costs of private burial services were interred here. Yet, during that period of historic battles and mass burials, no one foresaw that Arlington Cemetery would become this nation's greatest shrine to our fallen heroes.

Today, as visitors approach Arlington National Cemetery, they are awestruck by its grandeur even as they cross the Potomac River. Rising before them is Arlington House, standing majestically on a hillside like a proud sentinel diligently guarding those left in its charge. They travel along Memorial Drive, the broad avenue over which so many caissons have borne America's sons and daughters. And even before they enter the cemetery's gilded gates, they see monuments dedicated to those heroes.

This book helps you share the greatness of Arlington National Cemetery, from its checkered origin to its present glory. It guides you through the days when the land was purchased by the stepson of George Washington; when George Washington Parke Custis, Washington's adopted son, built Arlington House as a memorial to our first president; and when, as the home of Robert E. Lee, it was confiscated by the Union government and used as a burial ground during the darkest days of the Civil War. This book traces Arlington's history following the war, from the establishment of the Freedman's Village, through the successful Supreme Court battle waged by Lee's son to regain title of the property, to its development as this country's most important national cemetery.

Although the history of the Lee estate parallels the rich history of our nation, it is the collective story of the hundreds of thousands of men and women buried at Arlington that truly illustrates the colorful past of the American people. Within its walls Arlington perpetuates the memories of those who are famous and not-so-famous, known and unknown, honored or forgotten. Together on these hillsides overlooking the Potomac lie presidents and privates, officers and enlisted men, supreme court justices and unknown slaves, each with a past. It is impossible to tell the story of all those buried here yet it is both possible and important to gain a deeper knowledge of who these people are. Their lives tell the story of the spirit that has guided America for over two hundred years.

Walking among the gravestones at Arlington, a visitor discovers such names as Lingan, L'Enfant, Sheridan, Doubleday, Holmes, Lincoln, Westinghouse, MacArthur, Bryan, Delano, Taft, Pershing, Donovan, Hammett, Marshall, Bradley, Halsey, Forrestal, Dulles, Kennedy, Evers, Grissom, Stethem, and Scobee. It becomes increasingly clear while reading the names on these headstones that a visit to Arlington is like scanning the history shelves at the public library or browsing through the biography section of a good bookstore. To assist the reader in a better appreciation of Arlington's place in our nation's history, a collection of approximately one hundred short biographies are included in this volume. The stories of these people, many of them well-known and some not so well-known, illustrate the diversity of the more than 200,000 people buried at Arlington. With each biography, the grave's section and lot number is provided to help you find the grave's location.

Also within Arlington's 612 acres, there are numerous memorials dedicated not to an individual, but rather to the memory of a group or a collective cause. One complete section of this volume describes the history and purpose of thirty-five of those memorials. In addition, an extensive index is provided to allow the reader quick reference to the people, places, and events represented in the book. Any name appearing in **bold** type indicates that that person is buried at Arlington. To accommodate cemetery visitors, a specially-commissioned map is located inside the back cover. With this map, the reader can utilize the clearly-marked grid coordinates to assist him or her in locating a specific grave or memorial.

Today Arlington National Cemetery performs two very important functions. It maintains one of America's most revered historic sites and at the same time administers the growth of a modern cemetery where as many as twenty-five burials take place each weekday. The final chapter of this book explains the types of services regularly performed at Arlington, from military burials to the laying of wreaths by visiting dignitaries. Interment requirements, the new columbarium, and tombstone regulations are also discussed in this final section.

While many of the people buried at Arlington are not best known for their military careers, it is important to remember that Arlington is a military cemetery and, as such, military symbols and abbreviations are used on the headstones. A glossary is included explaining those military symbols and abbreviations, as well as religious designations. Other appendices provide information regarding the designation of military rank, the requirements for burial in Arlington, and the use of private headstones.

A person cannot casually visit Arlington National Cemetery and hope to view all its impressive sites. It is a vast, beautifully landscaped memorial to those Americans who have served our country and, in many cases, have sacrificed their lives in its defense. The story of Arlington is a wondrous one, no one volume could tell it all. Yet the reader will learn much about Arlington's past and present from this book, and in this it will have fulfilled its objective. Hopefully, everyone who reads it will visit Arlington National Cemetery. But if a personal visit to Arlington is not possible, then may this book fill you with the same tremendous sense of patriotic pride one experiences during a visit to our nation's most hallowed shrine.

FROM GEORGE WASHINGTON TO ROBERT E. LEE TO TODAY: ARLINGTON'S HISTORY

"When we assumed the soldier, we did not lay aside the citizen."

—George Washington

"Arlington...where my affection and attachments are more strongly placed than at any other place in the world."

—Robert E. Lee

"I could stay here forever."

—John F. Kennedy,
speaking at Arlington House
on November 11, 1963.

On a hillside rising above the Potomac River, overlooking Washington, D.C. stands Arlington House—the focal point of Arlington National Cemetery. For many of the millions of people who annually visit our country's most important national cemetery, it seems incongruous that this magnificent mansion should be located in the middle of a military burial ground. But in 1802, when construction of Arlington House began, it was not with the intent that it become the centerpiece of a cemetery. Rather, it was designed to be a living memorial to George Washington, the Father of Our Country. Here, on an 1100-acre estate, Washington's adopted son—George Washington Parke Custis—proudly housed the largest collection of Washington memorabilia in the world. Tragically, that collection and Arlington House itself became victims of America's bloody Civil War.

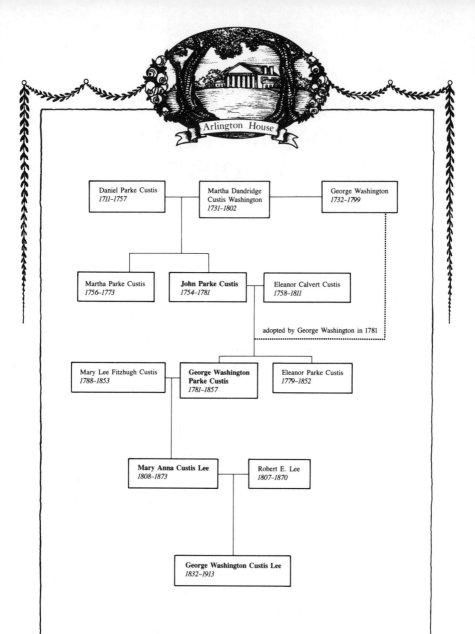

Arlington House

| Daniel Parke Custis *1711–1757* | Martha Dandridge Custis Washington *1731–1802* | George Washington *1732–1799* |

| Martha Parke Custis *1756–1773* | **John Parke Custis** *1754–1781* | Eleanor Calvert Custis *1758–1811* |

adopted by George Washington in 1781

| Mary Lee Fitzhugh Custis *1788–1853* | **George Washington Parke Custis** *1781–1857* | Eleanor Parke Custis *1779–1852* |

| **Mary Anna Custis Lee** *1808–1873* | Robert E. Lee *1807–1870* |

| **George Washington Custis Lee** *1832–1913* |

Names appearing in **bold** print signify holders of title to Arlington House.

Prior to the Civil War, Washington Custis occupied the home with his wife, their daughter, and their daughter's husband, Robert E. Lee — then a little-known but highly-respected Lieutenant Colonel. Arlington was Lee's home for nearly thirty years before it was confiscated by the Union Army at the outbreak of the Civil War. Today the restoration of the mansion is continuing in order to reflect its stature during that period before the war and has been dedicated as "The Robert E. Lee Memorial."

Evidence of Arlington's pivotal role in the Civil War is abundant. Not so clear, however, is the colorful history of the estate whose roots are tied to George Washington's life and which predate the American Revolution.

George Washington was an up-and-coming, twenty-seven-year-old Virginia planter when he married Martha Dandridge Custis, a widow one year older than he, on January 6, 1759. Martha Custis was rumored to be the richest woman in the colonies having inherited 15,000 acres and a considerable fortune from her late husband, Daniel Parke Custis. Her marriage to Custis had produced four children, but only two survived infancy, John Parke Custis and Martha Parke ("Patsy") Custis who were ages six and four respectively when their mother married Washington.

George and Martha's union produced no children of their own, but Washington worked hard to raise young John, or "Jackie" as he was sometimes called. As young John grew, he watched and learned from the manner in which his stepfather managed the large Mount Vernon estate, retaining what he learned for the day when he would own such an estate. In 1778 twenty-five-year-old John invested funds he had inherited from his natural father in an 1,100-acre tract of land about fifteen miles north of Mount Vernon. The property was purchased from one John Alexander. It was on this land, later known as Arlington, that Custis intended to build his home after the Revolutionary War.

During the siege of Yorktown in 1781 — while serving as an aide to General Washington — John Parke Custis died. He had contracted "camp fever," the name given to a wide range of maladies from malaria to tuberculosis. When John Parke Custis died, Washington and his family — like so many other wartime families — were devastated by the loss. John was survived by a wife and four children. To assist in the rearing of those children, George and

George and Martha Washington shown with young George Washington Parke Custis and Eleanor Parke Custis, who were adopted by Washington in 1781.

Martha Washington adopted the two youngest, George Washington Parke Custis and Eleanor Parke Custis.

George Washington Parke Custis, who as a child was known as "Tub" and later called "Washington," was only six months old when he was adopted by the future first President, and just as Washington had raised John Custis twenty years earlier, Washington again found himself in the position of role model, this time for his young adopted son. But the role Washington played was unlike any other in history, and constantly at Washington's heels, young Washington Custis was there to witness the historic events surrounding the birth of our nation. When prominent citizens and heads of state journeyed to Mount Vernon to call on the first President, young Washington Custis was ever present.

From an early age, Washington Custis was awestruck by his famous father and throughout his life he sought to emulate George Washington, not only in the way he managed his estate but in his political views as well. George Washington Parke Custis was only eighteen when President Washington died in 1799, but he promptly directed his energies to perpetuating the memory of the man whose name he bore. After Martha Washington died in 1802, Custis attempted to buy Mount Vernon to establish the first national historic site as a memorial to his adopted father. Unfortunately for Custis, Washington's nephew, Bushrod Washington, who had inherited the property from the former President, was unwilling to sell. So Custis looked elsewhere for a memorial site and discovered that among the 15,000 acres of land that he owned was the 1,100-acre tract north of Mount Vernon which his natural father, John Parke Custis, had purchased in 1778. Just across the Potomac River from the new federal capital, Washington City, Custis found the perfect site to build his home. He resolved that it would serve as a national memorial to George Washington and that he would serve as its self-appointed curator. Initially Custis wanted to name the property "Mount Washington," a title he deemed equal to its purpose, but he was persuaded by members of his family to settle on "Arlington House." That name was significant to the Custises since Arlington had been the name of their original family estate on Virginia's eastern shore.

Like many other Virginia planters at that time, Washington Custis was land rich but cash poor. Although he owned several plantations throughout Virginia and had inherited more than 200 slaves, he did not have sufficient liquid assets to build his home immediately. Undaunted, however, he forged ahead planning his home and collecting more Washington memorabilia to exhibit there. In 1802, when he moved to the site to begin construction of the house, Custis called upon George Hadfield for assistance in architectural and functional design. Hadfield was an English architect who had come to America in 1785 to help construct the U.S. Capitol. He provided Custis with plans for a Greek revival structure which, due to Custis' financial situation, would take sixteen years to complete.

Also contributing to Washington Custis' financial woes was his obsession with obtaining Washington relics. Although he had inherited many portraits, papers, and even clothes that had belonged to Washington, he acquired more. At one Mount Vernon auction, Custis bid over $4,500 for a variety of items that ranged from axes, corn drills, and a brick-making mold to Washington's coach, British and Hessian battle flags, and the red-trimmed tent that Washington used at Yorktown. It took him many years to retire the debt from that single auction alone. Nevertheless, he succeeded in acquiring the most extensive collection of Washington's personal effects in the country. Counted among Custis' possessions were such items as Washington's punch bowl, pocket telescope, umbrellas, and the very bed in which the first President had died.

All Custis lacked was the proper environment to display his collection. Unfortunately, the magnificent mansion he envisioned to house both himself and his treasures could only be built in stages. This was not only customary at that time but, considering Custis' poor cash situation, unavoidable.

The north wing of the house was the first structure completed, and Custis, who was a bachelor, made that section his home in late 1802. It consisted of only six rooms, a significant portion of which were used to store his Washington collection. By 1804 the south wing was finished, providing Custis with two additional rooms. The area that would ultimately contain the large center section and the now-famous portico was nothing more than an open yard and a home for Custis' chickens. Nonetheless, these two completed, but detached, wings of Arlington House were home to George Washington Parke Custis when he married Mary Lee Fitzhugh in July 1804.

Like her new husband, Mary was descended from old, established Virginia families; the Lees, Randolphs, and Fitzhughs. And though she was only sixteen years old when she married her "dear Washington", she assumed her position as lady of the house with grace and finesse. During the fourteen years it took to complete the entire house, the couple lived primarily in the north wing. The south wing served as an office for Mr. Custis and as a repository for the Washington relics, though it was also used for entertaining. Four Custis children were born to Washington and Mary Custis, but only one, Mary Anna Randolph Custis, would live to maturity.

As the mansion was being built, Custis was also developing the lands surrounding Arlington House using what he had learned from Washington at Mount Vernon. He rotated his crops and kept records to document his successes and failures. Custis also established a fine reputation in animal husbandry. He bred mules and developed a highly-acclaimed breed of woolly sheep known as Arlington Supremes (or Arlington Improved), encouraging other farmers to develop domestic breeds in light of the high cost of importing foreign sheep. It was his early agricultural successes that earned Custis the money necessary to improve the land and finish his mansion.

In 1818 the largest section of the house, the central section, was finished. Now the mansion stretched 140 feet from its north wing to its south wing. The newly completed section provided a large central hall on the first floor which served as a parlor during hot summer months. Between the hall and the old north wing now stood a formal dining room and a sitting room. Much of the area south of the hall was used for storage and Mr. Custis' studio. The vast portico with its eight majestic columns, each five feet in diameter at the base, stood like an honor guard greeting the many visitors to Arlington House. At last, Custis had completed his own "Washington monument" and he had succeeded in doing so more than sixty years before the towering obelisk monument was completed on the other side of the Potomac River. Arlington House could be seen for miles up and down the river prompting Robert E. Lee to later note that it was "a house that any one might see with half an eye."

With the completion of the house, visitors began coming in droves to view the Washington collection and to hear George Washington Parke Custis discourse on his famous father. The gregarious Custis welcomed any opportunity to tell stories about President Washington. Sometimes he would spot a group of picnickers gathered by the large spring on his estate and would canter down from the mansion with his violin tucked under his arm, ready to entertain his guests with music and his vast repertoire of stories. Often, to his own delight and that of his guests, he would even drag out and set up the huge tents Washington used at Yorktown.

Not only the local farmers and the folks from Washington came to Arlington House. Admirers of George Washington traveled from all over the globe to show their respect for the late President. The Marquis de Lafayette, who served with Washington during the Revolutionary War, twice made the pilgrimage to Arlington, and in 1825 during one of those visits, Custis presented him with an

Arlington House shown from "The Great Oak" shortly after the estate was designated a national cemetery.

umbrella and Masonic sash that had belonged to Washington. In honor of President Andrew Jackson's visit, Custis gave Jackson Washington's pocket telescope. Custis always enjoyed distributing souvenirs of Washington, often cutting Washington's signature from documents and giving them to guests as remembrances.

Arlington House was the scene of many colorful events during the life of George Washington Parke Custis, a man who was not only a famous farmer and teller of Washingtonian tales, but who was also an amateur artist and playwright. Several of his most accomplished battlescene paintings including the large work, *The Battle of Monmouth* (seven feet tall by eleven feet wide) can be seen at Arlington House. In 1827 Custis wrote his first play, entitled *Indian Prophecy*, but the best known of his plays is *Pocahontas*, which he finished three years later.

So it was in this antebellum environment filled with its receptions and cotillions, servants and socials, teas and tales that Washington Custis reared his daughter, Mary Anna Randolph

Custis. As his only surviving child, Mary Custis was the beneficiary of her father's undivided attention. She received an excellent education and life at Arlington House provided her with all the luxuries that a young woman of her age could have desired. Yet, her father did insist that she always remember one very important fact, she was the foster granddaughter of George Washington, and as his only heir, she alone would be entrusted with the preservation of this living memorial to him. Of course, the collection of Washington memorabilia and the many people who came to Arlington to see it, were constant reminders to Mary Custis of that responsibility which she accepted with pride. It was also one that later caused her overwhelming sorrow when she was unable to fulfill it.

In 1830 many young men sought to win the heart of Mary Anna Custis, but it was a childhood friend and distant cousin, Robert E. Lee, who finally captured her affections. Lee was the son of former three-term Virginia Governor Henry ("Light Horse Harry") Lee and had graduated from West Point in 1829. Mary's

George Washington Parke Custis, the man who built Arlington House as a memorial to his foster father, George Washington.

father, however, did not favor his only daughter marrying a career military man and voiced concern over the young Lee's ability to support Mary on a Second Lieutenant's salary. Nonetheless, the young couple found a strong ally in Mary's mother, Mrs. Custis. Mrs. Custis had known Robert E. Lee and his family since Robert was just a child and held him in the highest regard. But Mr. Custis remained reluctant. For him, the custody of his two greatest joys were at stake, his daughter and his memorial to Washington. However, finally succumbing to the overwhelming desire of his wife and daughter, Washington Custis blessed the marriage.

The wedding of Mary Anna Randolph Custis and Robert E. Lee was the grandest event ever to occur at Arlington House. June 30, 1831 was chosen as the wedding date and the house was decorated to reflect the magnificence of the occasion. Flowers from Mrs. Custis' famed gardens bedecked the halls. Friends and neighbors from all over Virginia and the Potomac Valley made their way up the hill to Arlington House. It was a grand day for the Custises and the Lees. Even the steady rain that fell in the afternoon could not dampen the spirits of those who had gathered to witness the ceremony. It was in this idyllic setting that Robert E. Lee realized he had married not only Mary Anna Custis, but Arlington House as well. And although his military career would lead them away from Arlington, it was on this estate that his life would be rooted for the next thirty years.

Lee readily shared his wife's custodial responsibility for the Washington memorabilia. Indeed, he welcomed the opportunity to preserve George Washington's memory. Having been raised himself in Washington's hometown of Alexandria, Virginia, Lee had long been an admirer of the first President, and except for his own father, he respected him more than any other man in the world. Of course Arlington and its Washington collection remained under the watchful eye of Washington and Mary Custis. Washington Custis continued to manage the estate for over twenty-five years after his daughter's marriage. The new Mrs. Lee usually accompanied her husband on his military assignments, but returned to Arlington House to give birth to six of their seven children.

Robert E. Lee served in the Army Corps of Engineers and, much to his family's pleasure, was given assignments near Arlington. His first major assignment away from the area came in

Mary Anna Custis Lee, the only child of George Washington Parke Custis, who married Robert E. Lee in 1831 and inherited Arlington House just prior to the Civil War. Colonel Lee is pictured during his days as Superintendent of West Point.

1837 when he was ordered to supervise engineering work for the harbor at St. Louis, Missouri. Knowing he would be gone for an extended period, he requested and received permission to take his family with him to the Far West. So in 1838 Robert E. Lee and his family left Arlington House and the Custises for St. Louis. Washington Custis was then fifty-seven years old and was no longer the aggressive estate manager that he had been thirty years earlier. Unfortunately, the condition of the estate declined markedly until Lee returned to assume its management.

Between 1841 and 1857 Lee was called away from Arlington for several extended periods. In 1846 he served in the Mexican War under General Winfield Scott, with whom he developed a lifelong friendship. It was during his service in Mexico that Lee distinguished himself as a brave and courageous engineer and soldier. The Mexican War has often been called the "training field" for the Civil War because so many of the Civil War's future officers got their training in the Mexican campaign. This was the case for Lee.

In 1852 Lee was appointed Superintendent of The Military Academy at West Point, his alma mater. He preferred a field command but instead accepted the opportunity to serve where his family could join him. No sooner had Mrs. Lee and their children arrived at West Point than Mrs. Lee was called back to Arlington to care for her ailing mother. Mary Custis Lee was at Arlington House when her mother died. Mary Fitzhugh Custis was buried in the family plot which continues to be preserved in Section 13 (Grid N-30) of Arlington Cemetery. Following her mother's burial, Mrs. Lee remained at Arlington for a time with her father, then in his seventies, before rejoining her husband at West Point.

In 1855 Lee was transferred from New York to Texas to command the Second U.S. Cavalry. While the transfer provided him with a promotion to the rank of Lt. Colonel and gave him the field command he sought, it also separated him from his family. Although Mrs. Lee and the younger children returned from West Point to the familiar surroundings of Arlington, Lee was very concerned for his wife's health. He knew that she suffered from chronic arthritis and was fast becoming an invalid. So, over the next two years, he returned home to Arlington to visit her as often as he could.

While in Texas in the fall of 1857, Lee received word from Arlington that Washington Custis had died and had been buried next to his wife. He had greatly admired and respected his father-in-law and this loss affected him deeply.

Custis had named Lee as executor of his estate and upon learning the terms of Custis' will, Lee quickly realized that this new responsibility would

The Custis Family plot as it exists today in Section 13. Only two graves are located within the plot— those of George Washington Parke Custis (on the left) and his wife, Mary Fitzhugh Custis.

demand his full attention. Immediately he applied for leave and returned to Arlington House to join his family. Upon his return Lee was dismayed to find the estate in a badly neglected condition, and he was even more shocked by his wife's rapidly deteriorating health.

Arlington House figured centrally in the terms of Washington

Custis' will. His daughter, Mary Anna Custis Lee, was given the right to inhabit and control Arlington House for the rest of her life. Upon her death, full title to the property would pass to her eldest son, George Washington Custis Lee. Contrary to what many people still believe, Robert E. Lee never owned the Arlington estate.

Further complicating Lee's burden as executor of the estate, Custis had bequeathed $10,000 to each of his four granddaughters and had left other plantations to his two remaining grandsons. However, Custis left no cash and was in debt at the time of his death. He had also provided that if there was not enough cash to fulfill the bequests to his granddaughters, the plantations should be sold to raise the requisite money. Custis did leave 196 slaves as personal property, but he had provided that they be emancipated within five years of his death. This left Robert E. Lee in a serious financial and familial quandary. To immediately raise the cash intended for his own daughters, he might have to sell the land left to his sons. In the alternative, he could have sold the nearly two hundred slaves which would have raised more than enough funds to satisfy the terms of Custis' will, but it was his strong belief that he should not raise the money in that manner. Lee, like his father-in-law, believed that the slaves should be educated, trained and freed. Therefore, under the terms of Custis' will—which provided for the manumission of the slaves within five years—Lee planned to utilize the slaves during that five-year period to earn the money necessary to satisfy the specific bequests.

Washington Custis had become completely indulgent in the last decade of his life. He had lived the comfortable life he sought, without enforcing fiscal discipline on himself or on his operators. Though Custis claimed to have despised slavery, calling it "the mightiest serpent that ever infested the world," he had always operated his lands with their extensive use, often renting them out to other farmers. As for the domestic slaves at Arlington House, he always referred to them as "servants," treated them with great affection, and demanded little of them.

After Custis' death, Lee attacked the complex problem before him with the same efficient methods he had used as an army engineer. He carefully plotted his strategy, attempting to cover every area in detail. He dealt with his field workers as if they were troops under his command, not indulging or coddling them as Custis had done. Lee himself also undertook the physical labors of restoring the estate. During daylight hours he could be seen repairing the roofs, replacing fences, or rebuilding roads, and after the sun had set, he literally burned the midnight oil doing the necessary bookkeeping.

In an attempt to ease the tremendous administrative and probate burdens, Lee's oldest son, Custis Lee, offered to convey his rights in Arlington to his father, but the elder Lee declined. It was Custis land and Custis land it would stay, he maintained. In one letter to his son, Lee did suggest that the best thing Custis Lee could do for Arlington was to marry a rich woman. Custis Lee never married.

The one benefit Lee allowed himself and his wife was to finish furnishing the house. The Lees redecorated most of the house in their own taste, especially the south rooms of the center section which had been used primarily for storage. Many of the furnishings which the Lees had purchased while living away from Arlington now found their way here. Among other pieces, the red velvet Victorian settee which had adorned his home at West Point was now placed in the large room just south of the central hall.

The study in Arlington House where George Washington Parke Custis wrote and painted.

By 1859 Lee had returned a semblance of order to the estate. The other plantations were showing profits, and even Arlington was breaking even. Also important to Lee, however, was the knowledge that the once-magnificent grounds of Arlington had been restored, its showplace stature redeemed. He was pondering the possibility of resuming his military career when in October of 1859, J.E.B. Stuart—a young officer who had been a cadet at West Point during Lee's superintendency—appeared at Arlington. He carried an urgent message from the War Department for Lee to appear there as soon as possible.

Without even changing his clothes, Lee headed with Stuart across the Potomac to Washington. There Lee was offered command of a detachment ordered to capture John Brown, who had just seized the federal arsenal at Harper's Ferry, Virginia. Without hesitation Lee accepted the command and ultimately captured Brown. The incident brought Lee considerable recognition and accelerated his return to duty. Lee also felt he could safely leave Arlington since he had secured a Washington assignment for his oldest son, Custis, which enabled Custis to oversee the estate. So in February 1860, Arlington House once again witnessed the departure of Robert E. Lee on a military assignment to Texas.

What greeted Lee upon his return to command in Texas disturbed him greatly. Throughout the entire South there was serious talk of secession. To Lee, secession was "nothing but revolution." For more than a year he bitterly argued against the destruction of the Union, even as he watched that possibility grow more likely each day. In December 1860 South Carolina voted to secede. There was talk in Congress and among members of President Buchanan's administration of an invasion of the South. To this apparent escalation of hostilities, Lee reacted by saying,

> A Union that can only be maintained by swords and bayonets, and in which strife and civil war are to take the place of brotherly love and kindness, has no charm for me. I shall mourn for my country and for the welfare and progress of mankind. If the Union is dissolved, and the Government disrupted, I shall return to my native state, and share the miseries of my people, and save in defence draw my sword on none.

The threat of secession became reality, the news of which arrived at Lee's doorstep on February 1, 1861 when Texas seceded. Less than two weeks later, on February 13, unsure of his fate or that of his country, Lee received orders to return to Washington. The next ninety days changed the course of life for the Lees, and Lee's decisions changed the course of our nation.

Lee arrived at Arlington on March 1, 1861 to find his ailing wife walking with a cane and his home state of Virginia threatening to secede. He awaited further orders from Washington. On March 28 word came that Lee had been promoted to full Colonel by Winfield Scott, General in Chief of the Army, with the approval of Abraham Lincoln, the newly inaugurated President. With this promotion came command of the First U.S. Cavalry. Scott, who was then seventy-five years old and nearly immobilized by obesity, looked to Lee as his choice as field commander should any action be required against the South. Lee accepted his promotion and waited. As war became more probable, Lee agonized over the position he would take. Virginia had still not taken any action toward secession and it was Lee's home state that claimed his first allegiance. He knew, however, that regardless of Virginia's decision, Arlington House would never be allowed to remain the serene and stately homestead it had been for him and his family. Its location on that strategic ridge overlooking Washington would make its occupation vital for either side of the conflict.

Events unfolded rapidly in April 1861 and, as Lee waited at Arlington, news arrived daily both from the Virginia state convention in Richmond regarding secession and from Washington as the Lincoln administration responded to the actions of the Southern states.

Friday, April 12. Soldiers of the new Confederacy fired the first shots at Union troops at Fort Sumter in Charleston Harbor.

Monday, April 15. President Lincoln called for 75,000 volunteers, and Virginia was called upon to furnish her share to suppress the rebel states.

Tuesday, April 16. An ordinance of secession was introduced into the Virginia convention in response to President Lincoln's call for volunteers from Virginia. The sponsors argued that they would rather secede than take up arms against fellow Southerners.

Wednesday, April 17. At the same time that the Virginia convention went into secret session to further debate secession, Lee received a letter to report to General Scott's office on the following day, the 18th. He was told to first call upon Francis P. Blair at his home on Pennsylvania Avenue before he appeared at the War Department to see Scott. Blair was considered an insider in the Lincoln administration although he held no official post.

Thursday, April 18. Lee left Arlington for Washington on what would be his last such journey. He went directly to Blair's house near the White House. Blair explained that President Lincoln had authorized him to offer Lee command of the new army that was being raised. This was the very command that Lee had waited a lifetime to attain but, without hesitation, he replied, "Though opposed to secession and deprecating war, I could take no part in an invasion of the Southern states."

With that, Lee left Blair House and proceeded across Pennsylvania Avenue to the War Department. There he met with his old friend, General Scott. He quickly related to the General the substance of his encounter with Blair, to which Scott uttered his famous reply, "Lee, you have made the greatest mistake of your life. But I feared it would be so."

A gray mood accompanied Robert E. Lee on his ride back to Arlington. The United States Army was his life. He had spent thirty-two years as an Army officer, protecting and defending the Union which his own father had fought to establish. With all his heart, he wanted to preserve that Union, but he did not want to fight against his fellow Southerners. How could he stay in the Army, but not be forced to fight? he wondered. And he wondered about Arlington House and its future.

Friday, April 19. Lee learned that Virginia had voted to secede, though it had not yet decided to join the Confederacy. It was springtime as Lee walked the grounds of Arlington pondering his next move. He could smell the flowers in the gardens and see the apple blossoms in the orchard near the river. From the front portico, Lee could also see across the river to the still-unfinished dome of the U.S. Capitol and the new Washington Monument, construction of which had been halted for lack of funds, both symbols of the Union he so strongly wanted to preserve.

That afternoon he went to his room on the second floor of Arlington House and remained there until after midnight. In the parlor below, Mrs. Lee and some of their family and friends waited quietly for his decision. They could hear his footsteps as he paced across the room's wooden floor, they could hear when he stopped, probably to ponder or pray, and they could hear him start to pace again. In the early morning hours of April 20 Lee reappeared downstairs and silently handed his wife a letter which he had written during the night. It was addressed to General Scott:

> General:
> Since my interview with you on the 18th instant I have felt that I ought not longer to retain my commission in the Army. I therefore render my resignation, which I request that you recommend for acceptance.
> It would have been presented at once, but for the struggle it has cost me to separate myself from a service to which I devoted all the best years of my life and the ability I possessed.
> During the whole of that time, more than 30 years, I have experienced nothing but kindness from my superiors, and a most cordial friendship from my companions. To no one Gen'l have I been as much indebted as to yourself for uniform kindness and consideration, and it has always been my ardent desire to meet your approbation.
> I shall carry with me to the grave the most grateful recollections of your kind consideration, and your name and fame will always be dear to me. Save in defence of my native State, I never desire again to draw my sword.
> Be pleased to accept my most earnest wishes for the continuance of your happiness and prosperity and believe me most truly yours,
>
> **R. E. Lee**

Later that same day, still tormented by his decision, Lee wrote another letter, this one to his sister:

> With all my devotion to the Union and the feeling of loyalty and duty as an American citizen, I have not been able to make up my mind to raise my hand against my relatives, my children, my home.

Monday, April 22. Upon the request of Virginia Governor John Letcher, Lee left Arlington House to catch a train for Richmond. He was unaware of the reason he was being summoned to the state capital, but, contrary to a widely held belief, it was not to take command of the Confederate Army. Virginia still had not joined the Confederacy and all Lee desired at this time was to offer his services to his native state. Of course, as he left Arlington that day, he could not have known that this would be the last time he would ever set foot on the grounds of the place he considered more dear to him than any other. It was still his hope that this matter that threatened the Union could be resolved and that he would be able to return to his home shortly.

Likewise, Lee did not know he would not see his beloved wife for more than fourteen months, during which time he would undertake a crusade that would reshape a nation. When next they met, Mary Custis Lee hardly recognized her husband because during that period of separation Lee, at the age of 54, had grown the stately gray beard that has come to characterize him. In fact, at no time during his nearly thirty years at Arlington House did Robert E. Lee ever wear a beard.

Late in the afternoon of April 22, 1861 Lee met with Governor Letcher in the Virginia state capitol. The Governor informed him that an ordinance had been passed calling for the appointment of a commander of Virginia's military forces to serve under the governor's authority and bear the rank of Major General. Letcher further stated that Lee had been recommended to him for the position. Lee accepted immediately. He had not resigned his U.S. Army commission in anticipation of this appointment nor was this an appointment to the Confederate ranks since Virginia was still not part of the Confederacy.

Wednesday, April 24. Virginia entered into a military alliance with the Confederacy. This alliance ultimately led to the state's formal incorporation into the newly formed confederation of states which occurred on May 24 when Virginia voters ratified the ordinance of secession.

Saturday, April 27. Although he had been gone for only five days, Lee was already deeply concerned about those members of his family still at Arlington. He was well aware of the estate's strategic importance to the Union Army, but feared that his wife did not appreciate the danger. Lee also knew what soldiers might do to the personal property found on occupied premises. With this worry weighing on his mind, Lee wrote to his wife:

> War is inevitable, and there is no telling when it will
> burst around you.... You have to move and make
> arrangements to go to some point of safety which you
> must select. The Mount Vernon plate and pictures
> ought to be secured. Keep quiet while you remain,
> and in your preparations....May God keep and
> preserve you and have mercy on all our people.

Mrs. Lee heeded her husband's warning, and began making
arrangements for her and for her daughters to leave Arlington.
She sent the portraits of President Washington and of some other
family members to relatives who lived in safer quarters farther
south. But other than those paintings and the family silver, she
shipped little more than her basic personal effects. No extensive
transfer of valuables was undertaken because she, like her husband, believed that they would ultimately return to their home and
that no one, whether Northerner or Southerner, would ever so much
as consider disturbing her treasured possessions.

Mary Custis Lee left Arlington House on May 15, 1861 for
temporary shelter at the plantation home of Anna Maria Fitzhugh
who was Mrs. Lee's aunt by marriage and a close friend of Robert's
since childhood. The plantation, known as Ravensworth, was
located in Fairfax County, Virginia.

Following the ratification of the ordinance of secession by the
voters of Virginia on May 24 of that year, federal troops crossed
the Potomac River into Virginia. Under the command of Brigadier
General Irvin McDowell, they took up positions around Arlington
House as well as at other points along the Potomac. From
Ravensworth, Mrs. Lee, ever mindful of her obligation to protect her home and to secure the Washington memorabilia, wrote
to both General McDowell and to General in Chief Winfield Scott
in Washington. In her letters she reminded both men that Arlington
was the home of George Washington's adopted son, that it should
be well protected, and that the slaves who were left there should
be looked after.

McDowell courteously replied to Mrs. Lee saying that she
could rest assured that the mansion would come to no harm and

Brigadier General Irvin McDowell (fifth from right with hand on sword) standing with his men on the steps of Arlington House during its occupation by Union troops in 1861.

that the personal possessions would be protected. Unfortunately, though that communication must certainly have given Mrs. Lee comfort, McDowell was unable to keep his promise. Arlington became a headquarters for the Union Army charged with the defense of Washington, and a great number of troops trafficked in and around the estate. At first, a few personal items belonging to the Lees began to vanish. Then later, when it became clear that great quantities of the Lees' property had disappeared, McDowell ordered that the remaining few items be packed and stored at the patent office in Washington under the label, "Captured at Arlington." Sadly, many irreplaceable heirlooms of the Washington, Custis, and Lee families were already gone.

Following the occupation of Arlington by Union soldiers, military installations were erected at several locations around the 1,100-acre estate, including Fort Whipple (on the site of present-day Fort Myer), Fort McPherson (now Section 11), and around the mansion. With the establishment of Arlington House as Headquarters for the defense of Washington, and with the large number of troops stationed on the land, the character of the once stately plantation changed. Instead of a productive, self-sustaining plantation which had always replenished the resources as they were used, Arlington was now occupied by military forces who were rapidly depleting its trees, crops, and other natural and man-made resources and making no effort to replace them.

General Lee foresaw the probable transformation of his home during the early stages of the war. In the fall of 1861, he wrote to Mrs. Lee about Arlington:

> It is better to make up our minds to a general loss.
> They cannot take away the remembrance of the spot,
> and the memories of those that to us rendered it
> sacred. That will remain to us as long as life will last,
> and that we can preserve.

Lee felt that he was still legally responsible for the estate under the terms of his father-in-law's will though the war made it impossible for him to exercise his authority. Nonetheless, he remained particularly concerned about the status of the slaves who had been left behind, and he continued to hope that they would be trained and freed within the five years prescribed in Washington Custis' will.

The appearance of the Arlington estate remained primarily that of a military camp until 1864. Prior to that time, however, actions taken by the government in Washington proved to have a direct impact on Arlington. On June 7, 1862 Congress passed "An Act for the Collection of Direct Taxes in the Insurrectionary Districts of the United States." Outwardly, the bill appeared to be a means to raise revenue from those areas of the Confederate states that were under Union control. In reality, however, the measure proved to be a method of confiscating private property for governmental use. That was exactly its affect on Arlington.

Under the act, the government established a commission charged with assessing "insurrectionary properties" and taxing them. The regulations further required that the legal titleholder of the property appear personally to pay the taxes. Since most property owners were Confederate soldiers or sympathizers and could come forth only under threat of arrest, they were forced either to place themselves in personal jeopardy or fail to pay the taxes. In most cases the taxes went unpaid, and the properties of the Confederate sympathizers were sold at public auctions.

The Arlington property had been assessed at a value of $26,810 against which a tax of $92.07 was levied. Because the law required that the legal owner appear personally, Mary Custis Lee would have had to travel behind Union lines to Alexandria to pay the taxes. Mrs. Lee, already wheelchair-bound and frail, could not physically make the journey, even if she chose to disregard the danger to her personal safety as the wife of the South's commanding general. So in her stead she authorized Philip R. Fendall, her cousin, to travel to Alexandria with the necessary funds to pay the taxes, including all interest and costs. This payment was refused and the taxes subsequently were declared delinquent. On January 11, 1864 the Arlington property was offered for sale at a public auction where the tax commissioners themselves were the only bidders. They "purchased" the property—consisting of 1,100 acres, the mansion, and all the outbuildings—for the exact assessed value of $26,810 "for Government use, for war, military, charitable, and educational purposes."

With Arlington owned by the government and used as a military installation, it came under the jurisdiction of Secretary of War Edwin M. Stanton. More specifically, it fell under the direct control of the Quartermaster General of the Army. Since the nation was in a state of war during that period, the Secretary of War and the Quartermaster General were given extraordinary powers. The Quartermaster General was charged with overseeing the use of government land for military purposes. He controlled the construction of barracks, depots, hospitals, cemeteries, and roads. He also supplied military units with food, clothing, and all equipment except ordnance, and he was responsible for providing transportation by pack animal, roads, rail, river, or sea. At this crucial time, the person in whom these extraordinary powers were vested was Brigadier General **Montgomery Meigs**.

Meigs, by all accounts, was a hard-working, efficient but vindictive man who tended to exaggerate his own importance. He espoused a particularly anti-Southern attitude, although he himself had been born in Georgia. **Meigs** had even served with some of the South's most eminent leaders, benefiting from his close association with Jefferson Davis while Davis was Secretary of War during President Pierce's administration. **Meigs** had served under Robert E. Lee in the Corps of Engineers while working on river improvements at St. Louis. Still, **Meigs** expressed deep hatred for the Southerners who left the Union, including his own brother who had become a Confederate soldier. He considered all of them traitors and repeatedly expressed his hostility toward General Lee.

At about the same time that the insurrectionary tax bill was passed by Congress, another piece of legislation found its way to President Lincoln's desk. Buried in an omnibus bill was a clause providing that "the President of the United States shall have power, whenever in his opinion it shall be expedient, to purchase cemetery grounds and cause them to be securely enclosed to be used as a national cemetery for the soldiers who shall die in the service of the country." It was signed into law on July 17, 1862 as the result of the inadequate preparations made for the burial of the massive number of Union casualties.

Early in the war much of the fighting centered around Washington, which became by necessity a city of hospitals where many wounded soldiers were cared for and where many of them died. Soon burial space became scarce and the public reacted to the haphazard and scandalous manner in which the burial of soldiers was conducted. This public outcry resulted in the passage of the cemetery authorization bill and in President Lincoln directing his Secretary of War to establish the necessary national burial grounds. During 1862 military cemeteries were established in Alexandria, Virginia and in the District of Columbia, but by 1864, with the continuation of the war and the heavy Union casualties, burial space had again become scarce. Therefore, to avoid another scandal, Secretary of War Stanton ordered his Quartermaster General to survey additional sites and to submit suggestions for his approval.

General **Meigs** made no surveys. To him it was obvious where the next military cemetery should be established: on the grounds of Arlington House. On June 15, 1864 he proposed Arlington as his suggested site. In his letter to Stanton, **Meigs** stated that "the grounds about the Mansion are admirably adapted to such a use." Stanton evidently shared **Meigs'** enthusiasm for this choice because he replied with uncharacteristic speed, informing **Meigs** the very same day:

> The Arlington Mansion and the grounds immediately surrounding it are appropriated for a Military Cemetery....The Quartermaster General is charged with the execution of this order. He will cause the grounds, not exceeding two hundred acres, to be immediately surveyed, laid out, and enclosed for this purpose.

Even if Arlington was the only available location capable of satisfying the need for additional burial space, there were many plots within its 1,100 acres that were clearly better suited for a cemetery than the two hundred acres surrounding the mansion. It was clear that **Meigs'** intention was to bury soldiers in the immediate proximity to Arlington House, rendering the mansion uninhabitable should the Lee family ever attempt to return. It is doubtful that this vengeful purpose was lost on Secretary Stanton, for he publicly declared his personal resentment of Lee.

There may also have been a secondary reason for **Meigs'** selection of the Arlington estate as a military burial ground. Historic records indicate that more than a month prior to his proposal to Stanton, **Meigs** had ordered the first burial of military dead on Arlington's grounds. On June 15, when **Meigs** had written to Stan-

The grave of the first soldier buried at Arlington National Cemetery—Private William Christman of Pennsylvania (Sec. 27, Lot 19, Grid CC–47/48). The "19" indicates a later designated lot number. Although not marked by the original headboard, Private Christman's original grave is still located in Section 27. At right, Union soldiers on the steps of Arlington House shortly after the estate was designated a national cemetery in 1864.

ton, more than a dozen soldiers already were buried there. To be exact, it was on May 13, 1864 that Private **William Christman**, a farmer from Pennsylvania and a member of Company G of the Sixty-seventh Pennsylvania Infantry, became the first soldier to be buried at Arlington National Cemetery. Today Private **Christman's** grave remains among other Civil War dead in Section 27 near the northern boundary of the cemetery.

Whatever the reason for General **Meigs'** decision to convert the grounds around Arlington House into a cemetery, it was his purpose to bury as many men there as quickly as possible. At first, the soldiers quartered at the mansion objected to the placement of graves near the house and ordered the burial details to inter bodies as far from the house as possible. But this did not meet with General **Meigs'** approval. When he visited the cemetery in August 1864, he expected to find the house nearly unapproachable due to the number of new graves. Instead, he found the mansion much as it had been when it was first occupied by federal troops. The graves had been neatly arranged some distance from the house. Furious, **Meigs** demanded that twenty-six bodies be brought immediately from Washington, and in the heat of that mid-August day, he personally supervised the burial of these fallen soldiers around Mrs. Lee's once famous rose garden only yards from the house. Those graves remain in their original locations and can be seen today encircling the restored garden.

Montgomery Meigs did not stop there. In April 1866, to assure the permanent destruction of Arlington as a habitable estate, he requested sealed proposals for a stone and masonry burial vault, twenty feet in diameter and ten feet deep, to be constructed in the rose garden of Arlington House. When this vault was built, **Meigs** placed in it the remains of 2,111 unknown soldiers who were found in trenches or scattered over battlefields within a twenty-five mile radius of Washington. Nearly 1,800 remains were collected from the battlefield at Bull Run, and it can only be assumed that these included the remains of Confederate soldiers as well since in some instances only a few bones or a skull were recovered. However, despite its checkered origin, this monument proudly stands today as Arlington's memorial to The Unknown Dead of the Civil War.

The vault that contained the remains of the Civil War unknowns was not the only structure that **Montgomery Meigs**

The Tomb of the Unknown Dead from the Civil War, a vault containing the remains of 2,111 soldiers. It was purposefully placed in the Lees' rose garden by Quartermaster General Montgomery Meigs. Meigs also erected the Temple of Fame (at right) as a monument to George Washington and eleven Union generals. Arlington House is at left.

placed on the site of Mrs. Lee's garden. He also constructed a colonnaded gazebo, called the Temple of Fame, which was dedicated to the memory of George Washington and eleven Union Generals. After approximately one hundred years, however, the gazebo had become structurally unsound and was removed to facilitate the restoration of the Arlington House grounds.

It is interesting to note that **Montgomery Meigs** is also buried within one hundred yards of the Lees' rose garden at Arlington National Cemetery. Buried with him are his wife, his father, and his son, Lt. **John Rodgers Meigs** who was, like his father, an Army engineer and who was killed late in the war. It has been reported that **Meigs'** son was killed in cold blood by Southern guerrillas. The manner of young **Meigs'** death further contributed to his father's bitter hatred toward the South.

From its establishment as an official military cemetery in June of 1864 until nearly the end of the nineteenth century, the Arlington estate served many purposes. Not only was it fast becoming one of the largest military cemeteries in the area, but it was the site of several permanent military installations (which today are part of Fort Myer), and the site of an encampment for freed slaves, known as Freedman's Village.

Freedman's Village resulted from President Lincoln's emancipation of all slaves living in the District of Columbia on April 16, 1862. With this action and given Washington's proximity to the Southern states, many fugitive slaves—as well as those liberated by advancing Union troops—found their way to Washington in search of a new life. Liberated slaves came to be known as "contrabands," following a precedent set by Major General Benjamin Butler. Butler refused to return fugitive slaves to their civilian owners in the belief that, like wagons or horses, they were property which might be used to support the Confederate war effort. As "contraband of war," he maintained, he was justified in releasing them.

These "contrabands" joined large numbers of free blacks already in Washington. They were housed in several camps, including one inside the U.S. Capitol building. Eventually, however, overcrowding and disease forced the government to relocate many of them. It was decided to establish a camp on the Arlington Estate in the area which now contains Sections 8, 47, and 25 along Eisenhower Drive. Its initial purpose was to provide a temporary refuge for freed slaves, but the camp grew to be known as Freedman's Village, providing permanent housing and other community services to liberated black men, women, and children for nearly thirty years.

By May 1863 the idea of a village to harbor freed slaves had gained widespread support within the Lincoln administration and construction of shelters began. When the village was dedicated on December 4, 1863, members of Congress, the Cabinet, and Army officials were present at the ceremonies. Throughout its early years, Freedman's Village entertained numerous government officials who took an interest in the welfare of the people living there. Vice-President Hannibal Hamlin, Secretary of the Treasury Salmon P. Chase, Secretary of the Navy Gideon Welles, and Secretary of State William H. Seward all spent time at the camp lending both their physical and moral support. Seward in particular demonstrated his interest in the intellectual wellbeing of the village residents by his personal support of its school.

At its inception, the village came under the jurisdiction of the U.S. Army and so was governed by a military commander. Many residents complained that life under military rule was not much better than slavery. In March 1865 the situation improved somewhat when the Bureau of Refugees, Freedmen, and Abandoned Lands (commonly known as the Freedmen's Bureau) assumed jurisdiction of the village. From its beginning as little more than a tent camp, the village grew into a large community not only for refugees from other states, but also for many of the former Arlington slaves who found a home here. The community counted among its institutions a school, a training center, a home for the aged and disabled, a hospital, and several churches and farms.

The first school opened soon after the camp was dedicated.

Students from the Freedman's Village school assemble on the grounds of the village which was established on the Arlington estate to provide refuge for former slaves.

Starting with 150 pupils, it grew to as many as 900 and classes were conducted not only for primary school age students, but for adults as well.

The training center, known as the Industrial School, provided training for blacksmiths, wheelwrights, carpenters, shoemakers and tailors. The carpenter trainees made the desks for the school while the tailor apprentices made clothing for the residents of the home for the aged and infirm. That "home" was a large structure which provided shelter for those people unable to care for themselves, including the very old, the permanently disabled, and those needing custodial care. Also assisting in the care of the residents was Abbott Hospital, which was established in November 1866. It provided fifty beds and a staff of fourteen medical officers who cared not only for hospitalized patients, but also for the health of the general village population.

In addition to providing for the cultural, intellectual, and physical needs of its residents, the village also established several churches to serve their spiritual needs. The first structures were small wooden facilities, but the residents built a brick church in 1878. People who did not work in the schools, the home, or the hospital worked as field laborers on the adjacent farms. These farms produced corn fodder, wheat, potatoes, and vegetables which were sold by the villagers for a profit.

While the village provided many necessary services to its residents, it was not without its problems. At first situated in a low-lying area, it was necessary to move the village to the higher ground of Section 4 when it was discovered that the water supply was contaminated by nearby marshes, causing frequent outbreaks of fever and disease. Also during its early days, the refugees were unhappy with the army rations they were fed. Known as "contraband" rations, they were smaller portions than those served to soldiers. Then, after the war, the desire to assist freed slaves lost a great deal of its support among the general public and fewer and fewer resources were made available to the villagers. Neighboring residents complained of the crime associated with the village and of the financial burden they were forced to assume as federal assistance to the villagers was reduced. All of these circumstances seriously threatened the existence of Freedman's Village, but it was a decision of the United States Supreme Court in 1882 which finally forced its closing. That Supreme Court decision resulted in the government obtaining legal title to the entire former Custis estate. The land—including the village and the cemetery—became a military reservation and federal law prohibited civilians from living there. On December 7, 1887 the residents were notified that they had ninety days to vacate the premises.

Nearly a generation had passed since the end of the Civil War and public sentiment in the United States had changed. No longer were the villagers considered refugees from slavery and, without the financial and moral support of the public, the village could not sustain itself. By 1890, after nearly thirty years, Freedman's Village was dismantled and the residents were forced to leave.

On April 9, 1865 General Lee surrendered to General Ulysses S. Grant at Appomattox Courthouse, Virginia effectively ending the Civil War, but as the head of the defeated Confederate Army, General Lee's future was uncertain. He and Mrs. Lee wanted desperately to return to their home at Arlington House, but were unaware of its current condition. They knew that the property had been confiscated by the federal government and that somewhere on the grounds there was a cemetery, although they did not know its precise location. The Lees did know that the house had been used as a military headquarters, but neither was yet aware of the nearly wholesale loss of their personal property, including the treasured Washington collection.

Neither Robert E. Lee, as executor of the estate of George Washington Parke Custis, nor Mrs. Lee, as titleholder to the property, ever attempted to publicly recover control of Arlington House. Lee did, however, contact Attorney Francis L. Smith of Alexandria to investigate the status of the property and to make private overtures regarding its recovery. These inquiries, however, were performed with the utmost discretion, were entirely unsuccessful, and were generally unknown during Lee's lifetime.

There were two major factors which governed Lee's decision not to bring an action against the government to reclaim Arlington. First, for more than three years following the cessation of hostilities between the North and the South, Lee considered his status as that of a "paroled prisoner of war." Under the law, as a former Confederate soldier Lee had no civil rights, including the right of suffrage. For this reason he believed he was without standing to bring any legal action in a Virginia state court or a Federal District court, and was not willing to test the point. However, there was an even greater concern deterring him from action. More than anything, Lee wanted to heal the wounds between North and South and to restore the Union envisioned by earlier Virginians such as Washington, Jefferson, and Lee's own father. He repeatedly advised his fellow Confederates to accept the outcome of the war and to "help build up the shattered fortunes of our old state." Lee recognized the important symbolic role that he played in rallying Southern support for reconciliation, and he did not wish to present even the appearance of contention between himself and the federal government. So his family's right to recover the Arlington estate was given secondary standing to the reunification of the country. He and his wife resigned themselves to never again living at Arlington.

Abandoning recovery of Arlington was not the only gesture Lee made to further advance his desire for national unity. He also rejected scores of business and political opportunities after the war which would have guaranteed his financial future. He wished to avoid any political or social position that might be used by others to rally opposition against the government and jeopardize national reconciliation. Instead he accepted the presidency of Washington College, a small institution in Lexington, Virginia where he could "be of some service to the country and the rising generation."

Lee and his wife did work to recover the personal effects that had been confiscated by the government in 1861 and were being stored in Washington. An opportunity presented itself late in 1868. On Christmas Day of that year, President Andrew Johnson proclaimed a general amnesty for all former Confederates. This action restored some of Lee's civil rights and lifted the indictment of treason that still shadowed the former Confederate General. Lee suggested to his wife that she write personally to the President appealing for the return of her personal property. Since the President was in the final weeks of his term in office, Lee believed Johnson might be free of political considerations and that he might be more disposed to release the property. His belief was affirmed. The President acceded to Mrs. Lee's request, and with the approval of his Cabinet, he informed the Secretary of the Interior to turn the items over to whomever Mrs. Lee designated to receive them. Included among the items held by the government were a set of china that Lafayette had given to Mrs. Lee's great-grandmother, Martha Washington, a mirror, a dresser, and some miscellaneous items including the Yorktown tents, and a strong box. Unfortunately, the transfer was discovered by a group of Radical Republicans before it could be concluded. Prompted by a story in the February 28 edition of the *Washington Evening Express*, the Republicans acted swiftly. The story had implied that "the Rebel General Lee" himself was going to invade Arlington National Cemetery amid the buried Union soldiers and was going to abscond with the priceless possessions of George Washington. This was all the fuel the Radicals needed for their *cause celebre* designed to again embarrass President Johnson. Led by Illinois Senator John A. Logan, a former Union General, the Radicals claimed that Johnson, who had survived their earlier impeachment attempt, was in collusion with his fellow Southerner, Lee, to deprive the nation of its rightful historic property. A resolution was passed by the Congress during the evening of March 3, the day before Johnson was to leave office, declaring that the property belonged to the federal government and that "to deliver the same to the Rebel General Robert E. Lee is an insult to the loyal people of the United States." That fateful resolution effectively ended any effort to regain any portion of the Arlington estate, either real or personal, during the lifetime of Robert or Mary Custis Lee. Lee later wrote with regard to the Washington relics:

> I hope their presence in the capitol will keep in the remembrance of all Americans the principles and virtues of Washington.

Today, many of these items, including George Washington's Yorktown tent, are in the permanent collection of the Smithsonian Institution.

Unable to return to Arlington, Robert E. Lee and Mary Custis Lee spent their remaining years on the campus of Washington College (today called Washington and Lee University), where he served as that institution's president until his death. General Lee never again visited Arlington House, though he did see the mansion from a distance during two trips to Washington after the war, in 1866 and again in 1869. Robert E. Lee died in Lexington on October 12, 1870, but he is not buried on the grounds of Arlington, his beloved home. Rather, he is interred in the chapel on the campus of the university that now bears his name.

General Robert E. Lee and his oldest son, George Washington Custis Lee, shortly after Lee's surrender at Appomattox. This photograph shows the last time Lee ever wore his Confederate uniform.

For Mary Custis Lee the fate of Arlington House caused even greater sorrow. She was the foster granddaughter of George Washington and never fully recovered from the loss of her ancestral home. Following her husband's death, Mrs. Lee was determined to once more see her home and the burial plot of her parents. In 1873, nearly three years after General Lee's death, Mary Custis Lee rode in a carriage up the winding road to Arlington House.

She could not help but notice the sad changes. Tombstones dotted the grounds; the rose garden she had cherished was now encircled with the graves of Union soldiers; and saddest of all, the mansion that her loving father had worked so long and hard to build, not only to house his family but also to enshrine the personal effects of his father, stood abandoned in dire disrepair. As she drew up to the front of the house, she was recognized by Selina Gray, a woman who had been a servant in her home. Selina offered Mrs. Lee a drink of water which she gratefully accepted, but was physically unable to leave her carriage to look inside her former home. Mary Custis Lee died within a few months of her visit, but before her death she wrote that she would not have recognized Arlington except for a few oak trees that the Union troops "had spared and trees planted on the lawn by the General and myself. . . . My dear home was so changed it seemed but as a dream of the past." Mary Anna Randolph Custis Lee died November 5, 1873 and is buried next to her husband in the chapel at Washington and Lee University.

Upon Mrs. Lee's death, the title to the property passed to her eldest son, George Washington Custis Lee under the terms of the will of Mary Lee's father, George Washington Parke Custis. George Washington Custis Lee, known simply as Custis Lee, graduated from the United States Military Academy in 1854. Like his father, he served in the U.S. Army Corps of Engineers until resigning his commission to join the Confederate forces. During the Civil War he served as an aide-de-camp to Jefferson Davis and attained the rank of Major General.

After the war, he was appointed a professor of civil and military engineering at the Virginia Military Institute. When his father died in 1870, Custis Lee was named to succeed him as president of the new Washington and Lee University, serving in that capacity until 1897. It was during his tenure as president of that university that he challenged the government's title to Arlington.

Lee had been advised by his legal counsel that, because of the questionable procedure used in obtaining the title, the government's claim to the Arlington estate was tenuous at best. He, therefore, made overtures to the government to recover the property or — if actual recovery of the land was impossible — to receive just compensation for it. In April 1874 his formal claim was presented to the United States Senate, where it received an unsympathetic reception. Lee's name still triggered a hostile response from the Radical Republicans, the same faction who had denied his mother recovery of her personal property five years earlier. The Radical Republicans contended that the government rightfully owned the property and that, as long as soldiers continued to be buried there, the government would not relinquish its title to the estate. After a failed three-year attempt to achieve a peaceful settlement of the dispute, Custis Lee filed suit against the United States of America. He brought an action for ejectment in the Circuit Court of Alexandria (today Arlington) County, Virginia, in April 1877. A host of defendants were listed in the suit because the law required every alleged trespasser be made a party to the action. This included all of the cemetery personnel, the Army personnel at Fort Whipple, and the residents of the Freedman's Village. This initial legal step began a process that would slowly wind its way through the Virginia State Court system into the Federal Courts, and would finally reach its climax before the United States Supreme Court five years later in December 1882.

To say that the case was complicated by procedural quagmires would be a gross understatement. The United States Attorney General opposed Custis Lee at every turn, attempting to derail the action before its scheduled jury trial. Eventually, however, the matter was presented to a jury in January 1879. After a six-day trial, the jury found in favor of the plaintiff Custis Lee. The government, dissatisfied with that judgment, appealed the verdict, and the matter was not resolved until the case reached the Supreme Court in October 1882. After only two months of deliberation, Mr. Justice Miller delivered the decision of the Court in a forty-six page opinion. By a 5–4 decision, the Court ruled that the United States had denied Mary Custis Lee her property without due process when its tax commissioners had refused to accept the payment of taxes from anyone but the owner. Accordingly, the Supreme Court granted Lee his request for ejectment and thereby reaffirmed his right to require all trespassers to leave the premises.

George Washington Custis Lee during his tenure as President of Washington and Lee College in Lexington, Virginia. It was also during this period that Custis Lee successfully challenged the United States government's title to the Arlington estate.

Of course the legal solution only raised the practical question of what was to be done with the nearly 16,000 graves and the military post located on the estate. Under the Court's ruling, Custis Lee could have ordered the government to dismantle the military post and disinter the remains of each and every soldier buried there. Fortunately, however, more reasonable minds prevailed. Custis Lee reissued his original offer to accept compensation for the property and, on March 3, 1883, the Forty-seventh Congress appropriated the agreed sum of $150,000 to be paid to Major General Custis Lee. Upon receipt of this payment, Custis

Lee executed the deed and following the approval of Secretary of War **Robert Todd Lincoln**, it was recorded at the Alexandria County Courthouse on May 14, 1883. At last, nearly twenty-two years after Union troops had first occupied the estate, Arlington became an official National Cemetery of the United States of America.

From the end of the Civil War, Arlington House served as the administrative center of the cemetery, as well as the residence of the superintendent of the cemetery. At the end of the war the cemetery consisted of only 200 acres and contained approximately 16,000 burials. In 1897 the area of the cemetery more than doubled, growing to 408 acres. By 1981 it had acquired the land formerly known as the South Post of Fort Myer and had grown to 612 acres. The number of persons buried at Arlington has increased significantly after every war. By 1957 nearly 93,000 American military personnel and their dependents had been buried at Arlington. In just less than thirty years, by 1986, that number had more than doubled again—to 200,000 burials.

The desire of Armed Services personnel and their families to be laid to rest at Arlington has been heightened by the significant number of famous Americans who have chosen to be buried here. This wish for an Arlington burial reflects the dramatic change in the cemetery's stature from its early days when it was considered little better than a potter's field. The original burials took place in Arlington by necessity, not by design.

In December 1899, 164 victims of the explosion which destroyed the USS *Maine* in February 1898 were reinterred at Arlington National Cemetery from Colon Cemetery in Havana, Cuba.

Few families chose to bury their dead here, but as more and more of the nation's heroes chose Arlington as their final resting place, more of those men and women who served with them followed their example. Today, burial in Arlington is restricted by official government regulation. A copy of the rules for eligibility for burial at Arlington can be found in Appendix III.

Also contributing to the honored status of Arlington Cemetery are the ceremonies that have been held here because of its close proximity to Washington, D.C. As early as 1868 the first Memorial Day services were held here in accordance with a declaration by the Commander of the Grand Army of the Republic, General John A. Logan, that May 30 be set aside as a day for memorial services to remember "comrades who died in the defense of their country." This early commemoration of a memorial day evolved into grand, day-long ceremonies which found thousands of people journeying to the cemetery to decorate graves and to listen to the nation's greatest speakers deliver their stirring orations in the Old Amphitheatre. This custom continues today as thousands of Americans visit Arlington each year on Memorial Day.

In 1922 former Confederate soldiers appeared at the Confederate Monument to remember their fallen comrades-in-arms.Completion of the Confederate Monument in 1914 symbolically brought North and South together, making Arlington truly a national cemetery.

Arlington also gained prominence as it became home to many celebrated memorials and monuments. In 1912 the mast of the battleship *Maine* became a permanent memorial to the 260 men who lost their lives in Havana Harbor when their ship exploded and sank in 1898. In 1914 the Confederate Monument was unveiled, honoring those soldiers who died fighting for the South during the Civil War. At its dedication it was hailed as the memorial that made Arlington, at last, a truly national cemetery.

The need for a larger, permanent gathering site prompted the construction of the Memorial Amphitheatre, dedicated in 1920. However, the most memorable ceremonies at Arlington have been the interments of the Unknowns. On November 11, 1921 an unknown soldier of World War I was buried with full military honors on the east plaza of the Memorial Amphitheatre. In 1958 that honored soldier was joined by unknown servicemen from World War II and from the Korean War, and in 1981 by an unknown member of the United States Armed Forces killed in Vietnam. In 1926 the daylight civilian Tomb guard was replaced with a military guard and in 1937 the guard became a twenty-four hour vigil. The Third United States Infantry undertook the full time guardianship of the Tomb in 1948.

In 1925 Congress designated Arlington House as a permanent memorial to Robert E. Lee. The War Department, which still had jurisdiction over the mansion, was instructed to restore the house to reflect its condition in the pre-Civil War period when the Lees had made the mansion their home. Arlington House, as the Robert E. Lee Memorial, was re-opened to the public in 1929. In 1933 the mansion and its immediate envi-

The East entrance to the Memorial Amphitheatre as it appeared at the time of its dedication in 1920. This photograph shows the East Plaza before it became the site of the Tomb of the Unknown Soldier the following year.

ons were transferred from the jurisdiction of the United States Army to the National Park Service in the Department of the Interior.

When George Washington Parke Custis began building Arlington House in 1802, he did so with the intent that the estate. would serve as a national shrine. Unfortunately, his dream of a memorial to George Washington was eclipsed by the tragedy of the Civil War and his monument to Washington was destroyed. However, that war forced the creation of a strikingly different national shrine—Arlington National Cemetery. Today Arlington is visited annually by nearly four million people who are drawn to the cemetery out of respect for the hundreds of thousands of men and women who are buried here, men and women who dedicated their lives to the preservation of this great nation. Although it is not the monument that Custis originally envisioned, Arlington proudly fulfills Custis' dream of honoring America and our nation's heroes.

AMERICAN HEROES AT ARLINGTON: PROFILES IN PATRIOTISM

On the Virginia hillsides overlooking Washington, D.C. lie the graves of hundreds of thousands of men and women who have dedicated at least a portion of their lives to the defense and preservation of liberty. Here at Arlington, lie Americans and friends of America; paupers and presidents; soldiers and civilians; warriors and peacemakers. Many we can never forget; most we will never know. The lives of these people reflect the history of our nation. Though it is impossible to collect in one volume the life stories of every man, woman, and child who now rest at Arlington, discovering more about even a few of them will illustrate the high calibre of people who have earned their place at Arlington. Therefore, outlined below are short profiles of more than one hundred of these patriots.

CREIGHTON WILLIAMS ABRAMS, JR.

Commander in Vietnam, Army Chief of Staff

(September 15, 1914–September 4, 1974)
Sec. 21, Lot S–33, Grid M/N–20

It was only after Creighton Abrams had faced combat in three wars and had climbed to the rank of General that he undertook a mission many military experts considered to be one of the most difficult in American military history.

After growing up in Springfield, Massachusetts, Abrams entered West Point where he gained a reputation as an outstanding athlete, known both as a horseman and as a football star. Following his graduation in 1936 he was commissioned a Second Lieutenant in the cavalry. By 1944 he had become a Lieutenant Colonel and was commander of the Thirty-seventh Tank Battalion, which he led into action in Normandy. His reputation as a tank commander earned him the praise of General George Patton, Jr., who said, "I'm supposed to be the best tank commander in the army, but I have one peer, Abe Abrams."

Abrams was an aggressive, fearless leader in combat, as evidenced by his conduct during the Battle of the Bulge. While commanding an armored task force advancing toward Bastogne, a concealed German antitank gun stalled their progress with heavy fire. Not to be deterred from his objective, Abrams went forward in his command tank, single-handedly destroyed the German weapon, and cleared the way for his task force's advancement. For this display of valor, Abrams was awarded his second Distinguished Service Cross.

Following World War II, he served as Director of Tactics of the Armored School at Fort Knox, Kentucky where he revised the Army's manual on armor tactics. He completed Command and General Staff College in 1949 and the Army War College in 1953. During the 1950s, while stationed in Europe, Abrams commanded the Sixty-third Tank Battalion and the Second Armored Cavalry Regiment. He also saw action in Korea as Chief of Staff of I Corps, IX Corps, and X Corps, an experience that later would serve him well in Vietnam. By 1960 he had advanced through the ranks to Major General to hold the position of Deputy Assistant Chief of Staff for Reserve Components, General Staff, Department of the Army.

From then on, Creighton Abrams was integrally involved in the major military events of that period of modern American history. During the Berlin crisis, he served as Assistant Commander of the Third Armored Division in Europe. When federal troops were sent to the University of Mississippi in September 1962 to quell rioting over the admission of James M. Meredith, its first black student, Abrams was in charge. Again in May 1963, when troops were placed on alert in the event of racial unrest in Birmingham, Alabama, Abrams commanded those troops. By 1964 he had achieved the rank of General and was named Vice-Chief of Staff, U.S. Army, in Washington, D.C.

President Lyndon Johnson appointed Abrams Deputy Commander of the United States Military Assistance Committee in Vietnam in April of 1967, issuing him orders to improve the fighting capability of the South Vietnamese forces. General Abrams directed the Allied military operations in Northern Vietnam during the grueling Tet Offensive of 1968 — North Vietnam's greatest attack of the war — and succeeded in recapturing the strategic city of Hue. The Tet Offensive, however, provided a major psychological victory for the North, one which forced a change of leadership of the American Forces. In July of 1968 Abrams assumed command of the American troops from General William Westmoreland, and soon was given the difficult responsibility of implementing President Richard Nixon's "Vietnamization" policy. Under intense scrutiny by both the world media and the American public, he undertook the task of reducing the involvement of American troops in Vietnam by training the Vietnamese to assume the defense of their own country. He pursued this policy until 1972 when President Nixon nominated him to be Chief of Staff of the Army.

Confirmed by the U.S. Senate on October 12, 1972, with only two dissenting votes, Abrams worked diligently to address the problems created by the Army's rapid reduction in size following the American withdrawal from Vietnam. An even greater challenge, however, was dealing with the political effects of that war, especially within the Army. Aware that his success both as commander in Vietnam and as Chief of Staff in Washington hinged upon his achieving the respect of the news media, he used character and candor to work toward healing the wounds of that unpopular war. He also sought to improve the Army's professional and ethical standards in the aftermath of Vietnam. Abrams worked tirelessly at these tasks for two years, until lung cancer claimed his life in Washington, D.C. in 1974. The General was buried with special military honors at Arlington National Cemetery.

THE APOLLO ONE ASTRONAUTS

Virgil I. ("Gus") Grissom

(April 3, 1926–January 27, 1967)
Sec. 3, Lot 2503–E, Grid Q–15/16

Roger Bruce Chaffee

(February 15, 1935–January 27, 1967)
Sec. 3, Lot 2502–F, Grid Q–15/16

Edward H. White II

Buried at The United States Military Academy,
West Point, New York

It was 6:31 P.M. January 27, 1967. The last traces of sunlight had disappeared over Cape Kennedy. Strapped into their command capsule atop the gigantic Saturn rocket, three Apollo One Astronauts prepared for a full-scale simulated liftoff. This was the dress rehearsal for the scheduled February 21 launching of the first Apollo mission, a mission that would carry the three Americans on a fourteen-day journey into space. With this mission, America would launch its program to put the first man on the moon.

Veteran astronaut Gus Grissom was in the command seat on the left, Ed White sat in the middle and Roger Chaffee, the rookie of the team, occupied the right-hand seat. They had been strapped into these positions for over five hours, testing various launch procedures and receiving commands from ground control, until only ten minutes remained before their simulated launch. All hatches were sealed as the men readied for liftoff. Suddenly, a bright flash erupted across the darkness atop the booster rocket. Communication with the astronauts went silent. Instantly, emergency crews scrambled to the capsule to investigate, but dense black smoke billowing from the cockpit blocked their approach. Even using a high-speed elevator, ten full minutes passed before the first rescuers reached the top of the rocket. Once inside the capsule they discovered that the three men had died, apparently instantaneously.

An intensive investigation by the National Aeronautic and Space Administration (NASA) revealed that the fire, which had been ignited by a spark from faulty wiring and had fed on nylon netting and other flammable materials, had swept through the cockpit's pure-oxygen environment with lethal speed. The emergency escape system had been rendered useless because it could only be triggered by an on-board astronaut. In this case, there had been no time to activate the escape system. As a result of this tragedy, NASA engineers undertook to redesign the entire spacecraft, installing more safety features and utilizing nonflammable or flame-retardant materials inside the cockpit.

On that fateful day in January 1967, Colonel Virgil I. ("Gus") Grissom, a native of Mitchell, Indiana, was preparing for his third space voyage. As one of the original seven Mercury astronauts, Grissom had eluded a disaster on his first flight in 1961. Returning to earth after becoming only the second American in space, he and his capsule splashed down in the Atlantic Ocean. The hatch opened, the capsule filled with water and began to sink. Grissom succeeded in scrambling out of the sinking capsule and was later rescued by a helicopter search team. His second space mission was the first two-man Gemini flight in 1965 during which he became the first person to make a second voyage into space.

Grissom graduated from Purdue University in 1950, majoring in mechanical engineering, then entered the United States Air Force. During the Korean War he served as a fighter pilot with the 334th Interceptor Squadron in 1951 and 1952, flying one hundred combat missions, and earning the Distinguished Flying Cross. By 1956 he had graduated from the Test Pilot School at Edwards Air Force Base, California and was assigned to Wright-Patterson Air Force Base, Ohio in the fighter branch. He remained with the fighter branch until his selection as one of the original Mercury astronauts in 1959.

Roger Bruce Chaffee was preparing for his first flight in space when the aborted test launch claimed his life. Born in Grand

Rapids, Michigan, he, like Grissom, was a graduate of Purdue University, and earned his degree in aeronautical engineering in 1957. During that same year, Chaffee undertook postgraduate work at the Air Force Institute of Technology at Wright-Patterson Air Force Base and joined the Navy. He became a Navy pilot, rising to the rank of Lieutenant Commander before being chosen for the third group of astronauts in 1963.

The third member of the Apollo One crew, Lt. Colonel Edward H. White II, a native of San Antonio, Texas, was the first man ever to walk in space. He accomplished this historic feat during his first flight in 1965. The Apollo flight was to have been his second mission in space. He is buried on the grounds of his alma mater, The United States Military Academy at West Point.

All America mourned the tragic loss of these three space pioneers as President Lyndon Johnson expressed the nation's sorrow at the burials of Colonel Grissom and Lt. Commander Chaffee in Arlington National Cemetery. Although they are buried in adjoining graves, their burial ceremonies took place four hours apart allowing each man to receive full military honors. Colonel Grissom's honorary pallbearers included many of the major figures in America's space program. John Glenn, Donald Slayton, Scott Carpenter, Alan Shepherd, Gordon Cooper, and Walter Schirra all escorted Grissom to his final resting place.

Roger Chaffee and Virgil Grissom rest side by side in graves

marked with simple government-issue headstones. Nothing on those stones tells the tragic story of how these men lost their lives. However, the decision to place them in Section 3 is significant: the two astronauts were assigned graves in this section to put them in close proximity to the grave of Lt. **Thomas Selfridge** who died on December 17, 1908 while testing a Wright brothers' plane at nearby Fort Myer. **Selfridge** was the first air fatality among American Armed Services personnel, just as Grissom, Chaffee, and White were the first fatalities of the American space program.

Two other astronauts — Commander **Francis (Dick) Scobee** and Captain **Michael J. Smith** — are also buried at Arlington. On January 28, 1986, they were among seven astronauts who became the first Americans to die during a space flight when their spacecraft — the Shuttle Challenger — exploded shortly after takeoff.

HENRY HARLEY ("HAP") ARNOLD

American Military Aviation Pioneer, Five-Star General

(June 25, 1886–January 15, 1950)
Sec. 34, Lot 44–A, Grid UV–11/12

The story of General Henry ("Hap") Arnold is the story of American military aviation. Learning to fly from the Wright brothers, he became the only man in American history to attain the rank of General in both the Army and the Air Force. It was largely through his efforts that the United States Air Force became a separate branch of military service. In fact, his role in transforming the old Army Air Corps into a modern air force won him the unofficial title of "Father of the United States Air Force."

Born and raised in Gladwyne, Pennsylvania, Arnold received an appointment to the United States Military Academy, where he was given the nickname "Hap" because of his cheerful disposition. His graduation from West Point in 1907 fatefully coincided with the birth of modern aviation. Four years later Arnold found himself assigned to the Aeronautical Division of the Signal Corps. Thereafter, for nearly forty years, his name would be synonymous with flying.

In 1911, after completing flight training under Orville and Wilbur Wright, Arnold became only the twenty-ninth pilot to be licensed in the United States. His career was highlighted by one first after another. In September of 1911 he carried the first U.S. air mail shipments; on June 1, 1912 he became the first person to attain the record altitude of 6,540 feet; and in October of 1912 he won aviation's first MacKay Trophy for a thirty-mile round-trip flight from College Park, Maryland to Fort Myer, Virginia. On that flight Arnold piloted an early Wright biplane powered by a forty-horsepower engine. It had two propellers driven by a chain-and-sprocket device. He also pioneered air refueling techniques, as well as airborne patrolling of forest fires. On July 6, 1924 Arnold established a new speed record of 113 miles per hour between Rockwell, California and San Francisco, and in 1934 he received a second coveted MacKay Trophy for outstanding achievement in flying—this time for commanding ten bombers on a round-trip flight from Washington, D.C. to Fairbanks, Alaska.

During World War I Arnold was appointed head of the Army's Aviation Training School and, following several flight-related commands, gained promotion to Lieutenant Colonel. By 1938 he rose to Major General, Chief of the Army Air Corps. By the time the United States entered World War II, the aircraft industry had increased its production capabilities sixfold, primarily due to Hap Arnold's influence and leadership. He was promoted to Lieutenant General in 1941 and was commissioned as aviation's first full General in 1943. Serving on both the Joint Chiefs of Staff and the Allied Combined Chiefs of Staff during World War II, he was recognized by President Harry Truman in 1944 with a promotion to the rank of Five-Star General of the Army, joining Douglas MacArthur, **George C. Marshall**, Dwight Eisenhower and **Omar Bradley**.

Hap Arnold retired to his farm in Sonoma, California in March 1946. Nevertheless, in 1949, in recognition of his unequalled contribution to the United States' flying forces, he was commissioned General of the Air Force, the first such commission ever given and one which made him the only person in American military history ever to attain that rank in both the Army and Air Force.

Arnold published his autobiography, *Global Mission*, in 1949 and died on his Sonoma ranch in 1950. His tomb is marked by a simple regulation tombstone, near the grave of another great American General, **John Pershing**.

WILLIAM WORTH BELKNAP

Impeached Secretary of War

(September 22, 1829–October 13, 1890)
Sec. 1, Lot 132, Grid O–33

William Belknap served with distinction during the Civil War and earned the trust and respect of his commanding General, Ulysses S. Grant. Yet less than ten years later, Belknap lost that trust and became the subject of a national public scandal. Ultimately, he was forced to resign from President Grant's Cabinet following his impeachment for accepting bribes.

Belknap, a native of Newburg, New York, graduated from Princeton University in 1852. He studied law at Georgetown University and following his graduation, moved to Keokuk, Iowa, where he entered private practice. While there, he served as a Democratic representative in the Iowa State legislature. When war broke out between the North and the South in 1861, Belknap volunteered for military service and was commissioned a Major in the Fifteenth Iowa Infantry.

Most of Belknap's combat experience was in the West—at Shiloh, Corinth, and Vicksburg. By 1864 his exemplary service had earned him promotion to Brigadier General of Volunteers. After serving under General William Tecumseh Sherman during the famous march through Georgia, he resigned from the Army in 1865 to accept appointment from President Andrew Johnson as revenue collector for the State of Iowa. By 1869 General Grant had been elected President, and cognizant of Belknap's outstanding service during the Civil War, Grant requested that Belknap serve as his Secretary of War. Acceding to the President's request, Belknap took his oath of office on October 13, 1869.

By 1875 allegations of impropriety surrounding Belknap's appointment of post traders (civilians authorized to sell merchandise on military installations) were being raised. Evidence surfaced showing that he had accepted payments from one John Rawlins in exchange for Rawlins' appointment as post trader at Fort Sill, Oklahoma. A Bill of Impeachment was introduced in the House of Representatives and quickly passed. However, before a trial could take place in the Senate, Belknap tendered his resignation to President Grant on March 7, 1876. But the scandal demanded resolution and in spite of his resignation, the Senate trial continued. Belknap was acquitted, though many Senators confessed to having voted in Belknap's favor simply because he had already resigned and they no longer had jurisdiction over the matter.

General Belknap remained in Washington where he resumed the practice of law. On October 13, 1890 he died suddenly in his Washington home.

CONSTANCE BENNETT

Stage and Screen Actress

(October 22, 1905–July 25, 1965)
Sec. 3, Lot 2231–A, Grid P–13

A military cemetery is an unusual place to find the final resting place of the glamorous movie queen of the 1930s, Constance Bennett. The whirlwind career of this film legend mirrored the Golden Age of Hollywood. Married several times during her life, Bennett's longest lasting marriage was to her fifth husband, an Air Force Colonel.

Daughter of silent film idol Richard Bennett and sister of Joan Bennett, another movie great, Constance Bennett was born in New York City. Samuel Goldwyn launched her movie career in 1924 with the silent film, *Cytherea*, the first of more than fifty films in which she was to appear. She survived the transition to "talkies" and played opposite many of Hollywood's greatest leading men, including Clark Gable, Frederick March, Joel McCrea, Herbert Marshall, and Cary Grant.

In *Topper*, the 1937 comedy hit, she and Grant were cast as a pair of well-intentioned ghosts who come to the aid of a downtrodden bank president, brilliantly portrayed by Roland Young. The same trio also starred in the film's sequel, *Topper Takes a Trip*. Her final picture was *Madame X*, which also starred Lana Turner, John Forsythe, Ricardo Montalban, and Burgess Meredith.

Bennett's private life was almost as entertaining as her movie roles. At age fifteen, she eloped with a University of Virginia student whom she met over Easter weekend. That marriage ended in divorce. At nineteen she married millionaire Philip Plant, and at twenty-six, divorced from Plant, she married the Marquis Henri de la Falaise, former husband of screen star Gloria Swanson. Ten years later she wed her fourth husband, movie actor Gilbert Roland. This, however, was not to be her last marriage. In 1946 she married Air Force Colonel John Coulter. An advisor for Air Force training films, Coulter met Bennett in Hollywood and persuaded her to try the life of a career military wife. That life seems to have agreed with her because she remained married to Coulter until her death in 1965 in New York City.

Filmmaking was not Constance Bennett's only forte. She was also known as a shrewd businesswoman, creating her own cosmetics firm and designing Constance Bennett originals for a Cincinnati dressmaker. When she died, Bennett was buried in Arlington National Cemetery, exercising her right to be interred with her husband, who had attained the rank of Brigadier General before his death. The plain black marble stone which marks her grave makes no mention of her sparkling film career or of her business successes; rather, it simply reads: Constance Bennett Coulter.

HUGO L. BLACK

U.S. Senator, Supreme Court Justice

(February 27, 1886–September 25, 1971)
Sec. 30, Lot 649 LH, Grid WX–39

During his thirty-four years on the Supreme Court, Justice Hugo Lafayette Black earned a solid reputation as a staunch defender of the Bill of Rights, but his position on the nation's highest court was jeopardized when it was disclosed that he had once been a member of the Ku Klux Klan.

Black, a native of Harlan, Alabama, was one of eight children whose father was a storekeeper and farmer. Young Hugo attended the University of Alabama where he received his law degree in 1906. He practiced law in Birmingham until he was selected as a police court judge in 1910. In 1915 he served as county prosecutor, but joined the U.S. Army when the United States entered the First World War. A member of the Eighty-first Field Artillery, Black served his entire tour of duty without leaving the country.

After the war Black resumed his law practice in Birmingham.

In 1926 he was elected to the United States Senate from Alabama and won praise for his investigation of utility lobbyists and for leading the drive for the Fair Labor Standards Act. He was also a staunch supporter of President Franklin Roosevelt's New Deal legislation and favored FDR's court-packing scheme. In 1937, when Justice Willis Van Devanter retired from the Supreme Court, President Roosevelt appointed Senator Black to fill the vacancy.

Black's nomination was quickly confirmed by the Senate, but came under fire shortly afterward when it was learned that during the 1920s he had been a member of the Ku Klux Klan. In a nationally broadcast radio statement—an act almost unheard of by a Supreme Court Justice—Black dramatically acknowledged that he had indeed been a member of the Ku Klux Klan, but that he had resigned many years earlier, prior to his election to the Senate. Following his broadcast, Black made no further comment on the subject and immediately undertook his duties on the Court. Within a short period of time, the furor over the disclosure calmed and Black's position on the Court was never again challenged.

On the bench Black became a strong advocate for the absolute authority of the Bill of Rights, especially the freedom of speech. Justice Black voted to strike down mandatory school prayer statutes, and to guarantee the right to legal counsel for suspected criminals. In 1971 his last major opinion upheld the right of *The New York Times* to publish the so-called Pentagon Papers.

Black suffered from ill health during the later years of his life, and was forced to resign from the Supreme Court on September 17, 1971. He died eight days later at Bethesda Naval Hospital in Maryland. President Richard Nixon nominated Lewis Powell, Jr. to succeed Black.

Government regulation tombstones mark the graves of Justice Black and his wife. Adorning the site is a small marble bench inscribed with the simple epitaph: "Here lies a good man."

OMAR NELSON BRADLEY

Five-Star General, World War II's "GI General"

(February 12, 1893–April 8, 1981)
Sec. 30, Lot 428-1, Grid AA–39

Omar Bradley did not have a field command in World War II until April of 1943. At that time, he assumed command of the II Corps from General George Patton and, following a successful D-Day landing at Normandy, marched the largest force ever commanded by an American field officer—1.3 million men—across Europe into Germany. Throughout his campaigns, he had a policy of keeping his own command posts near the front lines; he visited his troops regularly; and he cared greatly about the morale of his men. His conduct earned him the unofficial title of "The GI General." General **George C. Marshall**, Army Chief of Staff, in an official statement, called Bradley "the finest Army group commander" in the United States Army.

Born in the small Missouri town of Clark, Bradley moved to Moberly, Missouri as a child, living there until he left for West Point in 1911. Upon graduation from the military academy in 1915, in a class that included Dwight Eisenhower and James Van Fleet, he earned a commission in the Infantry. After various stateside assignments during World War I, Bradley was made a professor of military science at South Dakota State University in 1919, but was transferred to instruct at West Point the following year. By 1941 he had risen to the rank of Brigadier General and commandant of the Infantry School of the Eighty-second Infantry (later of the Eighty-second Airborne Division) at Camp Claiborne, Louisiana. After a year commanding the Twenty-eighth Infantry Division at Camp Livingston, Louisiana, Bradley was ordered to North Africa as an aide to General Dwight Eisenhower in 1943.

It was then, in April of 1943, that he was ordered to relieve General Patton of his command of the II Corps. Under his command, the II Corps captured Bizerte and Tunis, and Bradley became a Lieutenant General. From North Africa, he led his troops in a landing near Scoglitti, Sicily, then in September 1943, he was called to England to assist in the cross-channel invasion. While in England he was appointed commander of the Provisional First U.S. Army Group (FUSAG) for the historic D-Day invasion.

On June 6, 1944 he landed his First Army at Utah and Omaha Beaches. In July he directed the crucial breakthrough at St. Lo which allowed the advance of the Allied Forces and ultimately liberated Paris from Nazi control. During this advance, Bradley commanded the Twelfth Army Group, the largest force ever led by an American commander. Following the surrender of Germany, Bradley was appointed full General in August 1945. At that same time, because of his widely-publicized and widely-praised concern for enlisted men, he was also named Administrator of Veterans Affairs in what later became known as the Veterans Adminstration.

He stayed at the V.A. until February 1948, when he was named to succeed General Eisenhower as Army Chief of Staff. One year later he became Chairman of the first permanent Joint Chiefs of Staff in the new U.S. Department of Defense. In 1950 he was promoted to Five-Star General of the Army, joining **George C. Marshall**, Dwight Eisenhower, **Hap Arnold**, and Douglas MacArthur as the only persons to hold that rank.

In 1951 Omar Bradley published his memoirs, *A Soldier's Story*, and two years later retired from the Army. Following his retirement, he served as Chairman of the Board of the Bulova Watch Company. Omar Nelson Bradley died in 1981 while on a visit to New York City.

GEORGE SCRATCHLEY BROWN

World War II Fighter Pilot, Vietnam War Air Commander

(August 17, 1918–December 5, 1978)
Sec. 21, Lot S–34, Grid N–20/21

George Brown began his military career as a World War II flying ace and rose through the ranks of the Army Air Corps. When the Air Force became a separate service branch, he continued his rise and ultimately commanded the air war in Vietnam. Although Brown was at times a controversial officer, his skill and knowledge of the Armed Forces won him the highest position in the military — Chairman of the Joint Chiefs of Staff, making him the first Air Force officer to ever hold that position.

Brown, a native of Montclair, New Jersey, attended the University of Missouri before entering West Point, graduating in 1941. Commissioned in the Army Air Corps, throughout World War II he was a pilot in the Ninety-third Bombardment Group attached to the Eighth Air Force. Brown took part in the famed low-level bombing raid against an oil refinery at Ploesti, Rumania on August 1, 1943.

The raid called for a surprise attack by one hundred seventy-seven B-24 bombers. They were to evade German radar by flying all 1,200 miles, from their base at Bengasi, Libya to the oil refinery, at treetop level. However, a navigational error took them directly over Bucharest, the headquarters of the German Air Defense Command. The lead plane and ten others in Brown's group were shot down or crashed at Ploesti. Brown fearlessly took the lead, guiding the remaining planes back to their home base. For his courageous action under fire, he was awarded the Distinguished Service Cross.

After the war he returned to the United States to accept various assignments, including command of the Fifty-sixth Fighter Wing stationed at **Selfridge** Air Force Base, Michigan.

During the Korean War, Brown was Chief of Operations of

the Fifth Air Force. He later graduated from the National War College and was appointed Chief Executive Officer to the Chief of Staff of the Air Force. In 1959 Brown was promoted to Brigadier General, serving as military assistant to the Secretary of Defense.

By August 1966 Brown had become a Major General assigned to assist the Chairman of the Joint Chiefs of Staff, General **Earle G. Wheeler**. Perhaps his toughest assignment came in August of 1968 when he was promoted to General and named commander of the Seventh Air Force based in Saigon, Vietnam. In this post, Brown was responsible for air operations for the entire Southeast Asia region.

In July 1973 President Richard Nixon nominated General Brown to be Chief of Staff of the Air Force. During his confirmation hearings it was learned that he had overseen secret bombing raids into Cambodia while in charge of the air war in Vietnam. Brown maintained he was simply following orders from the Chairman of the Joint Chiefs of Staff and that no one with a "need to know" had been deceived. In spite of the controversy, Brown was confirmed and in July of the following year he was named Chairman of the Joint Chiefs.

Brown retained this chairmanship under President Gerald Ford, but not without further controversy. His outspoken personal views clashed with administration policy on several occasions, causing the administration political embarrassment. One incident occurred when Brown, addressing a seminar at Duke University in 1974, suggested that American Jews exerted undue influence in the U.S. because they "own the banks. . . and the newspapers." He also was sharply critical of the Jewish lobby in Congress.

Nevertheless, Brown retained his position until ill health forced his retirement from the Air Force in June 1978. He died of cancer on December 5 of that same year. General Brown is buried in Section 21 near his former commander in Vietnam, General **Creighton Abrams**.

WILLIAM JENNINGS BRYAN

Presidential Candidate, Secretary of State

(March 19, 1860–June 26, 1925)
Sec. 4, Lot 3121, Grids Y/Z–11

At age 36 William Jennings Bryan was the youngest person ever to be nominated for president by a major political party. Though he would be nominated twice more by his party, the nation's highest office would forever elude him.

A statue of William Jennings Bryan represents Nebraska in the United States Capitol's Statuary Hall because of his long association with that state, though he was born in Marion County, Illinois. He attended public schools in Jacksonville, Illinois and graduated from Illinois College in 1881. He returned to Jacksonville to practice law after completing his legal studies at Union College in Chicago in 1883. In 1887 Bryan moved to Nebraska, where he maintained his residence for nearly thirty-five years. After serving two terms in Congress from 1891 to 1895, he declined to be a candidate for reelection in order to run for the United States Senate in 1894, but he lost that election.

Following his Senate defeat, Bryan returned to Nebraska, becoming editor of the *Omaha World-Herald*. In 1896 he went to the Democratic National Convention in Chicago as a virtual unknown, but he left the convention as that party's nominee for president. This startling turn of events occurred as a result of the trait that made William Jennings Bryan one of the most famous men of his time: his dramatic talent as an orator.

During the convention's platform debate, Bryan addressed the question regarding the free silver plank. The resulting "Cross of Gold" speech is considered the most famous oration ever made before an American political convention. It left the convention hall in pandemonium and led to Bryan's nomination. He had to face Republican William McKinley in the general election and knew that he could not rely upon traditional campaign tactics to win.

Prior to that election, presidential candidates had not personally campaigned for votes, relying instead on surrogates to campaign for them. Bryan, however, knew that his most powerful weapon was his talent for communicating directly with people, so he stumped the countryside traveling 18,000 miles, facing five million voters along the way. The Republicans feared Bryan's ability to sway voters almost as much as they feared the populist positions he had taken. Therefore, the giants of industry rallied to McKinley's cause and outspent the Democrats and Bryan by more than twenty to one. The result was a victory for McKinley, though he garnered only four percent more of the popular vote than Bryan.

When war broke out with Spain in 1898, Bryan raised the Third Regiment of the Nebraska Volunteer Infantry and, while he saw no overseas duty, he was commissioned a Colonel. Two years later, Bryan was again ready to take on McKinley. He was again nominated by the Democrats, and again lost to McKinley, this time by a larger margin than in 1896.

In 1901 Bryan established *The Commoner*, a newspaper in Lincoln, Nebraska which he used as a forum for his political viewpoints. Theodore Roosevelt became President following the assassination of President McKinley, and enjoyed great popular support. Bryan chose not to challenge the popular President in 1904, believing that such a race could not be won.

During 1905-06, Bryan toured the world in recognition of the United States' new position as an international power and in preparation for his third try for the presidency. In 1908, again winning his party's nomination and hailed as "The Great Commoner," Bryan faced **William Howard Taft**. **Taft** won the election by a sizable margin.

Despite his three failed attempts at the presidency, Bryan continued to exercise great influence within the Democratic Party, playing a pivotal role in the nomination of Woodrow Wilson in 1912. Following Wilson's victory, Wilson named Bryan as his

Secretary of State on March 4, 1913. Bryan remained in that position, negotiating over thirty treaties during his tenure, until June 9, 1915, when he resigned in disagreement with President Wilson's strong protest against the German sinking of the *Lusitania*. Bryan felt that such a vehement response would only serve to pull the United States into the war already raging in Europe. However, once the United States entered the war in 1917, Bryan was a loyal supporter.

Out of office, Bryan resumed his writing and his popular lecture series in which he advocated the literal interpretation of the Bible and the prohibition of liquor. It was his fundamentalist religious beliefs that involved him in the famous Scopes monkey trial. John Scopes, a high school biology teacher in Dayton, Tennessee, was charged with teaching evolution, contrary to state law. Bryan, recruited to assist in the prosecution of the case, was put head-to-head against the country's foremost defense attorney, Clarence Darrow. Bryan was called to testify; Darrow, of course, relished the opportunity to cross-examine him. By the time the legal sparring ended, Darrow had humiliated Bryan, forcing him into ideological corners, often leading Bryan to contradict his own testimony. Immediately following the trial, Bryan set to work writing his rebuttal to Darrow, the rebuttal he did not have a chance to deliver at the trial. It was Bryan's intent to publish his remarks so that his position would be vindicated. Sadly, he died within a week of the trial's conclusion, the manuscript still incomplete.

William Jennings Bryan is buried on a hillside overlooking the southern sections of Arlington near Bryan Circle, named in his honor. Buried with him is **Mary Baird Bryan**, his "Wife and Helpmate." His tombstone bears the inscription: "Statesman, yet friend to truth! Of Soul sincere, In action faithful, and honor clear."

RICHARD EVELYN BYRD, JR.

Polar Explorer

(October 25, 1888–March 11, 1957)
Sec. 2, Lot 4969, Grid WX–32/33

Richard Evelyn Byrd, Jr. began his adventures at an early age. When he was only twelve years old, he took an unescorted trip around the world which convinced him that his life would be spent as an adventurer. By the time he died at age sixty-nine, Byrd had achieved what no other person had ever achieved. He had flown over both poles, led several extended expeditions into the Antarctic interior (one of which nearly cost him his life), received over

This statue of Admiral Richard E. Byrd, Jr., erected by the National Geographic Society, is located on Memorial Drive just outside the main gate to Arlington.

twenty commendations for bravery or conspicuous conduct, and won the hearts of his countrymen.

Born in Winchester, Virginia, Byrd attended the University of Virginia before entering the United States Naval Academy, from which he graduated in 1912. In 1915, after only three years of active service, Byrd was forced to retire, abandoning his dream of a Naval career. The Navy had determined that he was physically unable to serve because of a leg injury he had suffered while captain of the academy gymnastics team. However, upon the United States' entry into World War I, Byrd returned to duty in the Navy's aviation branch. He earned his wings in 1918 after he had flown solo with only six hours instruction. During the war, he served as commander of a Navy patrol squadron based in Canada.

After flying over sea, ice, and glaciers in western Greenland during an expedition with Commander D.B. MacMillan in 1924, Byrd set his sights on an airborne expedition to the North Pole. On May 9, 1926 he and his co-pilot, **Floyd Bennett**,(Sec. 3, Lot 1852, Grid ST–17) left their base in Spitsbergen, Norway, aboard their Fokker trimotor plane, the "Josephine Ford." They completed the 1,500-mile flight to the Pole, suffering no greater malfunction than a minor oil leak. The explorers returned home to a heroes' welcome and were each presented a Congressional Medal of Honor by President Calvin Coolidge, a rare peacetime achievement.

Next Byrd attempted an Atlantic crossing. In June 1927, with three companions, including Bernt Balchen, Byrd reached the coast of France, but was forced to crash-land his plane at Ver-sur-Mer after forty-two hours of flight. For this extraordinary flight he was named a Commandant in the Legion d'Honneur.

Searching for other uncharted skies, Byrd announced his intention to explore the unknown regions of the Antarctic from the air. In 1928 he sailed to the area known as Bay of Whales, Antarctica, and established Little America, the base that still exists today. On November 29, 1929, during the Antarctic spring, Byrd, Balchen, and two other men took off from their base at Little America and flew to the South Pole. The plane, named *Floyd Bennett* after Byrd's friend and polar companion, took nineteen hours to complete the world-record flight. For this achievement Byrd was promoted to Rear Admiral, Retired.

In 1933 Byrd headed yet another expedition to the Antarctic to map and to explore new regions around the Pole. During the winter of 1934, Byrd stayed alone in a weather observation shed 125 miles from any other human being. We know from Byrd's notes that with temperatures between $-58°$ and $-76°$ F. he could hear his breath freeze as it drifted from his lips, making crackling noises like little firecrackers. After five months in this self-imposed solitary confinement, in which he made no mention of any problems during his radio transmissions to the Little America base, Byrd became seriously ill. When members of the base camp crew became alarmed by incoherent reports from Byrd, a rescue team set out to investigate. They arrived to find Byrd suffering from frostbite and carbon monoxide poisoning, a result of an improperly vented oil-burning stove. Too weak to travel, Byrd was cared for in the hut for two months before he could return to Little America.

This episode permanently impaired his health and restricted his future activities. Admiral Byrd recounted this grueling adventure in his book, *Alone*, published in 1938.

Byrd went on to lead three more expeditions to the Antarctic as director of the newly established Antarctic Service. During World War II, he served on the staff of the Chief of Naval Operations, and in 1955 he was named head of "Operation Deepfreeze" which was the United States' contribution to the International Geophysical Year of 1957-58. It was during this project that Byrd took his last flight over the South Pole on January 8, 1956. He died in Boston the following year and was buried with full military honors at Arlington.

Two monuments honor Admiral Byrd at Arlington. The first marks his grave in Section 2. It is a regulation headstone, engraved in gold to signify his receipt of the Congressional Medal of Honor. The other monument is located on the north side of Memorial Drive along the approach to the cemetery's main gates. Erected by the National Geographic Society, it is a life-size statue of Admiral Byrd and the base is inscribed: "Upon this bright globe he carved his signature of courage." The sculpture was created by Felix de Weldon (who also sculpted the Seabees Monument and the Marine Corps Memorial) in 1961.

CLAIRE LEE CHENNAULT

Commander of the Flying Tigers of World War II

(September 6, 1893–July 27, 1958)
Sec. 2, Lot 872, Grid PQ–31

Claire Chennault was both a fighter and a flyer. And when World War II forced the forging of those two qualities, he became commander of one of the most famous flying groups in aviation history, The Flying Tigers.

Chennault's career started neither as a soldier nor as a pilot, but rather as a teacher and principal of a small rural school in Louisiana. Born in Commerce, Texas, Chennault attended Louisiana State Normal College (now Northwestern State College of Louisiana). When the United States entered World War I in 1917, Chennault enlisted, attending officers training camp at Fort Benjamin Harrison, Indiana. In November of that year he was commissioned a First Lieutenant in the Infantry Reserve and soon became both a pilot and flight instructor.

By 1929 Chennault had been promoted to Captain, and in 1931 he graduated from the Air Corps Technical School at Langley Field, Virginia. It was during this period that he and two friends formed a barnstorming-style air stunt show billed as "Three Men on a Flying Trapeze." He remained a flight instructor for six years until 1937, by which time his hearing had become so severely impaired that the Army forced him to retire. Disappointed, Chennault sought other skies, eventually being hired by Madame Chiang Kai-shek, wife of the Nationalist Chinese leader, to assume command of the Chinese air defenses against Japan.

In 1940, prior to the United States' declaration of war against Japan, Chennault recruited American pilots and mechanics to fight for the Chinese. In 1941 he began training what was known as the American Volunteer Group (AVG) at K'un-Ming. On December 20, 1941, just thirteen days after the attack on Pearl Harbor, the AVG flew their first mission. Their successes against the Japanese won them worldwide acclaim, and they became known as The Flying Tigers.

In 1942, disregarding his hearing impairment, the U.S. Army recalled Chennault to active duty as a Colonel in the Army Air Corps. Shortly thereafter, he was promoted to Brigadier General, and in July of that year the Flying Tigers officially became part of the Twenty-third Fighters Squadron, with Claire Chennault named Chief of Army Air Forces in China. By March of 1943 he had risen to Major General and had been placed in command of the Fourteenth Air Force. Following Japan's unconditional surrender on September 2, 1945, Chennault retired from the Army.

Chennault publicly criticized the United States for failing to support the government of Chiang Kai-shek. He rejoined the Nationalists in 1946 to organize the Chinese National Relief and Rehabilitation Air Transport. Later, he formed a contract cargo carrier known as the Civil Air Transport Service based on Taiwan. The Central Intelligence Agency eventually purchased this air transport company and Chennault continued in a management role with the service until ill health forced his retirement in 1955.

Returning to the United States in June 1958 to seek medical treatment for lung cancer, Chennault received an extraordinary recognition. By special legislation, Congress promoted him to Lieutenant General just nine days before his death in New Orleans on July 27th. He was buried with full military honors at Arlington and as a special tribute to his achievements, Chennault's tombstone bears his name inscribed in two languages: English on one side and Chinese on the other. His son, Colonel **John S. Chennault**, a veteran of World War II and Korea, was laid to rest next to his father in 1977.

As one final postscript, Claire Lee Chennault is buried in what was once part of the rose garden of his mother's distant cousin, Robert E. Lee.

JOHN LINCOLN CLEM

Drummer Boy of Chickamauga, Major General

(August 31, 1851–May 13, 1937)
Sec. 2, Lot 993, Grid S–32/33

On May 24, 1861 a nine-year-old boy ran away from his Newark, Ohio home to join the fighting that had recently erupted in what would become the Civil War. His mother had been killed in a train accident and he was now free to do his part to protect the Union. He was allowed by the Twenty-second Michigan Infantry to serve as their drummer boy, but within two years achieved the rank of Sergeant at the tender age of twelve. He was Johnny Clem, the youngest soldier ever to fight in the United States Army.

His proper name was John Joseph Klem but he was so enamored with Republican candidate Abraham Lincoln during the presidential campaign of 1860 that he changed his middle name to "Lincoln." It is unclear when he chose to start spelling his last name with a *C* rather than using the *K* which was used by his German immigrant family.

The first major action in which young Clem was involved was the Battle of Pittsburg Landing, near Shiloh, Tennessee. During a rout by Confederate troops, Union soldiers were rapidly retreating from their positions. With his drum rendered useless by Rebel gunfire, Clem picked up a musket with a sawed-off barrel and returned the Confederate fire. The Union troops, inspired by the young drummer boy's bravery, regrouped. Following the battle, Clem was cited for his valiant conduct, and officially inducted into the Army. During the battle of Chickamauga, Johnny wounded a Confederate Colonel, then eluded capture by playing dead. Once reunited with his regiment, he was promoted to the rank of Sergeant, becoming the youngest American soldier ever to hold that rank. The remainder of the war found young Johnny at Murfreesboro, Lookout Mountain, Missionary Ridge, and Atlanta. He was captured by Confederate forces shortly after Chickamauga, but was exchanged two months later. Twice ponies were shot from under the young soldier and once he was wounded in the hip by a shell fragment. But his military career did not end with the Civil War.

In 1869 an old wartime friend of his—Ulysses S. Grant— became President of the United States. Two years later, President Grant personally handed Clem his Second Lieutenant's commission, and Clem once again saw action during the Spanish-American

War. In 1915 he was promoted to Brigadier General; in 1916 he retired as a Major General. But when the United States entered World War I, sixty-five-year-old Clem sought permission to be reactivated and go to France to fight. President Woodrow Wilson flatly refused his request, sending the disappointed "drummer boy" into permanent retirement at his home in San Antonio, Texas. John Lincoln Clem, the youngest soldier ever to serve in the United States Army, died in 1937 at the age of eighty-six.

He is buried among many other great soldiers of that war, including **Sheridan**, **Wheeler**, **Schofield**, **Crook**, **Ord**, and 2,111 unknown Civil War soldiers. His stone proudly displays his military career in just three lines:

THE DRUMMER BOY OF CHICKAMAUGA
MAJOR GENERAL U.S. ARMY
1851–1937

GEORGE CROOK

Veteran of the Civil War and Indian Campaigns.

(September 9, 1830–March 21, 1890)
Sec. 2, Lot 974, Grid S–32

When he died at the age of fifty-nine, General George Crook was still on active duty after thirty-eight years. His career was highlighted by his courageous service to the North in the Civil War, as well as by his equitable treatment of Native Americans while stationed in the West after the war.

Born in Dayton, Ohio, Crook was a member of the West Point graduating class of 1852. He was first assigned to exploration and frontier defense duties in the Northwest where he began his lifelong study of Indians, their environment, cultures, languages, and ways of warfare. In 1857 he was wounded in a skirmish with the Pit

River Indians.

In September 1861 Crook was recalled from the western frontier to command a company of Ohio Volunteers in the Civil War. He took part in the battles of South Mountain and Antietam, earning himself a promotion to Brigadier General of Volunteers in 1862. In September of that year, he commanded a division of cavalry under General **William Starke Rosecrans** at Chickamauga; in October he pursued the Confederate cavalry under General **Joseph Wheeler** to Farmington, Tennessee where Crook defeated them. During the Shenandoah campaign in 1864, he saw action at Winchester under General **Philip Sheridan**; and in March 1865, while leading a cavalry division in the battle of Petersburg, Crook was captured and held at Richmond's Libby Prison. Following his release in an exchange of prisoners, he served with the Army of the Potomac.

Mounted on the tombstone of George Crook is a bas-relief depicting the 1883 surrender of Apache chief Geronimo to General Crook shown at the lower right.

Crook returned to the western frontier after the war and initially took a hard line against Native Americans. In 1871 he was ordered to Arizona to deal with the Apache Indians who, under their chief Cochise, had been terrorizing the white settlers the Apaches believed were encroaching on Indian territory. In 1875 Crook was commander of the Department of the Platte when gold was discovered in the Black Hills. Gold fever sparked an invasion of Indian territories by white settlers. Crook was heavily engaged throughout 1876 in trying to pacify the Sioux and Cheyenne Indians. On June 17 at Rosebud Creek, Crook fought nearly 1,500 Sioux and Cheyenne Indians under Chief Crazy Horse, but was forced to retreat.

This failed campaign changed Crook's attitude toward dealing with Indians. He felt that they needed protection from corrupt Indian agents and hostile frontiersmen, and over time he gained a reputation among the Indians as an equitable frontier army commander. In 1882 Crook returned to Arizona to quell an uprising by the Apaches under Geronimo. He chased the Indian warrior into the Sierra Madre Mountains of Mexico before capturing and returning him to his reservation. Geronimo escaped in 1885, but Crook was relieved of his command by General **Nelson A. Miles** before he could recapture the Apache Chief.

Crook spent his last years as commander of the Department of Missouri stationed in Chicago. He spent much of his time on public crusades criticizing government Indian policy because he came to feel that the Indians were often unjustly treated. George Crook died in Chicago and was brought back to Washington, D.C. for burial at Arlington.

General Crook's tombstone, erected by the Society of the Army of West Virginia, displays a bas-relief of the surrender of Geronimo as well as a list of Crook's Civil War campaigns. Like many of the tombstones of Union soldiers in Arlington, the Civil War is referred to as the War of the Rebellion. Also of note: The Crook Walk in Arlington Cemetery, which leads from Arlington House to the Tomb of the Unknowns, is named for George Crook.

CUSHMAN KELLOG DAVIS

Senator, Soldier, Statesman

(June 16, 1838–November 27, 1900)
Sec. 1, Lot 362, Grid L/M–36

Cushman Kellogg Davis was born in Henderson, New York and, like so many other Americans in the first half of the nineteenth century, moved with his family to the Midwest. They settled in Waukesha, Wisconsin where he attended the local public schools and Carroll College. He later transferred to the University of Michigan at Ann Arbor where he graduated in 1857. He continued his studies in law and began his legal practice in Waukesha in 1859.

During the Civil War, Davis served as a First Lieutenant in

the Twenty-eighth Regiment of the Wisconsin Volunteer Infantry and was assigned to the staff of General Willis A. Gorman from 1862 until 1864. Following the war, he moved to St. Paul, Minnesota where he was elected to the Minnesota House of Representatives in 1867. President Andrew Johnson appointed him United States Attorney for Minnesota in 1868, a position he held for five years. In 1874, as a Republican, he was elected Governor of Minnesota and in 1886 he was elected to the U.S. Senate where he served nearly three terms. President William McKinley named him to the special Commission which met in Paris in September 1898 to arrange the peace treaty ending the Spanish-American War. Cushman Kellog Davis died in office while visiting St. Paul in 1900. His grave in Arlington is marked by a bronze bust of himself atop a granite column. On the front of the column is a bas-relief depicting Davis in attendance at the historic Paris Peace Conference.

JANE DELANO

Army Nursing Pioneer

(March 12, 1862–April 15, 1919)
Sec. 21, Lot 6, Grid LM–20

During the first quarter of this century, Jane Delano was instrumental in providing qualified nurses for service in the United States Armed Forces. She personally supervised the training and preparation of more than 20,000 nurses who came to the aid of American troops during World War I.

Delano, a native of Montour Falls, New York, graduated from Bellevue Hospital of Nursing in 1886. The following year she became superintendent of nurses at a hospital in Jacksonville, Florida where she pioneered the use of mosquito netting to prevent the spread of yellow fever even before the mosquito was proven to be the carrier of the disease. She later established a

Full military honors accompanied the burial of Army nurse and former Red Cross official Jane Delano following her death in 1919.

hospital in Arizona for coal miners suffering from scarlet fever.

In 1902 Jane Delano returned to Bellevue Hospital to assume the position of Director of the School of Nursing. In 1909 she became chairman of the National Committee of the American Red Cross, simultaneously serving as President of the American Nurses Association and as Superintendent of the Army Nurse Corps. She authored the American Red Cross textbook, *Elementary Hygiene and Home Care of the Sick*.

During her tenure as Superintendent of the Army Nurse Corps, Jane Delano implemented a program which made the Red Cross Nursing Service a reserve for the military nursing corps. This plan resulted in the availability of 8,000 nurses ready for duty when the United States entered World War I. Delano was chosen to direct the wartime Department of Nursing, an organization established to select and assign all nursing units. Believing that she could better fulfill her obligations by being close to the nurses treating combat victims, she left her safe offices in this country and went to France.

She died at Savenay in 1919, but her body was returned to this country for burial with full military honors at Arlington National Cemetery.

JACOB LOUCKS DEVERS

World War II Sixth Army Commander

(September 8, 1887–October 15, 1979)
Sec. 1, Lot 149–F, Grid MN–33/34

When the United States entered World War I in 1917, Jacob Devers had been out of the Military Academy for eight years and was stationed in Hawaii. Not ordered to France during the First World War, he believed that his military career had suffered a fatal blow and that he would never realize his dream of renown as a military commander. Devers could not have known then that he would indeed command combat troops on French soil and that he would achieve military greatness, but that this would not come to pass for twenty-five years.

Jacob Devers grew up in York, Pennsylvania and had enrolled at Lehigh University in Bethlehem, Pennsylvania to study engineering when he accepted a last-minute appointment to West Point. Graduating from the Military Academy in 1909, and commissioned as a field artillery officer, he returned to the Academy as a mathematics instructor in 1912, during which time he also coached basketball and baseball for the West Point Cadets.

In 1917, when it seemed that everyone else was going to France, Devers was transferred from his post in Hawaii to Fort Sill, Oklahoma where he served in artillery training positions. Not until 1919 was his desire to serve in Europe realized. There, he attended a French artillery school and served in the Army of Occupation in Germany for several months.

Between the two world wars, Devers was stationed at Fort Sill, West Point, and Washington D.C., spending much of his time in the development of improved artillery tactics and techniques. Graduating with distinction from both the General Command and Staff School and the Army War College, he earned promotion to Colonel in 1939.

When war erupted in Europe during that same year, Devers was serving as Chief of Staff of the Panama Department. In May 1940 President Franklin Roosevelt named him senior Army member of the Military Board to locate suitable bases in the "Bases for Destroyers" deal with Great Britain. Then, in October of that year, he was named commander of the Ninth Division stationed at Fort Bragg, North Carolina, and seven months later—in July 1941—General **George C. Marshall** appointed Devers to head the Armored Forces Training Center at Fort Knox, Kentucky.

When Lt. General Maxwell Andrews was killed in an airplane crash in May 1943, the vacancy of overall commander of American forces in Europe needed to be filled immediately. Jake Devers was the man chosen to assume that important command. In his new capacity, Devers' primary responsibility was to train and organize the divisions of U.S. troops arriving in Britain for participation in the projected Channel crossing. By the end of 1943 Devers had been elevated to Deputy Supreme Commander in the Mediterranean Theatre. To his disappointment, this meant that he would see no combat duty. Yet in July 1944 his wartime orders changed when he was appointed head of the Sixth Army Group, including both American and French forces.

Devers led the Sixth Army in its charge across central Europe, a charge that began in March 1945. With twelve American divisions and eleven French divisions, he crossed the Rhine River and sliced his way through southern Germany, marching into Austria. On April 20 he took control of Nuremberg, and on May 4, 1945 he captured Berchtesgarten, Adolph Hitler's mountaintop retreat.

At the war's end, Devers had risen to full General and Commander of Army ground forces in Europe, a post he held until his retirement in 1949. He worked with the American Automobile Association until 1951, leaving that organization when he was named chief military advisor to the United Nations mission to India and Pakistan. Devers was associated with the Fairchild Engine and Airplane Corporation when he retired. He died at the age of ninety-two in Washington, D.C. in 1979.

SIR JOHN DILL

British Field Marshal,
World War II Allied Combined Chiefs of Staff

(December 25, 1881–November 4, 1944)
Sec. 32, Lot S–29, Grid X–33

British Prime Minister Winston Churchill visited Washington, D.C. in December of 1941 to confer with President Franklin Roosevelt soon after the United States entered World War II. Accompanying Churchill as a military advisor was Field Marshal John Dill. When Churchill returned to England, Dill remained in the United States as Chief of the British Joint Mission to the United States and as senior British representative on the Combined Chiefs of Staff.

Sir John was born John Greer Dill in Lurgan, Northern Ireland on Christmas Day 1881. He was educated at Cheltenham College in Sandhurst, England and joined the First Battalion Leinster Regiment in South Africa in 1901. He was promoted to Captain in 1911 and to Brigade-Major by 1914 when he served in France during World War I. Following the war, he was assigned to India and later commanded forces in Palestine in 1936 and 1937.

When Britain declared war on Germany in 1939, Dill was promoted to General and given command of the I Corps in France. He received his promotion to Field Marshal in 1941 and was named Chief of the Imperial General Staff. However, Prime Minister Churchill considered him to be obstructive and overly cautious in that position. At that time it was widely speculated that this was the reason Dill was assigned to the Washington. Nevertheless, he proved to be a valuable asset while in the United States capital. His services were of great importance in securing the necessary cooperation between the American and British armed forces, not only in Washington but at conferences in Casablanca, Quebec, Cairo, and Teheran. He earned the trust and confidence of everyone with whom he worked, especially President Roosevelt and Chief of Staff General **George C. Marshall**. Both the United States and Great Britain recognized the great contribution made by John Dill. On behalf of the British people, King George VI knighted Dill in 1942. The United States Congress, on behalf of all American citizens, granted Dill the Distinguished Service Cross posthumously.

Sir John died while stationed in Washington in 1944 and received the extraordinary honor—as a foreign soldier—of being buried at Arlington National Cemetery. His is one of only two equestrian statues in the cemetery.

WILLIAM JOSEPH ("WILD BILL") DONOVAN

World War I Hero, World War II Spymaster

(January 1, 1883–February 8, 1959)
Sec. 2, Lot 4874, Grid V–33

For fighting bravely in the trenches in World War I, William Joseph Donovan received the Congressional Medal of Honor; but when World War II started in Europe, he traded in his helmet and rifle for a cloak and dagger.

Donovan, the son of Irish immigrants, was born in Buffalo, New York. He entered Niagara College, then transferred to Columbia University where he played quarterback for the football team and became acquainted with classmate Franklin Roosevelt. He received his B.A. from Columbia in 1905, earned his law degree in 1907, and practiced law in Buffalo.

The cavalry troop which Donovan organized for the New York National Guard served under General **John Pershing** on the Mexican Border in 1916, then followed General **Pershing** to France during World War I. As part of the Twenty-seventh Division, Donovan became a Colonel of the 165th Infantry (formerly known as the Fightin' 69th). During the Meuse-Argonne Offensive, Donovan was wounded three times as he led his regiment against the seemingly impenetrable Hindenburg Line at Landres-et-St. Georges on October 14, 1918. He inspired his young recruits as he moved among his men in exposed frontline positions. For his uncommon valor in that war, Donovan was awarded the Congressional Medal of Honor.

Exactly when Donovan picked up his nickname, "Wild Bill," is unclear. Some reports place its inception during his college football days while others credit his conduct during the war as its source. One story claims Donovan, who was always a strong advocate of physical training, challenged his men during a rigorous workout: "I have fifty pounds on my back, the same as you do," he said, "and I'm twenty years older than any of you boys." Safely hidden in the ranks, a voice responded, "Yeah, but we ain't no wild man like you, Bill." Another report claims that one of his men quipped that "Wild Bill is a son of a bitch, but he's a game one." In any event, the press correspondents covering the First World War picked up the name, tagged him with it, and it remained his sobriquet for the rest of his life.

Throughout the war, Donovan was greatly respected by his men. Among his sergeants was the well-known poet, Joyce Kilmer. Speaking of Donovan, Kilmer, who was later killed in action, stated that he would rather be a sergeant under Donovan than "a lieutenant in any other regiment".

Donovan resumed his law practice in 1920 and actively involved himself in Republican Party politics. Serving as U.S. Attorney for Western New York from 1922 until 1924, then defeated in his bid for Lt. Governor of New York, he moved to Washington to serve as an Assistant U.S. Attorney General, a post he held for four years. Donovan worked hard in the election campaign of Herbert Hoover in 1928, hoping to be named Attorney General after Hoover's victory. However, because Donovan was a Catholic and an antiprohibitionist, Hoover did not name him to the post. A disappointed Donovan declined the President's offer to be Governor of the Philippines.

"Wild Bill" again sought public office in 1932 when he ran for Governor of New York against Herbert Lehman, but Lehman was swept into office in the Roosevelt landslide. Donovan returned to his law practice, devoting much of his time to assisting the American Legion in its efforts to find employment for military veterans.

As war ravaged Europe in 1940, Donovan undertook his first clandestine journey to Britain on behalf of President Franklin Roosevelt. There he met with Sir William Stephenson, the British intelligence agent known as "Intrepid," who was a confidant of Prime Minister Winston Churchill. Following their meeting, Donovan reported to Roosevelt that the British, with the aid of American ships and munitions, could survive the Nazi sweep across Europe. The United States ultimately provided that crucial military support.

It was also at this time that Donovan strongly urged the creation of an intelligence network for the United States. In July 1941 President Roosevelt appointed Donovan to head the Office of Coordinator of Information, charging him with the task of developing a comprehensive plan for a military intelligence agency to operate throughout the world. In June 1942 the Office of Strategic Services (OSS) was created and Donovan named as its director. He oversaw operations which gathered intelligence behind enemy lines in every theatre in World War II. He also participated in counterintelligence, sabotage, underground activities, propaganda, and psychological warfare. The legends credited to Donovan as "America's Spymaster" rival any fiction novel.

As head of the OSS, Donovan was privy to highly classified information and therefore not only required personal protection, but also carried the infamous OSS cyanide capsule, prepared to kill himself rather than face enemy interrogators. One feat credited to Donovan occurred after his office had perfected a quiet pistol. As the story goes, an excited Donovan eager to demonstrate his new discovery for the President, stormed into a startled FDR's office, tossed a sandbag on the floor, and proceeded to empty six rounds of ammunition into the sandbag.

WILLIAM J
DONOVAN

MEDAL OF HONOR
MAJ GEN
US ARMY
WORLD WAR I
JAN 1 1883
1959

After the war the OSS was dissolved, and when the CIA was created in 1947, Donovan held no position in the agency. He did serve as an aide to Robert H. Jackson, who was the chief prosecutor during the Nuremberg trials. In 1946 he ran unsuccessfully for the U.S. Senate and in 1953, at the age of seventy, he was appointed by President Dwight Eisenhower as Ambassador to Thailand, where he served for two years. Then in 1957, with his receipt of the National Security Medal, he became the first American to ever be awarded this country's top four decorations: The Medal of Honor, the Distinguished Service Cross, the Distinguished Service Medal, and the National Security Medal.

Donovan died on February 8, 1959 at Walter Reed Hospital in Washington, D.C. His grave in marked with a regulation government headstone, inscribed in gold to reflect his Medal of Honor status. Buried next to him is his son, **William James Donovan**, a U.S. Army veteran who served in Vietnam.

ABNER DOUBLEDAY

Inventor of Baseball?

(June 26, 1819–January 26, 1893)
Sec. 1, Lot 61, Grid NO–32/33

Although Abner Doubleday did establish the first cable car company in America, he did not—contrary to popular belief—invent baseball. In fact, Doubleday himself never claimed to have invented the game that has become our national pastime. He considered his greatest achievement to be his distinguished military career.

Doubleday was born in Ballston Spa, New York and grew up in Cooperstown. The grandson of a Revolutionary War veteran and the son of a newspaper editor, young Abner entered the United States Military Academy at West Point, graduating in 1842.

Like many other Civil War veterans, Doubleday got his first significant military experience in the Mexican War, where he served under General (and later President) Zachary Taylor. In 1856 he saw action again against the Seminole Indians in Florida. It was in 1861, after he was assigned to Charleston Harbor in South Carolina, that he was an eyewitness to the start of our nation's greatest domestic conflict. For it was at Charleston Harbor that soldiers of the young Confederacy first fired upon Union troops. The date was April 12, 1861, and Doubleday is credited with manning the first of Fort Sumter's guns to respond to this attack by the South.

Within two months he was promoted to Major and served with an infantry regiment in the Shenandoah Valley until the following year when he was assigned to assist in the defense of Washington, D.C. Promoted to Brigadier General of Volunteers in February of 1862, he took part in major battles in Maryland and Northern Virginia, including the Second Battle of Bull Run, Antietam, and Fredericksburg. In November of that same year, he became a Major General of Volunteers and was recognized for his command of the I Corps during the first day of battle at Gettysburg. Today a statue in his honor stands on the Gettysburg battlefield. Following his heroic performance at Gettysburg, Doubleday hoped for an even more important command, but his hopes were frustrated when he was reassigned to Washington, where he was stationed for the remainder of the war.

Following the Civil War, Doubleday reverted to the rank of Lieutenant Colonel, receiving a final promotion to full Colonel in September 1867. He retired from the Army in 1873 and moved to San Francisco where he started the first cable car company in America. Some years later he relocated to Mendham, New Jersey where he died in 1893.

Abner Doubleday's association with the invention of baseball is nearly a legend in itself. As our nation entered a new century, baseball had become widespread and a group of enthusiasts, led by former major leaguer and sporting goods kingpin Albert G. Spalding, established a commission under Spalding's direction to verify the origin of the sport. Relying upon very thin evidence, the commission decided that baseball had been founded in the United States and was "devised by Abner Doubleday at Cooperstown, New York in 1839." It is widely believed today, however, that a form of baseball had been played in the United States — and in England — long before Doubleday appeared on the scene. In Britain the sport was known as "rounders"; in colonial America it was called "townball." No doubt this information was discovered by Spalding's group, but they could hardly admit that the roots of our national pastime were found outside our own country, in Great Britain. What they did correctly verify was that Doubleday had codified some of the rules of the game, which they considered sufficient cause to declare Abner Doubleday, an American, the father of baseball.

Doubleday Field and The Baseball Hall of Fame and Museum at Cooperstown, New York were established in honor of Abner Doubleday during the celebration of baseball's centennial in 1939 by the citizens of Cooperstown. It is presently under the jurisdiction of Major League Baseball.

WILLIAM O. DOUGLAS

Supreme Court Justice, Environmentalist

(October 16, 1898–January 19, 1980)
Sec. 5, Lot 7004–B–1, Grid W–36

William O. Douglas served on the United States Supreme Court longer than any other Justice in history, and although his viewpoints during his lengthy tenure evoked fierce devotion from many supporters, he also twice faced impeachment by those who opposed his lifestyle and liberal viewpoints.

Born into an impoverished farm family just before the turn of the century in Maine, Minnesota, Douglas moved with his family to Yakima, Washington and spent his youth there. It was in Yakima that Douglas suffered an attack of polio. His therapy included hiking in the mountains near his home to strengthen his crippled legs and this therapy kindled his lifelong love of the outdoors.

Refusing to allow his polio to keep him from fighting for his nation during World War I, Douglas enlisted in the United States Army and fought in Europe. Douglas also refused to let poverty forestall his formal education, so he worked full-time to support himself and to pay his tuition at Whitman College in nearby Walla Walla. Following graduation in 1920, he was encouraged by his academic success to pursue a career in law and set his sights on Columbia University in New York City. Again working hard to support himself and to underwrite the costs of his own education, Douglas soon became one of Columbia's top law students and graduated Phi Beta Kappa in 1925.

Staying in New York, he joined a prestigious Wall Street firm, but realized after two years that corporate law was not what he desired. He returned to Yakima to enter private practice, but found that option undesirable as well. So the following year, Douglas returned to New York to join the faculty of Columbia University's School of Law. By 1933, as the Great Depression gripped the nation, he was teaching at Yale University Law School in New

Haven, Connecticut, and had developed a solid reputation as an expert in financial law. He had also gained the attention of President Franklin Roosevelt. Roosevelt, who was looking to staff the newly created Securities and Exchange Commission, turned to Douglas for his assistance. Joining the Commission in 1936, Douglas became its Chairman in 1937 and remained in that position until 1939.

On March 20, 1939 Roosevelt nominated Douglas to fill a vacancy on the United States Supreme Court, a vacancy created by the retirement of Justice Louis D. Brandeis. Within two weeks his nomination won confirmation by the Senate. However, despite this overwhelming initial display of Senate confidence, later members of that body twice attempted to impeach Justice Douglas.

Douglas became renowned as a champion of liberal causes and this reputation, coupled with his flamboyant personal lifestyle, fueled the fires of impeachment. Douglas married four times during his life; each of his first three marriages ending in divorce. In 1966, shortly after his third divorce, he married Cathleen Heffernan, a twenty-three-year-old summer waitress whom he met in Portland, Oregon. This marriage was viewed by some as utterly inappropriate for a Supreme Court Justice; others felt that marriage was a personal and private matter and that conservative critics of Douglas were exploiting his marriage for political reasons. The fourth Mrs. Douglas finished law school and was a prominent Washington attorney at the time of her husband's death.

Impeachment articles were first drafted against Douglas in 1953, but gained little support. Again in 1970 there was talk of impeachment. That threat of impeachment was spurred by resentment on the part of several conservative Senators of the rejection of two of President Richard Nixon's nominees for the Court. Like the earlier attempt, however, there proved to be little support to unseat Justice Douglas.

During the last years of his life, William O. Douglas suffered from ill health, relying on the use of a heart pacemaker, yet he refused to retire from the Court. It was widely reported that his reason for not stepping down was his unwillingness to allow President Nixon to name his successor. In January 1975, however, Douglas suffered a paralytic stroke. And, although he valiantly tried to continue his work on the bench, the burden was too great. In November of that same year he resigned. Seventy-seven years old, Douglas had served thirty-six years and seven months on the Supreme Court, eclipsing the career record of Justice **Oliver Wendell Holmes, Jr.** And if it was, in fact, Douglas' intent to deny President Nixon the nomination of his successor, Douglas succeeded. A year before Douglas retired, President Nixon himself resigned from office and Justice John Paul Stevens was named by President Gerald Ford to fill the vacancy on the Court.

Douglas' love of nature was memorialized in 1980 when the historic Chesapeake & Ohio Canal which runs along the Potomac River near Washington was renamed in his honor. He is buried near the graves of two other Supreme Court justices, **Oliver Wendell Holmes, Jr.** and **Potter Stewart**.

JOHN FOSTER DULLES

Senator, Secretary of State

(February 25, 1888–May 24, 1959)
Sec. 21, Lot 31, Grid MN–20/21

John Foster Dulles was the grandson of John Watson Foster, Secretary of State during the administration of President Benjamin Harrison and the nephew of Robert Lansing, President Woodrow Wilson's Secretary of State. So when President Dwight Eisenhower named him Secretary of State in 1953, it was a post for which, by his own account, he had trained and one he had sought throughout his lifetime.

Dulles, the son of a Presbyterian minister, was a brilliant student, both in the public schools of Watertown, New York and at Princeton University where he received his undergraduate degree. In 1908 he studied at the Sorbonne in Paris, then received his law degree in 1911 from George Washington University in Washington, D.C. That same year he joined the New York law firm of Sullivan and Cromwell.

Dulles' desire for a diplomatic career began early when in 1907, at the age of nineteen, he accompanied his grandfather, the former Secretary of State, to the Peace Conference at The Hague where the young Dulles served as a secretary to the Chinese delegation. Following his service as a Major in the United States Army in World War I, Dulles was appointed legal counsel to the U.S. delegation to the Versailles Peace Conference.

Soon Dulles returned to his international law practice with Sullivan and Cromwell, and by 1927 was head of the firm. His diplomatic portfolio further expanded in 1945 when he participated in the Dumbarton Oaks Conference at which the United Nations Charter was drafted. After chairing the U.S. delegation to the United Nations General Assembly in Paris in 1948, Dulles was chosen the next year by Governor Thomas Dewey of New York as interim United States Senator from that state to fill the term of Robert F. Wagner, who had retired due to ill health. In the subsequent election, Dulles sought to retain that Senate seat but was unsuccessful.

America's postwar diplomatic efforts were stalled in 1946. The United States could not successfully seal a peace treaty with Japan that would also include the Soviet Union. So President Harry Truman and his Secretary of State, Dean Acheson, charged Dulles with the extraordinary task of negotiating the Japanese peace treaty. Circumnavigating the globe, Dulles gained international acclaim for successfully managing the complex negotiations which resulted in a treaty signed by forty-nine nations.

Following Dwight Eisenhower's victory in the presidential election of 1952, the new President announced his first Cabinet appointment: John Foster Dulles, Secretary of State. During his tenure as America's chief diplomat, Dulles guided American foreign policy through the early days of the Cold War. A man of deep religious beliefs, he detested Communism, assailing its shortcomings at every opportunity. Dulles used his mastery of negotiating techniques to seek and conclude vital pacts which remain today as cornerstones of American foreign policy, including the Southeast Asia Treaty Organization (SEATO).

Critically ill with cancer, John Foster Dulles resigned his office on April 15, 1959. He was awarded the Medal of Freedom shortly before he died on May 24, 1959. His funeral at Arlington was attended by President Eisenhower, Vice-President Richard Nixon, and the entire foreign diplomatic corps.

MEDGAR WILEY EVERS

Civil Rights Activist

(July 2, 1925–June 12, 1963)
Sec. 36, Lot 1431, Grid BB–40

On June 12, 1963 President **John F. Kennedy** made a televised address to the nation on the subject of civil rights. Kennedy's message was clear: there must be equal rights and equal opportunities for all Americans, regardless of race. The President's statement was prompted by a variety of circumstances, but the most recent and most dramatic event had occurred just the day before when Alabama Governor George Wallace had denounced integration and had symbolically blocked the entrance to the University of Alabama. Across America that evening, people gathered in front of their television sets to hear President **Kennedy's** message. Many welcomed the President's steadfast commitment to civil rights, while others resented the President's interference in a local system they felt should be maintained. Joining the millions of Americans who watched the President's message that evening was Medgar Evers, field secretary of the National Association for the Advancement of Colored People (NAACP) in Mississippi. When the President finished speaking, Evers himself addressed a rally of civil rights proponents in Jackson, Mississippi. Just after midnight, on his way home from that rally, he was murdered.

At the time of his tragic death, Medgar Evers was not a nationally-known civil rights leader. In fact—though he worked tirelessly travelling across the state to recruit members, register voters, and organize economic boycotts—outside of Mississippi he was a relatively obscure figure. Born in Decatur, Mississippi in 1925, Evers was the son of a lumberjack. He attended segregated schools in Newton County and enlisted in the Army following his high school graduation. During the war, among other actions, Evers took part in the landing at Normandy on D-Day (June 6, 1944), and for his gallant service was awarded two Bronze Stars.

After being honorably discharged in 1946, Evers entered Alcorn A&M College in Lorman, Mississippi, paying for his education with the GI Bill. While there he played halfback on the football team and in 1952 earned a degree in business administration. Following graduation he embarked on a career as an insurance salesman. It was during this period that Evers began organizing local chapters of the NAACP on a part-time basis. In 1954 he left his insurance job and became the first full-time field secretary for the NAACP in Mississippi, dedicating his life to the advancement of the rights of black Americans. So it was with great interest that Medgar Evers listened to the words of **John Kennedy** on that June night in 1963.

The civil rights leader had just arrived home, parking his car in his driveway and turning toward the side entrance to his house which opened under the carport. The overhead light hanging under the carport silhouetted Evers, making him an easy target for the sniper who was hiding in nearby bushes. A bullet from a high-powered rifle struck Evers just below the right shoulder blade and passed entirely through his body. Evers staggered toward the doorway, but collapsed near the steps to the house. His wife and three children rushed to the door, their screams waking a neighbor. Together they lifted the wounded Evers into the neighbor's station wagon and rushed him to University Hospital in Jackson. There was little the doctors could do; Medgar Evers died of his wounds just after 1:00 A.M.

Byron de la Beckwith, a self-avowed segregationist was indicted for the murder of Medgar Evers and was twice tried for the crime. In both cases, however, all-white juries were chosen and were unable to reach a verdict. De la Beckwith was set free. However, in 1975 he was convicted of an unrelated weapons charge.

From relative obscurity, Evers became a nationally-known figure, the symbol of black pride and a martyr of the civil rights struggle in America. He was posthumously awarded the 1963 Springarn Medal of the NAACP. Medgar Evers was buried in June 1963 with full military honors at Arlington National Cemetery.

SIR MOSES J. EZEKIEL

Sculptor of the Confederate Monument

(October 28, 1844–March 27, 1917)
Sec. 16, Buried at the base of the Monument

Following his service in the Confederate Army, Moses Ezekiel studied art and music in Berlin, then took up residence in Rome for forty years. Yet, with roots steeped in Virginia soil, he was drawn back to America to design and sculpt what was—by his own account—his favorite work: The Confederate Monument at Arlington National Cemetery.

Born in Richmond, Virginia Moses Ezekiel's propensity for

art became evident at an early age. At ten, he was cutting out shadow pictures; by age fourteen, he was drawing and painting as well as writing poetry. Initially, Ezekiel's love of art was of great concern to his parents because—as Orthodox Jews—their religion forbade the creation of graven images. But young Moses' artistic talents could not be suppressed, and his parents came to recognize their son's extraordinary gifts.

Ezekiel was a cadet at the Virginia Military Institute when the Civil War began in 1864 and left school to fight for the Confederacy. Joining other VMI cadets, he took part in the battle of New Market, Virginia, under General, John C. Breckinridge. Ezekiel returned to graduate from VMI in 1868, then studied anatomy at the Medical College of Virginia. After living briefly in Cincinnati, Ohio, he went to Berlin in 1869 to study at the Royal Academy of Art.

While living in Berlin in the 1870s, Ezekiel supplemented his income by acting as a news correspondent during the Franco-Prussian War, but was arrested by the Prussians and imprisoned for a short time under suspicion of being a French spy. In 1874 the Jewish order, Sons of the Covenant, commissioned Ezekiel to execute a sculpture for display at the Centennial Exhibition in Philadelphia. The result was a marble group symbolizing religious liberty, considered one of his best and best-known works. While living in Europe, Ezekiel also studied music under Franz Liszt and eventually executed a bust of the music master.

After moving to Rome in 1874, Ezekiel was ultimately knighted by Italian King Victor Emmanuel for his outstanding contribution to art. Ezekiel received numerous international awards during his lifetime, including a decoration by the German Emperor.

On March 6, 1906 Secretary of War **William Howard Taft** approved plans of the United Daughters of the Confederacy to erect a memorial to the Confederate dead in Arlington National Cemetery. Ezekiel was chosen to design and sculpt the monument because, as a Civil War veteran, he brought to the work an unparalleled knowledge of the subject. The magnificent monument was dedicated on June 4, 1914.

Moses Ezekiel died in Rome on March 27, 1917, but because of the hostilities raging in Europe at the time, his remains could not be transported back to the United States. Four years later, on

March 30, 1921, funeral services for Ezekiel were held in the recently completed Memorial Amphitheatre at Arlington National Cemetery—the first ever to be held there. President Warren G. Harding called Ezekiel, "A great Virginian, a great artist, a great American and a great citizen of world fame." The Italian Ambassador, who participated in the funeral services, claimed Ezekiel as an "adopted son of Italy." Following the solemn services, Sir Moses Ezekiel was laid to rest at the base of the monument that he created.

JAMES VINCENT FORRESTAL

First Secretary of Defense

(February 15, 1892–May 22, 1949)
Sec. 30, Grave 674, Grid X–39

James Vincent Forrestal, a tireless worker and dedicated public servant, not only served valiantly as Secretary of the Navy during World War II, but also undertook the massive reorganization of the armed forces into the Department of Defense which he headed after the war. Tragically, the nonstop pace and hard-driving demands of his life finally took their toll. Suffering from severe fatigue and depression, Forrestal took his own life in 1949, becoming the highest ranking government official in American history ever to do so.

James Forrestal, the third son of Irish immigrants, was born in Beacon, New York. He entered Dartmouth College in 1911, but transferred to Princeton University the following year. Without explanation, he left school six weeks before graduation, never receiving his degree. However, the lack of academic credentials did not hinder his career. In 1916 he joined the well-known Wall Street investment firm of William E. Read & Company (later Dillon, Read & Company). A year later, when the United States entered the war in Europe, Forrestal enlisted in the Navy and won his aviator's wings, seeing action from several U.S. bases. He resigned in 1919 as a First Lieutenant and returned to Dillon, Read, where his career skyrocketed. Within weeks of his rejoining the firm, he made investment headlines resulting in his promotion to partner in 1923, vice-president in 1926, and ultimately president in 1938. His success did not escape the attention of President Franklin Roosevelt, another New Yorker, who appointed him the first Under Secretary of the Navy in 1940. In 1941 Forrestal represented Roosevelt in London, establishing a close liaison with the British Admiralty. Then, when **William Franklin Knox** died in April 1944, Forrestal succeeded him as Secretary of the Navy, a Cabinet level position at that time.

Applying proven business management techniques to his responsibilities as Navy Secretary, Forrestal established himself as a tireless administrator with an indefatigable drive to succeed. He continued as Secretary of the Navy under President Harry Truman, gaining special notoriety for his vocal opposition to Truman's decision to use atomic weapons against the Japanese toward the end of World War II. He was integrally influential in allowing the Japanese Emperor to retain his throne after the war to provide stability for the Japanese people.

On September 17, 1947 Forrestal accepted the position of Secretary of Defense, becoming the first person to serve in that capacity. He was charged with the immense responsibility of bringing all branches of the armed services under a single department head and at the same time coping with massive post-war demilitarization. Many believe the challenge to oversee these responsibilities was more than any one person could have managed. Forrestal was confronted with opposition from every direction. Military personnel, steeped in their own traditions, opposed the unification that Forrestal was mandated to achieve. He fought regularly with the President and Congress over the size of the budget he was given. The 1946 defense appropriation of

$45 billion shrank to $14.5 billion in 1947 and to $11.25 billion in 1948. Forrestal argued that this was inadequate to guarantee a strong national defense. He also waged a public campaign against the Truman administration's decision to recognize Israel, a stance which cost him widespread support.

By 1949 Forrestal's behavior was becoming notably erratic; his physical health was deteriorating. Increasingly irate in public and unwilling to make necessary decisions, he resigned on March 1, 1949. For his long and valued public career, he was awarded the Distinguished Service Medal by President Truman. Shortly thereafter he was admitted to Bethesda Naval Hospital for psychiatric care. Sadly, on May 22, 1949, after several prior attempts at suicide, James Forrestal threw himself from a sixteenth floor window to his death.

Forrestal was buried at Arlington with full military honors before a large crowd which included President Truman. His grave lies on a small hilltop beneath towering oak trees and is marked by a simple granite stone bearing the epitaph: "In the Great Cause of Good Government."

ADOLPHUS WASHINGTON GREELY

Arctic Adventurer

(March 27, 1844–October 20, 1935)
Sec. 1, Lot 129, Grid NO–32/33

Although Adolphus Greely lived to receive a Congressional Medal of Honor on his ninety-first birthday, he nearly lost his life during a treacherous adventure that killed eighteen other men and left him and his crew abandoned in the Arctic for nearly two years.

In their 1879 meeting at Hamburg, Germany the International Geographical Congress recommended the establishment of a chain of thirteen circumpolar stations in the Arctic. Following that recommendation, the United States Congress in 1881 authorized the appropriation of $25,000 to undertake the "Lady Franklin Bay Expedition." Granted command of the expedition was Lieutenant Adolphus Greely, who volunteered for the service and was authorized to take two officers and twenty-one volunteer enlisted men along with him on this dangerous journey. He was further authorized to charter a steam vessel for transport and to hire Eskimo hunters as guides.

The vessel he selected was the *Proteus*, an ironclad whaler which he felt would be able to negotiate the treacherous icy waters of the Arctic. This ship was to deliver the expedition to its proposed encampment and to return with supplies the following year. Because communication from the Arctic did not exist in the 1880s, it was necessary to arrange relief expeditions prior to getting underway so that if an expedition should run into difficulty, a rescue vessel would arrive...eventually. For Greely's expedition, arrangements had been made for the *Proteus* to seek them in 1882. If that mission should fail, then a second relief effort would be launched in 1883. Fully supplied, the *Proteus* set sail for the Arctic on July 4, 1881.

Greely's scientific expedition landed on the previously uncharted northeastern side of Ellesmere Island, north of Greenland in August 1881. Here they established Fort Conger where they conducted daily observations of weather and tides and collected samples of minerals, flora, and fauna for study. Sledge trips were made to the western side of the island during which Greely and his men set a new farthest north record by reaching 83 degrees and 24 minutes north of the equator. But sadly, the adventure ended in tragedy.

One year later, in August 1882, the party desperately awaited the arrival of the *Proteus*, but the ship never came. It was later learned that the ship had sunk in the Arctic waters on its way to meet Greely. Trapped then in the Arctic for another winter and with no new supplies, Greely and his crew rationed their food as they counted the days until the second relief vessel's scheduled arrival. When that vessel also failed to reach them in August 1883, the brave band of explorers abandoned their settlement and traveled southward in five small boats. In fifty-one days the party covered five hundred miles, landing at Bedford Pym Island in Smith Sound, still well within the Arctic Circle. Unable to travel farther, the weary crew, left with less than forty days rations, faced the long and brutal Arctic winter of two hundred fifty days.

During the journey, one Eskimo drowned; another was shot on Greely's orders for pilfering what was left of the meager rations. Throughout the ordeal, Lt. Greely kept a diary in the sad belief that if no one survived, someday someone might know their fate. The diary provides us with the gruesome details of their plight. Surviving the most arduous of conditions, the remaining crew members attempted to find what food they could to save their own diminishing food supplies. They ate frozen lichens and searched for any form of animal life. Occasionally, they killed a polar bear or a seal only to see it disappear beneath the floes. By April 3, 1884 their rations were reduced to five pounds of meat and three pounds of dried bread for a dozen men.

By June—without food of any kind, forced to eat their boots and the remnants of their seal skin clothing—only seven men were left alive. Finally Greely and his six crewmen, near death, spotted the *Thetis*, a relief ship, on June 23. Under the command of **Winfield Scott Schley**, the crew of the *Thetis* revived Greely and his men and returned them to a somber but happy welcome in the United States. For his extraordinary survival efforts, Greely was awarded medals from the Royal and the French Geographical Societies.

Greely was born in Newburyport, Massachusetts where he graduated from high school in 1860. Only 17, he bluffed his way into the Massachusetts Infantry as a volunteer private during the Civil War, seeing action in several major battles, including Antietam and Fredericksburg. During that war he was wounded three times.

After Greely's return from the Arctic, most of his military service was spent building telegraph lines throughout the Western United States, Cuba, Puerto Rico, and the Philippines. By 1906 he was promoted to Brigadier General—the first volunteer private ever to reach that rank—and was placed in charge of all relief operations after the San Francisco earthquake. He retired in 1908.

In 1911 President **William Howard Taft** selected Greely to head the delegation to the Coronation of King George V of England. He was also a founder of the National Geographic Society, serving on its board for forty-seven years. Years later, on his ninety-first birthday—March 27, 1935—Greely accepted a Congressional Medal of Honor, awarded to him for a "life of splendid service." Six months later, he died in his home in Washington, D.C.

WILLIAM FREDERICK ("BULL") HALSEY, JR.

Fleet Admiral of the United States Navy

(October 30, 1882–August 16, 1959)
Sec. 2, Lot 1184, Grid T-31

William Frederick Halsey, Jr. was the son of a career naval officer and, like his father, attended the United States Naval Academy at Annapolis. Graduating in 1904 Halsey was first assigned to the battleship *Kansas* which steamed around the world as part of President Theodore Roosevelt's Great White Fleet. During World War I, he served aboard patrol and escort vessels based in Ireland, earning a Navy Cross for his brilliant maneuvers in seas occupied by enemy submarines and laden with mines.

After the war, Halsey's career turned to diplomacy. He served as Naval Attache to the U.S. embassies in Germany, Sweden, Denmark, and Norway. Then in 1935 Halsey returned to active sea duty, commanding the carrier *Saratoga* and later completing flight training. He earned his wings as a naval aviator at the age of fifty-two, becoming the oldest American service personnel ever to do so. Subsequently, he was named Commandant of the Pensacola Naval Air Station, attaining the rank of Rear Admiral. By 1940, he was a Vice Admiral, commanding all aircraft carriers in the Pacific Fleet.

When the Japanese attacked Pearl Harbor, Halsey was with his force aboard the carrier *Enterprise*, 150 miles west of Oahu. He anchored the vessel at Pearl Harbor long enough to refuel, then set out to sea again by December 9 under orders to hunt Japanese submarines. He directed surprise forays against Japanese positions in the Marshall and Gilbert Islands, as well as on Wake Island. In April 1942 it was from one of his ships, under the command of Captain **Marc Mitscher**, that Colonel Jimmy Doolittle's famed B-25 Bombers were able to maneuver close enough to the Japanese mainland for air raids on the city of Tokyo.

In October 1942 Halsey was chosen to command the South Pacific Area Force and played an important role in the pivotal battles of Santa Cruz and Guadalcanal. Promoted to Commander of the Third Fleet in June 1944, Halsey teamed with the Seventh Fleet and provided support for Douglas MacArthur's invasion of the Philippines, defeating the Japanese Fleet in Leyte Gulf. With the Philippines liberated, Halsey's bombers conducted more raids on Tokyo and other naval installations, and when the Japanese surrendered the official surrender ceremonies took place aboard Halsey's flagship, *Missouri* on September 2, 1945 in Tokyo Bay.

In December of 1945, President Harry Truman elevated Halsey to five-star status, naming him Fleet Admiral of the Navy, and making him one of only five men in our nation's history to ever hold that rank. Retiring from the Navy in 1947 Halsey turned his attentions to the private sector where he served as president of International Telecommunications Laboratories for six years. He died in 1957 and was buried next to his father, **William Frederick Halsey, Sr.**, a Navy captain.

SAMUEL DASHIELL HAMMETT

Detective Novelist

(May 27, 1894–January 10, 1961)
Sec. 12, Lot 508, Grid YZ–23

"Samuel Spade's jaw was long and bony, his chin a jutting *V* under the more flexible *V* of his mouth. . . . He said to Effie

Perine: 'Yes, sweetheart?'" Thus Dashiell Hammett introduced his most famous detective in his most popular novel, *The Maltese Falcon*, published in 1930. Dash Hammett was himself no stranger to Sam Spade's lifestyle; he had been a detective during the 1920s, leading the same hard-boiled life he wrote about.

Hammett was born in St. Mary's County, Maryland and grew up in Baltimore. By age thirteen he had dropped out of school, choosing to work at low-paying jobs from messenger boy to stevedore. At twenty-one he joined the Pinkerton Detective Agency, interrupting his eight-year detective career to serve in World War I. Although Hammett reached the rank·of Sergeant during his military career, he also contracted tuberculosis and spent much of his time in Army hospitals immediately after the war.

It was in 1928 that Hammett emerged as a pioneer of the "hard-boiled" detective novel. His first books, *Red Harvest* and *The Dane Curse* set the stage for his finest work, *The Maltese Falcon*. That book which was the basis for the classic 1941 film starring Humphrey Bogart, propelled Dashiell Hammett into literary stardom as a fiction writer. Another of his works which spawned a motion picture and later a television series was *The Thin Man* (1934), in

The government headstone marking the grave of Samuel D. Hammett yields few clues that this is the grave of detective novelist Dashiell Hammett.

which Hammett introduced witty amateur detectives, Nick and Nora Charles. Hammett also tried his hand at creating comic strips for a time, but his "Secret Agent X-9" could never match the success of Dick Tracy.

During the 1930s Hammett began to take interest in left-wing political activities and in the defense of civil liberties. His appearance at Marxist rallies prompted the FBI to place him under surveillance. Nevertheless, Hammett—who bitterly opposed Hitler and Mussolini—enlisted for military service in World War II. It is reported that under suspicion by the Army, he was assigned to the remote Aleutian island of Adak, eight hundred miles off the

Alaskan coast. There, on that barren island, he edited a military newspaper for nearly two years.

After the war, he resumed his political activities and became a trustee of the Civil Rights Congress. As such, he knew the names of persons who had contributed to its bail bond fund. Amidst the widespread anti-Communist furor of the postwar period, he was subpoenaed and questioned about these contributors. When he refused to divulge their names, he was sentenced to six months in jail, a sentence which he dutifully served. Commenting on his sentence, Hammett displayed some of Sam Spade's defiance: "If it were more than jail, if it were my life, I would give it for what I think democracy is, and I don't let cops or judges tell me what I think democracy is."

Throughout his adult life Dash Hammett maintained a close, romantic relationship with playwright Lillian Hellman, who he acknowledged as the model for his fictional character, Nora Charles. At age thirty-nine, he virtually stopped writing, and his later years were marked by chronic ill health. By the time he died in 1961 he had become a veritable recluse in his cottage in Katonah, New York. Hammett's burial at Arlington National Cemetery prompted objections from the FBI, but burial here was what Dashiell Hammett wanted; and it was an honor he had earned. His grave is marked by a standard government tombstone, just one in a long line of similar stones. It reads simply, "Samuel D. Hammett."

LEWIS BLAINE HERSHEY

General, Director of the Selective Service System

(September 12, 1893–May 5, 1977)
Sec. 7, Lot 8197–D, VW–24

General Lewis B. Hershey remained on active duty in the United States Army for more than sixty-two years, rising to the rank of Four-Star General and serving as Director of the Selective Service System through three wars. Yet, to those who opposed the war in Vietnam, this Four-Star General—the only one in American history never to serve in combat—became a symbol of American involvement in a tragic war.

General Hershey began his military career when he left his home in Steuben County, Indiana to join the National Guard. There he won election to First Lieutenant just as his unit was called for duty in 1916 along the Mexican border. In October of 1917 he was promoted to Captain in the Guard, but was commissioned in the regular Army in 1920.

Hershey entered the Command and General Staff School in August of 1931, despite the loss of vision in his left eye from being struck by a mallet during a polo match in 1927. He completed study at the Army War College in 1933 and reported for duty as Secretary to the Joint Army and Navy Selective Service Committee in 1936. Hershey's first assignment was planning for a possible wartime mobilization of manpower. One result of his committee's work was the passage of the Selective Training and Service Act in 1940. In July 1941 President Franklin Roosevelt appointed then Brigadier General Hershey to be Director of the Selective Service System, a position Hershey held for nearly thirty years.

Under Hershey's system, thirteen million men were drafted during World War II. After the war when the draft laws expired, Hershey—who had risen in rank to Major General—remained as Director of Selective Service Records and dedicated himself to the planning of future mobilization.

Because of threats by the Soviet Union and other potential adversaries, the Selective Service System was reestablished in 1948 and did not again expire during Hershey's tenure in the Army. The large scale drafting of young men was renewed during the Korean War in the early 1950s, but it was not until the escalation of the war in Vietnam in the mid-1960s that Hershey's position became controversial. Then in his midseventies, Hershey's support for restricted deferments, his advanced age, and his strong support of the Vietnam War made him an issue in the 1968 presidential campaign. Democratic candidate Hubert Humphrey threatened to fire Hershey and Republican Richard Nixon considered the General a political liability. After Nixon was elected, he removed Hershey as Director of the Selective Service but named him a presidential advisor on manpower and promoted him to full general. This promotion made Hershey the first full General never to have served in combat. Because Hersey refused to retire on his own, the army retired him in April 1973 after sixty-two years of active duty. He died four years later.

OLIVER WENDELL HOLMES, JR.

Civil War Veteran, Supreme Court Justice

(March 8, 1841–March 6,1935)
Sec. 5, Lot 7004, Grid VW–36

To say that Oliver Wendell Holmes, Jr. had a long and distinguished career is to grossly understate the achievements of a man whose career saw him wounded during the Civil War, teach law at Harvard, sit on the Massachusetts state supreme court for twenty years, sit for another thirty years on the United States Supreme Court, and resign only to advise President Franklin Roosevelt on the appointment of his successor.

As a child growing up in Boston, Holmes was the product of an aristocratic environment which stressed character and accomplishment. The descendant of two established Boston families, he was the maternal grandson of Charles Jackson, a justice of the Massachusetts supreme court, and the son of Oliver Wendell Holmes, Sr., the physician and celebrated poet who penned such noted works as "Old Ironsides" and "The Autocrat of the Breakfast Table." The senior Holmes exercised a great deal of influence over his eldest son, especially by acquainting him with a circle of friends that included such literary giants as Ralph Waldo Emerson, Nathaniel Hawthorne, Henry Wadsworth Longfellow, and Herman Melville.

Oliver, Jr. attended private schools· and entered Harvard University at age sixteen. During his last year at Harvard the Civil War began and, expecting to be called before he could graduate, he enlisted in the Army. Holmes was, however, able to receive his degree and was chosen class poet, just as his father had been thirty-two years earlier. Upon graduation Holmes was commissioned as a Lieutenant in the Twentieth Massachusetts Regiment of Volunteers and began a wartime experience that affected his entire life.

During the Civil War Holmes was wounded three times. The first was near Leesburg, Virginia at the Battle of Ball's Bluff, where he was shot in the chest. Survival meant a treacherous trip down the bluff above the Potomac and across the river in the midst of enemy gunfire. Miraculously Holmes survived, only to be wounded again at Antietam, this time in the throat. Slower to recover from this wound, Holmes nonetheless returned to the front and was wounded a third time at Chancellorsville when his foot was hit with shrapnel.

The best-known tale of Holmes' Civil War experience occurred later in the war. In July 1864 Confederate General Jubal Early's forces were threatening Washington, D.C. Holmes, now under the command of General **Horatio Wright**, was chosen to escort President Abraham Lincoln to Fort Stephens on the outskirts of the city. Lincoln, anxious to witness his first battle confrontation, was so intrigued by the fighting that he climbed up on the rampart to get a better view. The sight of the tall, lanky President in his stovepipe hat immediately drew fire from the Confederate troops, but Lincoln was unfazed. In a gentlemanly and subordinate manner, General Wright attempted to convince the President to take cover, but he met with little success. It was obvious to Holmes that the President was not going to guard himself against the clear and present danger of the Confederate gunfire. Exasperated, Holmes shouted at Lincoln, "Get down, you fool!" The President immediately obeyed the command and later expressed his gratitude to Holmes. "Captain," he said, "I'm glad that you know how to talk to a civilian."

The war finally over, Holmes returned to Harvard to study law, his wartime experiences having irrevocably deepened his passion for life. He was admitted to practice law in 1867, but found a certain rigidity in the precedent-oriented law of the midnineteenth century. To Holmes too many concepts were kept alive long after they had lost their relevance. Addressing this problem, he published his classic treatise, "The Common Law," in 1881. In this legal masterwork, he advocates a legal system which is fluid and flexible enough to change with the needs of society instead of being bogged down by antiquated precedents.

In December 1882 Holmes was appointed to the Supreme Judicial Court of Massachusetts, becoming its Chief Justice in 1899 and serving in that position until 1902 when a vacancy occurred on the United States Supreme Court. President Theodore Roosevelt was looking for a successor to Justice Horace Gray who had resigned. He had asked then-Governor of the Philippines, **William Howard Taft**, to accept the appointment, but Taft declined. Next, Roosevelt turned to Holmes. The President was impressed with Holmes' opinions in corporate antitrust cases, as well as his progressive labor views at a time when the labor movement was rapidly expanding. Holmes, at age sixty-one, accepted the appointment.

For twenty-nine years Holmes remained on the Court and although he disappointed Roosevelt with many of his opinions, he became one of the most respected jurists in American history. Justice Holmes was known as "the Great Dissenter," not because he frequently dissented (fewer than one in ten of his opinions were in the minority), but because of the brilliant legal reasoning found in his written opinions. He strongly advocated the doctrine of "judicial restraint," which discourages judges from allowing their personal opinions to influence their legal decisions. "Judicial restraint" is now a dominant force in the American judicial system.

Oliver Wendell Holmes, Jr. remained on the Supreme Court

of our nation until January 12, 1932, just two months short of his ninety-first birthday, the oldest man to ever sit on the bench. Amazingly, most legal scholars agree that many of Holmes' best decisions were written when he was well past eighty years of age.

For twenty-five years Holmes did not miss a single session of the Court, walking every day the two and one-half miles from his home to the Capitol building, where the Supreme Court met until its present building was completed in 1935. Also, even though Justices were exempted, he voluntarily paid federal income tax every year. Regarding taxes, he said, "Taxes are what we pay for a civilized society." That statement now is inscribed on the frieze of the Internal Revenue Service building in Washington, D.C.

After Holmes retired in 1932, President Franklin Roosevelt called upon the former Justice to discuss a possible successor. The President found Holmes reading Plato and, wondered aloud why a ninety-two-year-old man would read Greek philosophy. Without missing a step, Holmes quipped, "To improve my mind, Mr. President." Roosevelt appointed Benjamin Cardozo to the Court.

Holmes and his wife, Fanny Dixwell Holmes, had been married for fifty-seven years when she died in 1929. Upon her death Chief Justice **William Howard Taft** made arrangements for her burial at Arlington, knowing that Justice Holmes desired to be buried there himself but was too shy to request it. Holmes died six years later on March 6, 1935, just two days before his ninety-fourth birthday. He was buried with full military honors, next to his wife, a privilege he had earned seventy years earlier during the Civil War.

JULIET OPIE HOPKINS

Florence Nightingale of the South

(May 7, 1818–March 9, 1890)
Sec. 1, Lot 12, Grid N–33

Juliet Opie Hopkins was a genuine Confederate heroine. So great was America's respect for her, that twenty-five years after the Civil War she was awarded full military burial honors by the United States Army at Arlington National Cemetery.

Born in Jefferson County, Virginia, she was married at the age of nineteen to A.G. Gordon, a Navy Lieutenant who died in 1849. She later met Arthur F. Hopkins, a justice of the Alabama Supreme Court, and although he was twenty-four years her senior, they were married in 1854. Living in Mobile, Alabama at the outbreak of the Civil War, Juliet Hopkins offered her services to the state and was sent to Richmond, Virginia where she took charge of the Alabama section of the Chimborazo Hospital.

In November 1861 the Alabama legislature named Judge Hopkins to be State Hospital Agent, though that state's true intent was for Mrs. Hopkins to fulfill the duties of the office while her husband held the title. Immediately she set about the task of staffing, supplying, and managing base and field hospitals, proving herself to be an effective and resourceful administrator. Juliet Hopkins was so dedicated to her cause that she expended much of her personal fortune and that of Judge Hopkins to staff and equip the hospitals she established.

Her care and concern were not confined to the hospitals alone. She frequently left the security of her hospital office to go onto the battlefields to treat the wounded. On May 31, 1862, at Seven Pines (Fair Oaks), while assisting a wounded Confederate soldier, she was hit by a wayward bullet that left her with a permanent limp.

The high quality of health care in the hospitals under Hopkins' supervision won widespread acclaim. She received the profound gratitude of many commanding generals, including Robert E. Lee who once wrote to her: "You have done more for the South than all the women." Hopkins is now buried on the grounds of Lee's former home. She was further honored when her likeness was put on the $100 bill issued by the Confederate state of Alabama.

In 1890 Juliet Hopkins died while visiting her adopted daughter in Washington, D.C. She is buried with her son-in-law, General **Romeyn E. Ayers**, who preceded her in death. For nearly one hundred years the grave of Juliet Opie Hopkins was marked only by the headstone of her son-in-law. Finally, in 1987 the oversight was corrected when a new government regulation headstone was erected to mark the grave of the woman known as the Florence Nightingale of the South.

ROBERT GREEN INGERSOLL

Nationally Known Orator, Agnostic Philosopher

(August 11, 1833–July 21, 1899)
Sec. 3, Lot 1620, Grid S–16/17

Robert Ingersoll became one of the best known men in the latter half of the nineteenth century for openly criticizing religion and espousing a humanistic philosophy that endorsed both civil rights and sexual equality. He was both greatly admired and greatly despised.

Born in Dresden, New York Robert Ingersoll, the son of a Congregational minister, discarded the teachings of the Bible when he was still a boy. After growing up in Illinois, and despite a lack of formal education, he was admitted to the Illinois bar and began a lucrative law practice in Peoria. His masterful oratory in the courtroom contributed to his reputation as an outstanding trial lawyer. Yet even his own profession was not exempt from his cutting barbs. For example, after commenting on the luxury of a gas-lighted office, he stated, "Gas, you know, is an excellent thing in law; in fact, indispensable."

During the Civil War Ingersoll was commissioned a Colonel

in the cavalry and was captured near Corinth, Mississippi. Although soon released, he still made time to treat his captors to a rousing antislavery speech.

After the war Ingersoll turned to politics, becoming a staunch Republican. He served as Illinois Attorney General from 1867 to 1869, and stumped for the party's presidential candidates, making notable contributions to the Republican cause. He hoped for but was never awarded a Cabinet post. Quite simply, the Republican administrations, while quick to accept his oratorical contributions to their campaigns, were afraid of his unorthodox religious views. They viewed him as a political liability.

Ingersoll never hesitated to acknowledge his agnosticism or to cast doubt on the Bible. He was decried as a "moral leper" by clergymen at the same time as he was lauded by such literary giants as Mark Twain and Walt Whitman who hailed Ingersoll's fresh attitude toward humanity. The cornerstone of his beliefs was the family; he revered his own wife and daughters.

Ingersoll strongly advocated equal rights for blacks and women. He defended Susan B. Anthony from hecklers when she spoke in Peoria; when every hotel in the city refused to house Frederick Douglass, Ingersoll welcomed the black journalist into his home. Despite his highly unorthodox views on religion and social order, Ingersoll enjoyed great popularity as a public speaker. He died in Dobbs Ferry, New York in 1899 at the age of sixty-five. His writings, published posthumously, fill twelve volumes.

IWO JIMA MARINES

On February 23, 1945 Associated Press photographer Joe Rosenthal was nearby as a group of six Marines planted the United States flag atop Mount Suribachi on the tiny island of Iwo Jima. The resulting photograph has become the single most famous photograph taken during World War II. The six men captured in that photo became instant celebrities. Those six Marines are Corporal Harlan H. Block, PM2/C John H. Bradley, PFC **Rene Gagnon**, PFC **Ira Hayes**, PFC Franklin R. Sousley, and Sgt.

Michael Strank. Three of these men are buried in Arlington National Cemetery. They are:

RENE ARTHUR GAGNON

(March 7, 1926–October 12, 1979)
Sec. 51, Lot 543, Grid DD–47/48

FOR GOD AND HIS COUNTRY
HE RAISED OUR FLAG IN BATTLE

A bronze plaque which recreates the famous flag-raising on Iwo Jima Island during World War II is mounted on the grave of Rene Gagnon, one of the six men shown and one of three who are buried at Arlington.

Rene Gagnon was born in Manchester, New Hampshire where he attended local schools before leaving high school to work in a textile mill. On May 6, 1943 Gagnon was inducted into the Marine Corps Reserve and sent to Parris Island, South Carolina. Promoted to First Class on July 16, 1943, he was assigned to the Twenty-eighth Marines at Camp Pendleton on April 8, 1944.

Gagnon was with the Twenty-eighth Marines when they assaulted the beaches of Iwo Jima on February 19, 1945, and he was atop Mount Suribachi on the 23rd when the United States colors were planted. Following the Marines' victory on Iwo Jima, Gagnon was ordered to Washington, D.C. because of the public interest generated by Rosenthal's photo. He joined the other two survivors to make public appearances in connection with the Seventh War Loan Drive which featured the photo on its publicity poster. When the tour was completed, Gagnon was married in Baltimore and reassigned to San Diego.

Gagnon was again sent overseas on November 7, serving in China until he was discharged on April 27, 1946 after three years in the Marines. After his discharge he returned to Manchester, New Hampshire where he resided until his sudden death on October 12, 1979. Gagnon was buried in Mount Calvary Mausoleum in Manchester until permission could be obtained to allow his reinterment at Arlington. Since Corporal Gagnon did not meet burial requirements for Arlington at the time of his death, a waiver of policy was necessary. It was granted on April 16, 1981, and on July 7th of that year he was buried at Arlington.

IRA HAMILTON HAYES

(January 12, 1923–January 24, 1955)
Sec. 34, Lot 479A, Grid U–11

Ira Hayes is probably the best known of the six men in Joe Rosenthal's famous photo of the flag-raising on Iwo Jima in 1945. His Native American heritage added an additional dimension to his background that intrigued a public already very interested in the six men. Unfortunately, Hayes could not cope with the celebrity status that was thrust upon him. On January 24, 1955, suffering from alcoholism, he was found dead from exposure near his home in Arizona.

Hayes, a Pima Indian, was born on the Gila River Indian Reservation in Arizona. He left high school after two years to serve in the Civilian Conservation Corps in 1942 and then worked as a carpenter. On August 26, 1942 he enlisted in the United States Marine Corps Reserve and, following boot camp in San Diego, was assigned to the Parachute Training School. He was promoted to First Class and sailed for New Caledonia on March 14, 1943. Hayes took part in the Bougainville campaign, but was ordered back to San Diego on February 14, 1944 when he was reassigned to the Twenty-eighth Marines.

With the Twenty-eighth when they landed on Iwo Jima on February 19, 1945, Hayes joined five of his comrades to plant the colors on Mount Suribachi on the February 23. When it became clear that those six men were becoming the focus of international attention, Hayes tried very hard to conceal his identity, even swearing the other five men to secrecy. He was inordinately shy and came to dread the notoriety. He remained on Iwo Jima until it was secured on March 25, 1945 but after his identity became known he was ordered to Washington, D.C. to take part in the promotional tour for the Seventh War Loan Drive. Hayes remained with that public tour for less than three weeks, at which time he was returned to the Twenty-eighth in Hawaii. On December 1, 1945 Ira Hayes was honorably discharged.

Following his military career, Hayes had difficulty keeping

a steady job because of the widespread discrimination against Indians and because of his alcoholism. When the U.S. Marine Corps Memorial was dedicated in the fall of 1954, he was working as a cotton picker and was again pulled unwillingly into the national limelight. His indigent status was widely publicized; two months later, Hayes was found dead of exposure.

After his tragic death, Ira Hayes' body lay in state in the Arizona State Capitol before he was buried with honors at Arlington National Cemetery. Hayes' life story later became the subject of a motion picture. He now rests in Section 34 very near the grave of General of the Armies, **John J. Pershing**.

MICHAEL STRANK

(November 10, 1919–March 1, 1945)
Sec. 12, Lot 7179, Grid ZAA–25/26

Sergeant Michael Strank was the oldest of the six men in Joe Rosenthal's famous Iwo Jima photograph. He was twenty-six years old when they planted that flag on February 23, 1945 but Strank soon became one of the nearly 6,000 men who lost their lives on the island. On March 1, during fighting on the northern side of Iwo Jima, he was killed; the very same day that another of the six men, Harlan Block, died.

Michael Strank was born on November 10, 1919 in Conemaugh, Pennsylvania, the son of Czechoslovakian immigrants. Following high school, he spent nearly eighteen months with the Civilian Conservation Corps and then worked as a laborer for the state highway department. Strank enlisted in the United States Marines on October 6, 1939 for a four year term. During 1942 and 1943, he participated in campaigns in the Wallis Islands, the Russell Islands, and on Bougainville Island. On January 12, 1944 he was reassigned to the Twenty-eighth Marines and stormed ashore with them at Iwo Jima on February 19, 1945. After helping to capture Mount Suribachi, Strank moved northward on the island with his unit. While attacking Japanese positions on March 1, Strank was fatally wounded by enemy artillery fire. He was initially buried in the Marine Cemetery on Iwo Jima, but he was reinterred in Arlington National Cemetery on January 13, 1949, nearly six years before the Marine Corps Memorial was dedicated.

DANIEL ("CHAPPIE") JAMES, JR.

First Black American Four-Star General

(February 11, 1920–February 25, 1978)
Sec. 2, Lot 4968-B, Grid V–33

At the end of his military career in 1977 Daniel James, Jr. reflected on his life in the Air Force, stating that early in his career he had realized the importance of setting an example for younger recruits to follow, especially young black Americans who wished to pursue military careers. James had experienced firsthand some of the obstacles encountered by blacks in the military. When he entered the Army in January 1943, he did so as a member of a segregated unit in Alabama. Once he was barred from leaving the base in his uniform so that white enlisted men would not have to salute a young black flight officer. Nevertheless, he held firm to his dream of a military flying career, choosing to fight the racial inequality in the U.S Armed Forces and to change the system from within. When James retired from the Air Force, he had become the first black American in our nation's history to achieve the Four-Star rank of General.

Raised in a family of seventeen children, "Chappie," as he was known, left his home in Pensacola, Florida to attend Tuskegee Institute in Alabama. Following his graduation in 1942, he continued his education in the field of civilian flight training until he received his appointment as a cadet in the Army Air Corps in January 1943. Assigned to a segregated

unit in Alabama and remaining with that unit throughout World War II, he trained pilots for the all-black Ninety-ninth Pursuit

Squadron. During the Korean War he flew 101 missions in fighter planes and from 1953 until 1956 he commanded the 437th and then the Sixtieth Fighter Interception Squadrons. In 1957 James graduated from the Air Command and Staff College and was assigned to duty in Washington, D.C. After tours of duty in England and Arizona, James was ordered to Vietnam in 1966. There he flew seventy-eight combat missions, earning promotion to Colonel. When he left Vietnam the following year, he was named Vice-Commander of the Thirty-third Tactical Fighter Wing at Elgin Air Force Base, Florida. His rise in rank continued. In 1969 he was promoted to Brigadier General and given command of Wheelus Air Force Base in Libya. Returning to the United States in 1970, he served as Deputy Assistant Secretary of Defense for Public Affairs and achieved the rank of Major General. In 1974 climbing to the rank of Lt. General, he became Vice-Commander of the Military Airlift Command at Scott Air Force Base, Illinois.

The pinnacle of James' distinguished career was reached in December 1975 when he became the first black American in any branch of the service to gain promotion to full General. At that time, General Daniel James, Jr. was named commander of the North American Air Defense Command (NORAD), a distinction which gave him responsibility for all aspects of the air defense of the United States and Canada.

Unfortunately, James suffered from heart problems which forced his retirement from the Air Force in 1977. He died in Colorado Springs, Colorado on February 25, 1978 and, following a funeral mass attended by military and civilian leaders at the National Shrine of the Immaculate Conception in Washington, D.C., General James was buried with full military honors at Arlington National Cemetery.

PHILIP KEARNY

Mexican War Hero, Civil War Hero

(June 1, 1814–September 1, 1862)
Special Lot S–8, Grid OP–32

The lifelike equestrian statue of Philip Kearny in Arlington Cemetery dramatically tells the story of this man who was determined to be a professional soldier. Sculptor E. C. Potter has captured the scrappy little General poised in his saddle, practically standing in his stirrups. His horse appears caught in midstride, its tail and mane blowing in the wind. With the reins in his only hand, Kearny seems ready to bark orders to his men as he leads the charge. His proud military career is graphically summarized by the inscription on its base:

Gave his left arm
at
Churubusco, Mexico
August 18, 1847
and his life at Chantilly, Va.
September 1, 1862.

Kearny was born in New York City to a very wealthy family, but was orphaned as a young child. Although reared by a grandfather who wanted a career in the ministry for his grandson, Kearny's heart was set on being a soldier. As soon as he was old enough he left for France to become a student at the French Cavalry School at Saumur. He later served with the Chasseurs d'Afrique, returning to the United States to enlist in the Army and serve on the western frontier.

Kearny always believed that in order to be a good soldier you must look like a good soldier. So, while commanding a troop of dragoons during the Mexican War, he purchased matching dapple gray horses for his men with his own funds. It was also during that war that Kearny lost his left arm. While leading an assault in the battle of Churubusco, Kearny's arm was shattered by gunfire and later required amputation. Yet he could do with one arm what many men could not do with two.

Following the Mexican campaign, undaunted by the loss of his arm and searching for more battles, Kearny returned to France to take part in the Franco-Italian War under Napoleon III. When the Civil War broke out in the United States, he came back to fight for the Union. Initially unwilling to offer him a commission, the Army relented and Kearny took command of the First New Jersey Brigade as part of the Third Division of the Army of the Potomac.

Kearny demanded strict discipline of his men, but he demanded even more of himself. He was often seen holding his reins in his teeth and directing his men with his free right arm. Kearny's men, fiercely loyal to him, could always count on the General leading the charge, not following it as so many other commanders did. But his unbridled gallantry cost Kearny his life. Just prior to the Second Battle of Bull Run, Kearny inadvertently crossed the Confederate lines and was killed.

Even among the Confederate soldiers Kearny commanded such deep respect that, under a flag of truce, General Robert E. Lee immediately ordered the return of Kearny's body and later returned his horse and sword. Kearny is now buried in what was once part of Lee's garden at Arlington.

Following his death, Kearny's men decided to establish a tribute to their fallen leader. For that reason, Kearny's successor, Major General David Birney, created the Cross of Honor, also known as Kearny's Cross, to be awarded to noncommissioned officers and privates for exceptional valor in battle. That commendation has evolved into the Medal of Honor, the highest decoration that can be given to American military personnel.

Major General Philip Kearny was buried in Trinity Church Yard in New York City following his death at Chantilly, Virginia at the age of 48. His remains were reinterred in Arlington Cemetery on April 12, 1912. He was later placed in his current grave when his statue was completed in 1914 during the centennial of his birth. Kearny is one of only two persons honored with an equestrian statue in Arlington. The other is Sir **John Dill**.

WILLIAM PITT KELLOGG

Nebraska's Chief Justice, Louisiana's Governor

(December 8, 1830–August 10, 1918)
Sec. 3, Lot 2538, Grid P–16/17

The diverse career of William Pitt Kellogg led him to every corner of the United States. From his birthplace in Vermont he moved to Illinois, where he practiced law and befriended Abraham Lincoln. He was later appointed Chief Justice of Nebraska, but resigned that high post to enlist in the Union Army. After the Civil War, he returned to the bench in Nebraska before moving to Louisiana, where he was elected Senator, Governor, Senator once again, and then elected to the House of Representatives.

After his graduation from Norwich College in Vermont in 1848, Kellogg moved to Peoria, Illinois where he taught school while studying law. He was admitted to the bar in 1853 and practiced law in Canton, Illinois. It was at this time that he befriended another Illinoisan, Abraham Lincoln, an association which served him well.

During the presidential election of 1860 Kellogg was a member of the Illinois delegation to the electoral college which "elected" the Republican ticket of Abraham Lincoln and Hannibal Hamlin. Shortly after the inauguration, Lincoln appointed Kellogg as Chief Justice of the Supreme Court of the Territory of Nebraska. Kellogg resigned that post immediately after hostilities broke out between the North and the South. He returned to Illinois and was commissioned Colonel of the Seventh Regiment of the Illinois Volunteer

Cavalry. He served under General John Pope in Missouri and at the battle of Corinth, Mississippi until ill health forced him to resign.

Lincoln next appointed Kellogg as Collector of the Port of New Orleans on April 13, 1865, just one day before Lincoln became the target of an assassin's bullet at Ford's Theatre. Kellogg remained in that post until July 1868 when, following Louisiana's readmission to the Union, he was elected to represent that state in the United States Senate. He resigned from the Senate in November 1872 to become Governor of Louisiana. Following one term in the statehouse, he was again elected to the U.S. Senate, remaining there until March of 1883 when he declined to stand for reelection. He did, however, run for election to the U.S. House of Representatives where he served for a single term. In 1885 he retired from public life, taking up permanent residence in Washington, D.C., where he died in 1918.

JOHN FITZGERALD KENNEDY

35th President of the United States

(May 29, 1917–November 22, 1963)
Sec. 45, Grid U-35

It was 12:30 P.M.CST on November 22, 1963 when President John F. Kennedy was assassinated in Dallas. Word of that tragedy spread quickly throughout the world and for anyone who heard that shocking news, that moment was frozen in time forever. It seems that anyone old enough to remember that day recalls exactly where he or she was when the first report of the President's death was broadcast.

President Kennedy had traveled to Dallas to forge a united political front in Texas in anticipation of the 1964 presidential election. Kennedy knew that a win in the Lone Star State would help him secure a near-landslide victory in 1964 and give him the mandate he sought for his social programs. While riding in an open limousine, two bullets shot from a high-powered rifle struck John Kennedy and he slumped helplessly into his wife's lap. He was raced to Parkland Memorial Hospital for emergency treatment, but our nation's thirty-fifth President was pronounced dead on arrival. Vice-President Lyndon Baines Johnson took the oath of office as President at 2:38 P.M., November 22, 1963.

The life that ended so tragically in Dallas began so hopefully and with such promise in Brookline, Massachusetts, a suburb of Boston, in 1917. "Jack" Kennedy, as he was known to his family and friends, was the second son of Boston banker and financier Joseph P. Kennedy and his wife, Rose, who was the daughter of Boston mayor John F. ("Honey Fitz") Fitzgerald, after whom John was named. Young Jack was raised in a very affluent environment and, like each of his eight brothers and sisters, was given a million dollar trust fund by his father. His life, however, was not a pampered one.

Joseph Kennedy, who served as Chairman of the Securities and Exchange Commission in the mid-1930s and later as U.S. Ambassador to Great Britain, was a strict disciplinarian who taught his children to be fiercely competitive in all aspects of their lives, whether they were playing touch football or running for public office. John did not foresee a political career for himself; that career had been reserved for his older brother, Joseph, Jr. When Jack graduated from Harvard in 1940, his eye was on a career in Academe or journalism. In fact, during the year of his Harvard graduation, he expanded his senior thesis on the subject of British military unpreparedness prior to World War II into a best-selling book, *Why England Slept*.

In the spring of 1941, more than six months before the Japanese attack on Pearl Harbor, Jack Kennedy attempted to enlist in the United States Navy, but was denied because of a back injury which he suffered while playing football at Harvard. He underwent physical therapy and treatment and was finally accepted into the Navy in September 1941. In August 1943 Lieutenant John Kennedy was in command of a torpedo boat—PT-109—patrolling the waters off the Solomon Islands. Running with lights out through heavy fog, Kennedy's boat was rammed and ripped in half by a Japanese destroyer. The impact threw the young Lieutenant and his crew into the Pacific Ocean. Kennedy risked his own life to save the lives of his men, even towing one injured sailor for three miles by holding that man's life-jacket between his teeth. For this heroic deed, Jack Kennedy was awarded the Navy and Marine Corps Medal, but he was also hospitalized with further injury to his back.

While recuperating from this injury, Kennedy learned of the death of his older brother, Joe, a Naval aviator shot down over the English Channel. It was Joe who was to have carried the family's political standard; John knew that now that responsibility was passed on to him. This special family belief regarding public service was later expressed by Kennedy after he was elected to the Senate: "Just as I went into politics because Joe died, if anything happened to me tomorrow, my brother Bobby would run for my seat in the Senate. And if Bobby died, Teddy would take over for him."

Kennedy's first campaign for elective office came in 1946 when he ran for Congress from Massachusetts. He easily won the primary and registered a landslide victory in the November general election. He had won his first election at age 29; he was never to lose one. After serving three terms in the House of Representatives, he chose to give up his safe House seat to tackle the popular incumbent Senator from Massachusetts, Republican Henry Cabot Lodge. With his brother **Robert** managing his campaign and with his family working in full force, Jack Kennedy succeeded in unseating Lodge, even while Dwight Eisenhower recorded a statewide presidential victory. Kennedy entered the Senate in January of 1953, and eight months later married Jacqueline Bouvier.

In 1956 Kennedy underwent one of three major surgeries on his back. While convalescing he conceived of *Profiles in Courage*, an anthology of eight great American political leaders that was awarded the 1957 Pulitzer Prize. Also in 1956 Kennedy was considered as a running mate for Democratic presidential candidate Adlai Stevenson. When Kennedy was not selected for Vice-President in favor of Estes Kefauver, some politicos felt this was a blow to Kennedy's desire for national office. However, given the national exposure he received, Kennedy found himself the front-runner for his party's presidential nomination in 1960.

John F. Kennedy formally announced his presidential can-

A horse-drawn caisson bears the body of President John F. Kennedy during his burial services in 1963 (top left); representatives of every branch of the Armed Services carry the slain President to his grave in Section 5 (top right); Mrs. Jacqueline Kennedy is escorted by the President's brothers, Robert and Edward, while the President's mother, Mrs. Rose Kennedy, and other members of his family follow (center left); the flag which draped the casket throughout the services for President Kennedy is folded as part of the Combined Armed Forces Honors (center right); having received the flag (lower left), Jacqueline Kennedy prepares to light the eternal flame which continues to light the permanent memorial to John F. Kennedy.

didacy in January of 1960 and undertook the drive to win the nomination from his chief rivals, fellow Senators Hubert Humphrey and Lyndon Johnson. In overcoming their challenge, he dealt effectively with the question about his religion (Roman Catholic) and won the nomination on the first ballot. Then, with Senator Johnson as his running mate, he faced Vice-President Richard Nixon and Henry Cabot Lodge in the general election.

The 1960 campaign introduced several new campaign techniques to American political life, including extensive use of air travel, heavy reliance on television advertising, and televised debates between the candidates. Analysts uniformly agree that the four televised debates greatly aided Jack Kennedy who appeared poised and demonstrated a firm grasp of the issues. By contrast Vice-President Nixon suffered from poor make up and a fatigued appearance. It was early on the morning after the election before all the votes were counted when Kennedy was declared the winner by a razor-thin margin of victory, winning by just over 100,000 votes out of a total of nearly 69,000,000 votes cast nationwide.

John F. Kennedy was inaugurated President of the United States on January 20, 1960, becoming the youngest man ever elected to that office and the first Roman Catholic. His administration was a relatively short one, lasting only 1,037 days. Yet during that time, President Kennedy faced several major foreign policy tests and proposed wide-ranging domestic legislation. Kennedy also began the televised press conferences—which have since become commonplace—where he often disarmed his critics by displaying an unusually candid sense of humor.

Soon after his inauguration the CIA sponsored an invasion of Cuba by a brigade of Cuban exiles intent on inciting rebellion against Fidel Castro. John F. Kennedy had allowed the covert operation on the recommendation of the Joint Chiefs of Staff and accepted full responsibility when the rebel forces failed in their objective and every member was either killed or captured by Castro's troops. The most serious challenge of Kennedy's administration, however, came in October 1962 when it was learned that the Soviet Union had installed missiles in Cuba. President Kennedy demanded that the missiles be removed. When his warnings went unheeded, he ordered the U.S. Navy to blockade the island. For thirteen days the two superpowers appeared on the brink of

A never-before-published photograph of John F. Kennedy's grave, taken on November 27, 1963, two days after his burial. More than eight million people visited Arlington National Cemetery during the first year after the death of John F. Kennedy. The large number of visitors required a redesign of the area around the Kennedy gravesite and a prohibition of vehicular traffic in the cemetery.

war, but then the Soviets yielded, agreeing to withdraw their missiles and handing President Kennedy a major foreign policy victory. In his own estimation, his greatest foreign policy achievement was the Nuclear Test-Ban Treaty, signed by Great Britain, the Soviet Union, and the United States in December 1962.

Domestically, Kennedy envisioned greatly expanded civil rights and social programs. The President knew he could not marshal the support he needed unless he could win a strong mandate in his bid for reelection. This was his purpose for visiting Dallas in November 1963. After John Kennedy's assassination, President Lyndon Johnson did win the mandate Kennedy had sought, and many Kennedy-authored programs became part of Johnson's "Great Society."

Following reports of President Kennedy's assassination in Dallas, the world watched for three days as our nation prepared to bury its fallen leader. On Monday, November 25, 1963, as a worldwide television audience viewed the proceedings, John Fitzgerald Kennedy was laid to rest on the hillside below Arlington House. Today that grave is the single most visited site in Arlington National Cemetery.

The gravesite of John Kennedy consists of a circular walkway which approaches a small elliptical terrace. From this terrace visitors can look over a low wall toward the Lincoln Memorial across the Potomac. The wall is inscribed with passages from President Kennedy's speeches. President Kennedy's grave lies on a slightly elevated terrace, marked by a marble tablet which simply proclaims:

John Fitzgerald Kennedy
1917-1963

Above his grave stands the Eternal Flame which was lit by

Mrs. Jacqueline Kennedy at her husband's burial service. Two infant children—a boy, **Patrick Bouvier Kennedy**, and an unnamed baby girl who predeceased the President—were reinterred on either side of him on December 4, 1963. When this permanent gravesite was completed, the bodies of President Kennedy and his two children were removed to their final resting places on the evening of March 14, 1967 and were blessed by Richard Cardinal Cushing the following morning.

John Kennedy's brother, **Robert Francis Kennedy**, is also buried at Arlington, a short distance away from the President's tomb in a grave marked by a simple white cross.

ROBERT F. KENNEDY

Attorney General, Senator, Presidential Candidate

(November 20, 1925–June 6, 1968)
Sec. 45, Grid U–33/34

After Robert Kennedy graduated from Harvard University in 1948, he foresaw a career dedicated to advancing the political ambitions of his older brother, John. Having already managed John's successful campaign for Congress, Robert Kennedy looked forward to working toward seeing his brother elected President of the United States. It was only during those dark days following John Kennedy's assassination that Robert Kennedy decided to consider elective office for himself.

Robert F. Kennedy was the seventh of nine children born to Joseph and Rose Kennedy, a wealthy and prominent Boston couple. Joseph Kennedy was a banker and financier who had accumulated great wealth in the stock market before its crash in 1929. The elder Kennedy ultimately chaired the Securities and Exchange Commission in the mid-1930s during the Franklin Roosevelt administration and then served as U.S. Ambassador to Great Britain. Rose Kennedy was the daughter of John F. ("Honey Fitz")

Fitzgerald, the long-time mayor of Boston.

Robert Kennedy's early years were spent developing the fierce competitive drive for distinction which typified his father and the love, compassion, and serenity that were the result of his mother's influence. Spared the economic hardships that befell many American families in the 1930s, Robert grew up in an affluent environment. With his three brothers and five sisters, Robert enjoyed touch football, sailing, and tennis. After entering Harvard University, he interrupted his studies to serve in the U.S. Navy during World War II. Following the war, he returned to graduate from Harvard in 1948 and continued his education at the University of Virginia Law School, graduating in 1951.

It was no surprise that Robert joined the successful congressional campaign of his older brother, John, in 1946. Following John to Washington, D.C., Robert was named Assistant Counsel to the Senate Permanent Committee on Investigations, a powerful committee chaired by Senator Joseph McCarthy. Robert stayed in that position for only a short time, resigning because of the nature of the investigations undertaken by the committee. He returned the following year as Majority Counsel when McCarthy was no longer chairman. Then in 1957, Robert was Chief Counsel for the special Senate committee investigating labor racketeering. It was in this position that he first encountered Teamsters' Union leader, Jimmy Hoffa. This encounter led to a longstanding feud between Kennedy and Hoffa, a battle which continued into Kennedy's days as Attorney General. It was during Kennedy's tenure as Attorney General that Hoffa was imprisoned for jury tampering, fraud, and conspiracy.

In 1960 Robert Kennedy directed his brother's successful campaign for President of the United States. Subsequently, Robert was named as JFK's Attorney General amid loud public cries of nepotism. Although Bobby, as he became universally known, was only thirty-five years old at the time, President Kennedy brushed aside criticism of his appointment with such quips as "I can't see that it's so wrong to give him a little legal experience before he goes out to practice law." The President's confidence was confirmed by his younger brother's performance. Bobby established a record which advanced civil rights across our country, fought relentlessly against organized crime, and improved life for underprivileged

Americans. When he resigned from that post in 1964, *The New York Times* (which had criticized his appointment three years earlier) editorialized about Robert Kennedy:

> He named excellent men to most key posts, put new vigor into protecting civil rights through administrative action, played a pivotal role in shaping the most comprehensive civil rights law in this country...Mr. Kennedy has done much to elevate the standard.

When John Kennedy was assassinated in Dallas in 1963, Robert was overcome with grief. He and his brother had spent much time together, working closely on many issues as national leaders and sharing personal thoughts and feelings as friends. After considerable soul searching, Robert resigned from the Justice Department in September of 1964 to enter the race for the United States Senate from New York.

In that election Kennedy easily defeated incumbent Senator **Kenneth Keating** (Sec. 5, Lot 141) and became a major political figure in the Democratic Party, championing liberal causes and opposing President Lyndon Johnson's wartime policies in Vietnam. As a younger man, Robert had never viewed himself as potential presidential material. He had left that to his older brother, Joseph, who had been killed during World War II, and then  to John. But Robert Kennedy believed America was heading away from the ideals set by his brother, so on March 16, 1968, he announced his candidacy for the Democratic nomination for President.

Embarking on an uphill fight against incumbent President Lyndon Johnson, the race opened up for Kennedy when President

Johnson announced that he would neither seek nor accept his party's nomination. Kennedy's campaign gained great momentum, as he won five of six primary contests, including the final and most important preconvention election, the delegate-rich California primary on June 4, 1968.

It was a Robert Kennedy filled with hope and confidence who addressed his supporters following his victory in California. As he stood before them at the Ambassador Hotel in Los Angeles just after midnight on June 5, he exhorted his followers, promising to take the fight for the nomination to the floor of the National Democratic Convention in Chicago. He left them cheering in the ballroom as he slipped out through a kitchen hallway. There, with the cheers still echoing in the air, Robert Kennedy was met by Sirhan Sirhan, a Palestinian immigrant, who shot and critically wounded him. Senator Kennedy died the following morning. Surviving Kennedy were his ten children and his wife, Ethel, who was expecting another child. Sirhan Sirhan was convicted of murder and was sentenced to death by a California court, but his sentence was commuted to life imprisonment when the United States Supreme Court declared the death penalty unconstitutional.

At Robert's funeral Senator Edward Kennedy said of his older brother, "Some men see things as they are and ask, 'Why?' He saw things that never were and asked, 'Why not?'" Robert is now buried at Arlington in a grave which is marked by a simple white cross near his brother, John. Passages from Robert Kennedy's speeches are inscribed on a wall above a fountain which forms a part of the burial site.

WILLIAM FRANKLIN KNOX

Rough Rider, Newspaper Publisher,
Secretary of the Navy

(January 1, 1874–April 28, 1944)
Sec. 2, Lot 4961, Grid WX–32/33

The inscription on his tombstone reads "Secretary of the Navy," leaving unlisted the other remarkable achievements of William Franklin Knox. Nowhere is it engraved, for example, that Knox was with Teddy Roosevelt on San Juan Hill, or that he saw combat in World War I, or that he published the *Chicago Daily News*, or that he ran for Vice-President of the United States.

Born in Boston, Knox moved to Michigan at an early age. He attended Alma College in Alma, Michigan and when war broke out with Spain in 1898, enlisted in the First U.S. Volunteer Cavalry—better known as the Rough Riders. Knox was sworn into the Army by Theodore Roosevelt himself and not only did he fight at Las Guasimas, but also saw action in the battle up San Juan Hill near Santiago de Cuba. Sunstroke and malaria forced Knox to return home before the conclusion of that war. He received his honorable discharge in September 1898.

Following the war, he began a successful career in journalism, publishing the *Sault Ste. Marie (Michigan) News* in 1902. He launched his political career in 1910 when he successfully managed the Michigan gubernatorial campaign for Republican Chase Osborn. Unfortunately, he would never again be associated with a successful campaign, although he tried on several different occasions, including the 1912 election in which he supported Teddy Roosevelt in his unsuccessful bid for another term as President.

When World War I erupted across Europe in 1917, Knox—then 43 years old—volunteered for active service again. Following completion of Officer's Training School, he was commissioned a Captain and took part in the battles of the St. Mihiel Salient and the Meuse-Argonne. The war's end marked his return to journalism and politics.

In 1920 Knox went to work for publisher William Randolph Hearst, taking charge of Hearst's paper, *The Boston American and Advertiser* seven years later. While handling Hearst's newspapers in New England in 1924, Knox ran for Governor of New Hampshire but lost in the Republican primary. In 1931 Knox purchased the *Chicago Daily News* and remained its publisher until 1940. In 1936, governor Alf Landon of Kansas, the Republican nominee for President, picked Knox as his running mate, but their ticket lost overwhelmingly to Democrat Franklin Roosevelt in the November general election.

In spite of his defeat by Roosevelt and his staunch Republican ties, Knox supported FDR's military and foreign policies regarding the war in Europe in 1939. At that time, Roosevelt asked Knox to join his Cabinet as Secretary of the Navy. Knox refused, however, claiming that it would take more than one Republican to make a good Cabinet. Following the German successes in Denmark, Norway, and the Low Countries during the spring of 1940, FDR again asked Knox to take the Navy post. This time Knox accepted and was sworn in on July 11, 1940.

His term as Secretary of the Navy, then a Cabinet-level position, was highlighted by his frequent and candid press conferences which reflected his journalistic background. He tied American survival with the survival of Great Britain, and played a key role in arranging the "Destroyers for Bases" exchange with Britain in 1940. FDR credited him with winning the necessary support for the war effort among Republicans just prior to America's entry into World War II.

Knox died while Secretary of the Navy in Washington, D.C. in 1944. He was succeeded by **James V. Forrestal**. Knox was buried with full military honors on the slope below the mansion at Arlington Cemetery.

WILLIAM D. LEAHY

Five-Star Fleet Admiral of the Navy

(May 6, 1875–July 20, 1959)
Sec. 2, Lot 932, Grid R–31/32

Though William D. Leahy's long naval career spanned four decades, it was not until he retired from the Navy that he undertook the task which earned him the highest rank ever conferred upon a U.S. Navy officer.

Leahy's father, a Civil War veteran, moved his family from their home in Hampton, Iowa to Ashland, Wisconsin where young Leahy attended high school. Entering the Naval Academy and graduating in 1897, William Leahy was on board the *Oregon* when it made its famous dash around Cape Horn to join the American fleet under the command of **William T. Sampson** and **Winfield Scott Schley** at Santiago, Cuba during the Spanish-American War.

After various assignments took him to the Philippines, China, Santo Domingo, Mexico, and Nicaragua, Leahy received his first command of the transport *Dolphin*. It was during this period that Leahy became acquainted with the Assistant Secretary of the Navy, Franklin Roosevelt, who often traveled on the *Dolphin*. Then, when the United States entered World War I, Leahy took command of an expropriated German liner, the *Princess Matoika*, and undertook the dangerous task of transporting troops and supplies to France. For his courageous and successful efforts, he was awarded the Navy Cross.

Leahy's career eventually turned to administrative duties but not before he spent two years on the faculty of the Naval Academy in the Department of Physics and Chemistry. In 1927 Leahy earned promotion to Rear Admiral and was named Chief of the Bureau of Ordnance. In 1933 he was appointed Chief of the Bureau of Navigation, becoming one of the few people ever to hold both positions. Elevated to Vice Admiral in 1935, he was promoted to Admiral the following year. On January 2, 1937 Leahy was awarded the highest command in the Navy, Chief of Naval Operations, becoming only the second person in American history ever to attain that position after heading both Navy Bureaus. He retired from the Navy in August 1939 and was awarded the Distinguished Service Medal.

His retirement was short-lived. Immediately, Leahy was called upon by his old friend and now President, Franklin Roosevelt, to serve as Governor of Puerto Rico. He accepted the appointment, serving only until the next year when he resigned to assume the delicate diplomatic post of U.S. Ambassador to the Vichy government. This was the government established at Vichy in that part of France not occupied by the Germans after the French defeat early in World War II. Here Leahy walked a diplomatic tightrope, dealing with the Petain government while under close scrutiny by the Germans. When the United States went to war against Germany in December 1941, Leahy returned to the U.S. to assume the newly created position of Chief of Staff to the President.

In this position Leahy advised President Roosevelt on military affairs. He also served as a member of the U.S. Joint Chiefs of Staff and as U.S. representative on the Allied Command Combined Chiefs of Staff. In December 1944, in recognition of Leahy's invaluable service to our country, the President elevated him to the venerable rank of Five-Star Fleet Admiral of the Navy, placing him in the elite company of only four other men to ever hold that position—George Dewey, Chester Nimitz, Ernest J. King and **William F. Halsey, Jr.**

Upon FDR's death in 1945 Leahy retained his position under President Harry Truman until March 1949, at which time he retired for the second time. Completing his memoirs in 1950, he continued to advise the Secretary of the Navy on international strategic matters. Fleet Admiral William D. Leahy died in Bethesda, Maryland on July 20, 1959 at the age of eighty-four.

PIERRE CHARLES L'ENFANT

Designer of the United States Capital

(August 2, 1754–June 14, 1825)
Sec. 2, Lot S–3, Grid S–34

The tombstone of Pierre Charles L'Enfant invites comparison between his original plan for the new federal city and present-day Washington, D.C. L'Enfant's design of the nation's capital is permanently embossed in stone atop a table-like monument which marks his grave. From its position near Arlington House on the hilltop overlooking Washington, the comparison between his original concept and today's Washington is simple. But it was not always so. When L'Enfant was called upon by our nation's first President to plan this city, this area was little more than wilderness.

Pierre L'Enfant was born in Paris and studied art under his father at the Academie Royale de Peinture et de Sculpture. In 1776 he left France to join the American fight for independence against Great Britain. At age twenty-two, he enlisted in the Corps of Engineers; by the end of the war he had risen to the rank of Captain. *(The tombstone indicates he was a Major, but this error in engraving was not changed for fear of disfiguring the stone.)*

Following the Revolutionary War, L'Enfant joined other veterans headed by General Henry Knox to form the Society of the Cincinnati, a military and fraternal society. L'Enfant designed the Certificate and Insignia of the Society and is one of three founding members buried at Arlington.

L'Enfant eventually returned to France, but remained there only a short time, finally settling in New York in 1784. In 1787 he renovated New York's old city hall under authority from the United States Congress. It was on the steps of the new Federal Hall that George Washington took his first oath of office. In 1791 Congress authorized the new President to hire a designer to plan the new federal city, which was to be built on the banks of the Potomac River on land ceded from Virginia and Maryland. Trying to build a nation's capital out of this one hundred square miles of wilderness promised to be a difficult task. President Washington entrusted Pierre Charles L'Enfant with this historic undertaking.

While L'Enfant drew ideas from the great cities of Europe, his concepts and designs were uniquely his own. In a prophetic pronouncement, he promised President Washington that he was going to design a city magnificent enough not for just "thirteen states, but fifty." The focal points of his city were the "Congress House" and the "President's House" with a grand mall connecting them. There would be wide avenues crisscrossing and encircling the city to form squares, circles, and triangles where parks, fountains and monuments could be placed.

In 1792, while much of L'Enfant's plans were still only on paper, President Washington dismissed him. L'Enfant had become defiant of the city commissioners and highhanded in his methods, especially in removing a prominent citizen's house to make way for one of his avenues. L'Enfant further enraged the populace when he pressed a claim for payment of his fees totalling $95,000. Congress authorized $3,800 to be paid to him, but he continued throughout his life to demand more money, alienating many former friends in the process.

Pierre L'Enfant spent his last days residing at Chilham Castle Manor, the estate of his friend and benefactor, William Dudley Digges, located in Green Hills, Maryland. L'Enfant died there penniless on June 14, 1825 and was buried on the estate.

Like many great artists, however, the value of L'Enfant's creations was appreciated only many years after his death. In 1908 the Board of Commissioners for the City of Washington made overtures to remove his body from its resting place in Prince Georges County, Maryland to a suitable site in Arlington National Cemetery and requested the Secretary of War to make such a site available. On April 28, 1909 his remains were conveyed by military escort to the United States Capitol where they lay in state for three hours. During that time, thousands of Americans paid their respects to the man who had planned this nation's capital city. At noon on that date, the military escort carried the body of the Revolutionary War veteran to the hilltop in front of Arlington House in Arlington Cemetery. There, overlooking the magnificent city, Pierre Charles L'Enfant was buried with the full military honors due an officer of the United States Army.

On May 22, 1911, with President **William Howard Taft** presiding, the tombstone that now marks his grave was dedicated. By Act of Congress the stone was designed and sculpted as a belated tribute to L'Enfant. The focal point of the monument is the reproduction of L'Enfant's original plan for the city sculpted into the white marble top. Accompanying the map on top of the stone is a tribute to L'Enfant: "Engineer – Artist – Soldier."

The monument remains as a visual testament to the achievement of L'Enfant's dream. The city he planned stands proudly across the Potomac and the comparison between the dream and the reality is simple. The Capitol rises majestically above Jenkin's Hill where L'Enfant envisioned the "Congress House" and across the wide expansive mall can be found the "President's House" just as L'Enfant had dreamed.

JOHN ARCHER LEJEUNE

World War I Field Commander,
Marine Corps Commandant

(January 10, 1867–November 20, 1942)
Sec. 6, Lot 5682, Grid VW–22/23

John Archer Lejeune was known as "The Greatest of All Leathernecks," and he earned that sobriquet the hard way. After surviving a deadly hurricane that wrecked his ship and killed several of his fellow crew members, he became the first Marine to command an Army division, ultimately serving as Commandant of the Marine Corps under three Presidents.

Lejeune was born in Pointe Coupee, Louisiana, the son of a former Confederate officer who had lost his home during Reconstruction. The younger Lejeune attended Louisiana State University, which at that time was both a military preparatory school and college. After three years at L.S.U. he attempted to gain entry to West Point, but finding no openings in his class, he chose instead to attend the United States Naval Academy at Annapolis, Maryland, graduating in 1888.

Sent to sea aboard the *Vandalia*, Lejeune and his shipmates suffered through a devastating hurricane near Samoa that destroyed their vessel in March 1889. Convinced that sea life was not for him, he applied for a transfer into the Marines. His initial request was denied, but his continued pleas resulted in his eventual transfer to the Corps in July 1890.

Promoted to First Lieutenant in 1892, Lejeune was given command of the Marine attachment aboard the *Cincinnati* during the Spanish-American War. While in that post, he took part in the occupation of Puerto Rico. By 1903 he had advanced through the ranks to Major and had been given command of the Marine Battalion attached to the Atlantic fleet.

In 1905 Lejeune was named commander of the Marine Barracks in Washington, D.C., but was sent to the Philippines in 1907. In 1909, having risen in rank to Lt. Colonel, Lejeune became the first Marine officer admitted to the Army War College, graduating in 1910. He was then granted the prestigious command of the New York Navy Yard, a command he retained until 1913 when he gained promotion to full Colonel and took command of the Advanced Base Brigade at New Orleans in his home state. Among his military credits, he led the Marine brigade that occupied Veracruz, Mexico in 1914. Then in August 1916, promoted to Brigadier General, he served as assistant to the Marine Corps Commandant, General George Barnett.

In 1917 Lejeune assumed the critically important post of commander at Quantico, Virginia. This base served as a training center and staging area for Marines on their way to the European front in World War I. Lejeune himself went to France in June of 1918 to take command of the Fourth Marine Brigade, the only Marine brigade in the American Expeditionary Force. In July he was promoted to Major General, succeeding General Omar Bundy as commander of the Second Infantry Division, and becoming the first Marine ever to command an Army division. He led that Division in the St. Mihiel Offensive in the battle of Blanc Mont Ridge on October 3, 1918 and throughout the Meuse-Argonne operation.

Following the war, Lejeune served with the Army of Occupation in Germany, returning in 1919 to resume command of the Quantico Marine base. Named Thirteenth Commandant of the Marine Corps in June 1920, he is credited with modernizing the Corps, as well as with establishing the Marine Corps School at Quantico. Lejeune retained his command throughout the terms of three U.S. Presidents: Wilson, Harding, and Coolidge. Upon his retirement from the Marine Corps in 1929, he accepted the position of Superintendent of the Virginia Military Institute, serving in that capacity until 1937.

General John Lejeune died of cancer in Baltimore, Maryland on November 20, 1942. The sprawling Marine base in North Carolina has been named in his honor.

ROBERT TODD LINCOLN

Lawyer, Secretary of War, Diplomat, Son of the President

(August 1, 1843–June 26, 1926)
Sec. 31, Lot 13, Grid Y–38

During his lifetime, Robert Todd Lincoln often wondered if history might have been different had he accepted his father's invitation to accompany the President and Mrs. Lincoln to Ford's Theatre the night his father was assassinated. Instead, the young soldier, fresh from the battlefields of the Civil War, chose to visit friends that fateful April night.

Robert Lincoln returned to Washington to visit his parents on April 13, 1865, just four days after Lee surrendered to Grant at

Appomattox Courthouse. Lincoln, who was a member of Grant's staff, was present at the courthouse as Lee offered his sword in surrender. The grueling Civil War that had crippled the country was finally over and the nation's capital was filled with the sights and sounds of celebration. Young Lincoln commented that even his father, normally drawn and weary, seemed noticeably relieved. Having recently graduated from Harvard College, the twenty-one-year-old Robert had been commissioned a Captain and had joined the staff of General Grant in February 1865.

President Lincoln mentioned to his son that General and Mrs. Grant would be joining the Lincolns on the evening of April 14 at a performance of *Our American Cousin* at nearby Ford's Theatre. When the afternoon papers reported that both the Lincolns and the Grants were going to be at the theatre that same evening, tickets to the performance sold out. However, later in the day Grant informed the President that he and Mrs. Grant would be unable to attend and were planning instead to take an afternoon train to Burlington, New Jersey to visit their children. The President then asked Robert to accompany him and his mother, but Robert declined, having previously planned to visit with friends in Washington.

It was nearly midnight before Robert learned that his father had suffered a single gunshot wound to the head and lay dying in a house at 453 10th Street in northwest Washington. He rushed to the site to find his father near death, stretched diagonally across a single bed in a rear bedroom, and his grieving mother secluded in a front parlor. Robert kept vigil with his mother throughout the night, but the man known as The Great Emancipator died the following morning at 7:22 A.M. He became the first American President to be killed in office.

Robert Todd Lincoln was the eldest of President Abraham Lincoln's three sons and the only child to live to maturity. He shared his father's Midwestern roots, having been born and raised in Springfield, Illinois. In 1859, seeking the education denied his father, Robert attempted to enter Harvard but was unsuccessful, failing fifteen of the sixteen subjects in the entrance examination. Following a year at Exeter Academy in New Hampshire, Robert again attempted and gained admission to Harvard where he was studying when his father became the President in 1860.

Following the Civil War Robert studied law in Chicago and

The gravesite of Robert Todd Lincoln, Mary Harlan Lincoln, and their son Abraham Lincoln II assumes a parklike aura in this photograph taken in 1932, six years after Robert's death.

was admitted to practice in 1867. The following year he married **Mary Harlan,** daughter of Iowa's Senator. Lincoln became a well-known and skillful lawyer, representing many major corporations and railroads. He was named Secretary of War by President James Garfield in 1881, and retained that position under President Chester Alan Arthur after Garfield's assassination. From 1889 to 1893 he served as Minister to Great Britain, the last American to serve with that title. All later envoys to the Court of St. James were elevated to the rank of Ambassador. Upon returning to this country, Lincoln resumed his legal practice and was ultimately named president of the Pullman Company of Chicago, one of his major clients. Lincoln served as Pullman's president from 1897 until 1911.

Robert Todd Lincoln's life was filled with many ironies. Prior to his father's assassination, young Lincoln was saved from falling from a speeding train by Edwin Booth, the brother of his father's assassin. Lincoln was also present when two other presidents were assassinated. While serving as Secretary of War, he was waiting on the platform at a Washington railroad station to greet President Garfield when Garfield was shot in 1881. In 1901 Lincoln was at the Buffalo Pan-American Exposition when President McKinley was fatally wounded. This series of events later led Lincoln to refuse a presidential invitation with the comment, "No, I'm not going, and they'd better not ask me, because there is a certain fatality about presidential functions when I am present."

After 1912 Robert Todd Lincoln lived in Washington and was present during the dedication of the memorial to his father in 1925. He died at his retreat "Hildene" in Manchester, New Hampshire on June 26, 1926.

Mary Harlan Lincoln (1846–1937) is buried with her husband on this hillside in Arlington. Their grave is marked by a pink marble stone which bears another familiar name. Buried here with his parents is the namesake of our sixteenth President, **Abraham Lincoln II**, who was the only son of Robert Todd Lincoln and who died at the age of seventeen in 1890. Robert Lincoln was survived by two daughters. The last direct descendant of Abraham Lincoln, a great-grandson, died in 1985 at the age of eighty-three.

JAMES McCUBBIN LINGAN

American Revolutionary, Defender of Free Speech

(May 13, 1751–July 28, 1812)
Sec. 1, Lot 89–A Grid JK–32

James McCubbin Lingan fought alongside thousands of other colonists during the American Revolution to gain independence for this nation and to insure certain basic freedoms, including the right of free speech. Although he was held by the British as a prisoner of war for over three years, Lingan survived the Revolution. Later, in 1812, he again fought for the right of free speech, this time defending a newspaper editor's right to publish antiwar sentiments. But this battle for freedom of the press was not against the British; it was against a violent mob of Americans and it cost Lingan his life.

On July 13, 1776, just nine days after the United States of America declared its independence from Great Britain, twenty-five-year-old James McCubbin Lingan was commissioned a Second Lieutenant in the Rawlings Additional Regiment. Four months later on November 16, during a battle at Fort Washington, he was stabbed with a bayonet and taken prisoner. For nearly three and one-half years he was held captive aboard the British prison ship *Jersey*.

During his imprisonment, Lingan was approached by British Admiral Sir Samuel Hood, Lingan's distant cousin, who offered Lingan ten thousand pounds and a high commission in the British Army if he would renounce the revolution and support King George III. Sitting in his cell, a space in which he could neither stand up nor lie down, Lingan unequivocally replied, "I'll rot first."

On another occasion while Lingan was aboard the prison ship, a fellow prisoner died during the night. When the guards arrived to retrieve the body, they brought along a coffin which was too short to hold the remains. One of the guards suggested that they simply cut off the dead prisoner's head and be done with it. At that, Lingan stood astride the body, stating in no uncertain terms that he would kill with his bare hands any person who would dare to touch the man's body with a knife. The guards found a larger coffin.

By the end of the American Revolution, Lingan had risen to the rank of General. Following that war, he was appointed by President George Washington to be Collector of the Port of Georgetown, which is now a part of the District of Columbia. He was also a founding member of the famed Revolutionary War veterans group, the Society of the Cincinnati.

During the War of 1812 Lingan found himself defending the First Amendment to the U.S. Constitution which he had fought so hard to establish over thirty years earlier. But this time he was not fighting against British soldiers; instead it was American citizens who opposed the freedom of the press. On June 19, 1812 the United States declared war on Great Britain, a decision which did not have the unanimous backing of the American people, including Alexander Contee Hanson. Hanson, a close friend of Lingan, was the editor of the *Federal Republic*, a newspaper in Baltimore, Maryland which ran an editorial denouncing the call to arms against Britain. That editorial ignited the fierce opposition of several readers who felt that Hanson's opinion was treasonous. A large group of angry citizens congregated in front of the newspaper's office. Excited by loud denunciations of Hanson, the mob began raiding the offices and destroying its presses. Hanson was forced to run for his life.

James McCubbin Lingan's tombstone proudly displays his record of service in the Revolutionary War. He is one of eleven veterans of that war reinterred at Arlington.

On July 27, 1812 Hanson resumed publication of his paper from a house in Georgetown. Within a few hours a mob again gathered and shots were fired. Among the supporters who had come to the defense of Hanson were James Lingan and "Light Horse Harry" Lee, another famous General of the American Revolution and former Governor of Virginia. Only the arrival of the militia prevented further bloodshed. For their own protection, Hanson and his supporters were escorted to the jail in Baltimore where they intended to stay until the mob dispersed. However, the mob did not disperse. Instead they broke into the jail during the night where a fierce battle ensued. Although Alexander Hanson survived the attack, James McCubbin Lingan was beaten to death. Harry Lee, father of Robert E. Lee, was severely beaten, but miraculously managed to escape almost certain death by remaining motionless as several of the rioters rummaged among the victims. One of the scavengers even poured hot wax into Lee's eye, searching for any sign of life. Lee, left blinded and permanently disabled by the episode, never fully recovered.

Lingan's death produced great public indignation. St. John's Church in Georgetown was to have been the site of his funeral but the size of the crowd forced the ceremony to be held outside. Called upon to deliver Lingan's eulogy was the son of George

Washington, **George Washington Parke Custis**. Custis acknowledged that he only knew Lingan by reputation, but quickly pointed out that President Washington had held Lingan in the highest regard. Praising Lingan for his defense of freedom of the press, Custis—his voice trembling with emotion—chastised every citizen for having allowed this massacre to have taken place, "Oh, Maryland! Would that the waters of the Chesapeake could wash this foul stain from thy character!" No one knew at that time that James McCubbin Lingan's final resting place would be on Custis' former estate. Lingan was originally buried in a private burial ground in Georgetown. His body was later reinterred in Arlington National Cemetery on November 5, 1908.

JOE LOUIS (BARROW)

"The Brown Bomber,"
Heavyweight Champion of the World

(May 13, 1914–April 12, 1981)
Sec. 7A, Lot 177, Grid U–24

During the 1930s and 1940s, the name of Joe Louis was probably as well known as that of the President, Franklin Roosevelt, because between 1937 and 1949, Joe Louis was boxing's "Heavyweight Champion of the World." He held that title longer and defended it more often than any other boxer in history, becoming the first great black idol for a whole generation of Americans.

Joe Louis' proper name was Joe Louis Barrow, but when he fought his first amateur fight, he signed up as "Joe Louis." His career skyrocketed and he became universally known. Born in Lexington, Alabama Joe moved with his six older brothers and sisters and their widowed mother, Lilly Barrow, to Detroit when he was a young boy. He was working in Detroit as an automobile assemblyman when he won the U.S. Amateur Athletic Union crown in 1934 and turned professional that same year.

Joe Louis suffered only one defeat in his first sixty-nine fights, and that was at the hands of Germany's great Max Schmeling, the reigning world heavyweight champion, on June 19, 1936. Schmeling knocked out Louis in the twelfth round of that title fight. Louis became world champion one year later, on June 22, 1937, when he knocked out James J. Braddock in the eighth round of their bout. While defending his title twenty-five times, more than any other champion in boxing history, Joe scored knockouts in twenty of those fights.

On June 22, 1938, in what was touted as "the fight of the century," a rematch between Joe Louis and Max Schmeling drew a crowd of 70,000 to Yankee Stadium in New York. This time it was Louis who entered as champion and Schmeling as challenger. President Roosevelt met with "the Champ" before the fight to wish him well; everyone knew that more was at stake on that night than just the title. In that ring Joe Louis represented America's best, and he was squaring off with Schmeling, the pride of Nazi Germany, at a time when the Nazis were professing to be a superior race. While none of the American spectators were disappointed in the outcome, they may have been disappointed that the fight did not last longer. Louis pummeled Schmeling, knocking him to the canvas in just over two minutes into the first round. Schmeling was hit so hard and so often in that short time that he spent a full week in a New York hospital.

When the United States finally went to war against Germany in 1941, Louis enlisted in the Army, serving in the same segregated unit as Jackie Robinson, the first black man to play major league baseball. During the war Louis fought ninety-six exhibition matches before over two million troops. He also donated more than $100,000 to Navy and Army relief efforts. When he left the Army, he had reached the rank of Sergeant.

Joe Louis retired from boxing on March 1, 1949 with a record of sixty-eight wins and one loss. During his fabled career he had earned about $5,000,000, most of which he either gave away or spent. In the late 1940s the Internal Revenue Service assessed Louis over $1,000,000 in back taxes and penalties. This arose as a result of a divorce settlement in which Louis agreed to pay his ex-wife a portion of the purse from his biggest fight, $650,000. It was based upon a percentage of his winnings, as a manager's fee would be computed, but the IRS considered it to be "alimony," ruling that Louis owed taxes and considerable penalties on that money. Louis knew only one way to earn that kind of money, so he returned to the ring.

Coming out of retirement on September 27, 1950, he challenged the new champion, Ezzard Charles, but was beaten decisively in fifteen rounds. He attempted another major bout on October 26, 1951 against future champion Rocky Marciano; this time Louis was knocked out in the eighth round. He never fought again, ending his extraordinary seventeen-year career with a record of sixty-eight wins and three losses, winning fifty-four of his fights by knockouts.

Louis is remembered for the famous "Bum-of-the-Month" tour during which Joe defended his title with a fight each month for a full year. He spent his last years confined to a wheelchair as a result of open heart surgery. He also worked as a greeter at a Las Vegas hotel.

When Joe Louis died on April 12, 1981, exactly thirty-six years to the day after Franklin Roosevelt's death, Louis had not been champion for more than thirty-two years. But still people throughout the world paid him homage. To them he would always be "the Champ." President Ronald Reagan waived the technical requirements for burial at Arlington in order to allow Joe Louis to be interred there. During a service with full military honors, the hundreds of people who came to the funeral heard three volleys fired into the quiet, spring air as a salute to the former boxing great, signalling his last round. Since his death thousands of visitors have come to view the tombstone that bears a bas-relief of the famous fighter and the inscription "The Brown Bomber."

MELVIN J. MAAS

Congressman, Disabled Veteran Commander

(May 14, 1898–April 13, 1964)
Sec. 34, Lot 4–A, Grid VW–12/13

After serving eight terms in the United States House of Representatives, Melvin J. Maas returned to active military duty during World War II. During the Okinawa campaign, a bomb explosion resulted in the loss of his sight. Undaunted by his impaired vision, Maas served tirelessly after the war for fifteen years on the President's Committee on Employment of the Handicapped.

Born in Duluth, Minnesota, Maas grew up in St. Paul, graduating from St. Thomas College in 1919. He received an appointment to the United States Military Academy in 1917, but was so anxious to join the World War I effort, that he enlisted in the Marine Corps as a private. Though he did not see combat during the war, Maas did earn his wings as a pilot, and in 1925 was commissioned an officer in the Marine Corps Reserve.

Elected to Congress as a Republican in 1926, Maas served on the House Foreign Affairs Committee, where he expressed great concern about the air defenses of Washington, D.C. To dramatize his point, Maas rented a biplane in 1929 and buzzed the Capitol dome during a joint session of Congress. Upon landing, he stated that with one bomb he could have wiped out the entire government.

Maas caused another stir in the House in 1932. This time, however, it was for his heroics. While Maas was speaking on the floor, a man brandishing a handgun rose to his feet in the House gallery and demanded that he be allowed to address the House regarding some personal business. Maas, holding the floor with his authoritative presence, calmly but sternly informed the gentleman that no one was allowed to address the House while carrying a weapon and ordered him to drop the handgun. The man complied and immediately was taken into custody. For his coolness in this tense situation, Maas was awarded the Carnegie Silver Medal.

Congressman Maas lost his bid for reelection in 1932, but staged a comeback victory, rejoining the House in 1934. While still in Congress, Maas served in the South Pacific as a Colonel in the Marine Corps. In 1944, after sixteen years in the House, Maas was defeated for reelection and so chose to remain on active duty in the Pacific. It was during the attack on Okinawa that Maas suffered damage to his optic nerve from fragments of an exploded bomb. The incident caused permanent damage that led to total blindness in 1951.

Maas was not discouraged by his impairment. In 1949 President Harry S Truman appointed him to the President's Committee on Employment of the Physically Handicapped, a committee Maas chaired from 1954 until his death in 1964. During that period, Maas dedicated his efforts to assisting disabled veterans and served as National Commander of the Disabled American Veterans and the Blinded Veterans Association. In 1952 he retired from the Marine Corps Reserve with the rank of Major General. Congressman Maas died at the Bethesda Naval Hospital on April 13, 1964.

ARTHUR MacARTHUR

Medal of Honor Winner, Highest Ranking Army Officer

(June 2, 1845–September 5, 1912)
Sec. 2. Lot 879, Grid P–31

Arthur MacArthur foresaw a military career for himself but was unable to secure the appointment to West Point which he so strongly desired. Not to be deterred, he volunteered his services to his country, earning a Congressional Medal of Honor for gallantry during the Civil War and, by 1906, becoming the highest ranking officer in the Army. His proud military record set an example for his son, Douglas MacArthur, who was able to enter West Point and who rose to the rank of Five-Star General.

Arthur MacArthur was the son of a prominent Scottish immigrant who had settled in Springfield, Massachusetts. The elder MacArthur developed a successful law practice by the time Arthur was born in 1845. In 1849 the family moved to Wisconsin where the senior MacArthur continued his legal and political interests becoming Lieutenant Governor and then Governor of the state. Arthur attended Milwaukee public schools and sought an appointment to West Point but was unable to obtain one. Nevertheless, Arthur volunteered for service during the Civil War with the Twenty-fourth Wisconsin Volunteer Infantry.

MacArthur saw combat at Perryville; Kentucky where his conduct earned him a citation for bravery and a promotion to Captain although he was still just seventeen years old. During the siege of Murfreesboro in December 1862, MacArthur quickly assumed command of the troops when his regimental commander fell. Issuing timely orders, MacArthur held the Twenty-fourth together. He lead the assault on Missionary Ridge, planting the regimental colors and giving confidence and direction to his men. For his action, he was awarded the highest military combat decoration, the Congressional Medal of Honor, although it was not presented until June 30, 1890.

On January 24, 1864 MacArthur was given command of his regiment and was later wounded during the Battle of Kennesaw Mountain on June 27 of that year. On November 30, 1864 MacArthur was wounded again in the Battle of Franklin, Tennessee, the result of hand-to-hand fighting. His injuries were so severe that he was unable to return to active duty for the remainder of the war. Nonetheless, he was promoted to Lt. Colonel of Volunteers and when he mustered out of the Army in June of 1865, he was an experienced field commander carrying the title, "Boy Colonel of the West." He had just celebrated his twentieth birthday.

MacArthur began the study of law but soon realized that his real love was the military. He reenlisted in February of 1866 and received a commission as a Second Lieutenant in the regular Army. By the end of 1866 he was a Captain and began a three-year tour of the western frontier. During the next thirty years, MacArthur's tour of duty found him in New York, the Utah Territory, Louisiana, Pennsylvania, and New Mexico where he took part in the campaign against Geronimo in 1885. MacArthur became an instructor at the Infantry and Cavalry School at Fort Leavenworth, Kansas in 1889 and was promoted to Lt. Colonel in 1896. He had finally reached the same regular Army rank at the age of fifty-one that he had achieved as a volunteer more than thirty years before.

Arthur MacArthur was stationed in the Dakotas when the Spanish-American War started in 1898. On May 27 of that year, he was commissioned a Brigadier General and assigned as Adjutant General of III Corps. He ultimately commanded a brigade of Volunteers headed for the Philippine Islands and took part in the capture of Manila in August. President William McKinley named him Military Governor of the Philippines on May 6, 1900 which ultimately put him at odds with the civilian governor appointed the following year, **William Howard Taft**. MacArthur combined an aggressive military presence with humane civic actions such as establishing public education and revising the harsh Spanish civil code. Nevertheless, MacArthur favored military rule for at least another decade, an idea which ran contrary to **Taft's** desire for a quick return to civilian government. By this time, however, **Taft's** good friend and mentor, Theodore Roosevelt, was President and **Taft** remained as civilian governor while MacArthur was transferred back the United States.

During the next eight years, MacArthur held several commands and toured American posts overseas. He went to Manchuria in 1905 to observe the final stages of the Russo-Japanese War and served as Military Attache to the American embassy in Tokyo. He returned to the U.S. in 1906 to resume his previous post as commander of the Pacific.

In 1906 the position of Army Chief of Staff, the highest position in the Army, became vacant. At that time MacArthur was the highest ranking officer in the Army and would normally have been elevated to the post. Instead, he was overlooked by his former nemesis and now Secretary of War, **William Howard Taft**.

Although he was promoted to Lt. General, the highest rank available at the time, MacArthur never achieved his dream of being Army Chief of Staff. He retired from the Army on his sixty-fourth birthday, June 2, 1909. On September 5, 1912 MacArthur returned to Milwaukee to address a reunion of veterans of the old Wisconsin Twenty-fourth Volunteer Regiment from the Civil War. He suffered an attack while on the dais and died. He was buried with full military honors at Arlington National Cemetery.

GEORGE C. MARSHALL

Five-Star General, Secretary of State, Nobel Laureate

(December 31, 1880–October 16, 1959)
Sec. 7, Lot 8198, Grid VW–24

As a soldier, he was more than a victor, he was a healer; in government, he was greater than a politician, he was a statesman; and in international affairs, he rose above routine diplomacy to become a peacemaker. President Harry S Truman called him "the Greatest of the Great." He is General of the Army George C. Marshall.

George Catlett Marshall, Jr. shared his birthplace – Uniontown, Pennsylvania – with another American General, Revolutionary War hero **Thomas Meason**. A distant cousin of early Supreme Court Chief Justice John Marshall, George Marshall entered Virginia Military Institute in 1897. When he graduated in 1901, Marshall held the position of First Captain of the Corps of Cadets. He applied for a commission in the United States Army and was named First Lieutenant of Infantry in February 1902.

Marshall's first assignment was in the Philippines, his station until 1903. In 1906 he entered the Infantry School, graduating first in his class, then went on to serve as an instructor at Fort Leavenworth, Kansas. In June 1917 Captain Marshall accompanied the First Division to France at the outbreak of World War I. His mastery of military logistics allowed him to move hundreds of thousands of troops in the Meuse-Argonne Salient and earned him recognition from the commander of the American Expeditionary Force, General **John J. Pershing**. **Pershing** was so impressed with this young Lt. Colonel that he made Marshall his aide and kept him in that position until he himself retired as Army Chief of Staff in 1924. When Marshall married in 1930, he chose **Pershing** to serve as his best man.

Following his assignment with **Pershing**, Marshall spent three years in Tientsin, China as Executive Officer of the Fifteenth Infantry Regiment. Returning to America in 1927, he was placed in charge of instruction at the Infantry School at Fort Benning, Georgia where, in the following five years, 165 future generals passed under his command, among them **Omar Bradley** and **Walter Bedell Smith**.

From 1933 through 1936 Marshall served as senior instructor of the Illinois National Guard and was promoted to Brigadier General. Two years later he was head of the War Plans Division (WPD) in Washington, D.C., rising to Deputy Chief of Staff. Ironically, Marshall was promoted to full General and sworn in as Army Chief of Staff on September 1, 1939, the same day that Nazi troops invaded Poland to begin the Second World War.

When Marshall assumed the position of Chief of Staff, it was clearly with an eye on the events in Europe. Although the U.S. did not enter that war until two years later, Marshall directed his efforts toward preparing for our nation's entry. In 1939 the United States forces numbered less than 200,000 men. Under Marshall's direction, that number increased to over 8,000,000 men and women in less than four years. Not only did he oversee the expansion of our Armed Forces but the improvement of their training and equipment as well.

It was George C. Marshall who coordinated the U.S. military efforts throughout the world during World War II. Every theatre of operation—whether in Europe, the Pacific, or the Far East—benefitted from Marshall's influence and presence. He traveled throughout the world, meeting with Winston Churchill and Allied commanders in London and with Douglas MacArthur in the Pacific. From Washington he planned and directed the successful invasion of Normandy on D-Day, though sharing very little in the glory given to the generals who were present on the beaches of France.

On December 16, 1944 President Franklin Roosevelt elevated Marshall to the Five-star rank of General of the Army. Only five men were so honored in that war; three of them now rest at Arlington: Marshall, **Omar Bradley** and **Henry "Hap" Arnold.** The others were Dwight Eisenhower and Douglas MacArthur.

Marshall resigned as Chief of Staff on November 21, 1945; just one week later, President Truman persuaded him to tackle the challenge of resolving the difficult political situation in China. As President Truman's special envoy, Marshall returned to the country where he had lived during the 1920s and dedicated himself to bringing the Nationalists and Communists together. After a full year of unsuccessful diplomatic maneuvering, he returned to the United States in 1947 to accept another top-level assignment from the President.

President Truman appointed him to succeed James F. Burns as Secretary of State. Marshall assumed the Cabinet post during a period of international realignment in the aftermath of the war. During his two-year tenure, the U.S. provided support for the anticommunist forces in Greece and Turkey, and the State of Israel was recognized as an independent nation. He began the discussions which led to the formation of the North Atlantic Treaty Organization (NATO) and the Organization of American States (OAS); in 1949 he oversaw the Berlin Airlift, the action that defused the threat of a Soviet Union blockade of West Berlin.

Marshall's greatest triumph, however, was his European Recovery Program, universally known as "The Marshall Plan." Proposed in a commencement address at Harvard University in June 1947, this plan contributed billions of dollars toward the economic recovery of sixteen war-torn European nations. It was

Marshall's belief that the Soviet Union was simply awaiting the economic collapse of Western Europe before attempting to expand its sphere of influence in Europe. As a testament to his efforts, Marshall was awarded the Nobel Peace Prize in 1953, becoming the only professional soldier ever to receive that most coveted award.

George Marshall resigned as Secretary of State in 1949 following surgery to remove a kidney and became President of the American Red Cross. As war in Korea neared, President Truman again summoned Marshall to his Cabinet, this time as Secretary of Defense. Nearly seventy years old, Marshall agreed to serve for one year. Special legislation was passed by Congress waiving, in Marshall's case alone, the prohibition against a military man serving as head of the Defense Department. During his tenure, Marshall rebuilt American military manpower and increased production of war materials before permanently resigning from public service in September 1951.

Marshall adamantly refused offers to publish his memoirs, including one offer for a million dollars. It was his belief that such memoirs would require the truthful recitation of events and he did not wish to tarnish the image of people he would have felt compelled to include. In addition to the numerous decorations presented by this country, Marshall received recognition from at least a dozen other nations, including the Soviet Union. These awards and his many honorary degrees are housed at the George C. Marshall Research Library in Lexington, Virginia.

Early in his career, it was clear that George C. Marshall possessed the attributes of command. Those who served with him recognized his quiet self-confidence and his desire to shun flamboyance. He could communicate effectively with soldier and civilian alike and could inspire any subordinate to do his or her best. Few Americans have done more to further the cause of democracy and world peace than he did. George Marshall died at Walter Reed General Hospital in Washington, D.C. on October 16, 1959 and was buried with honors at Arlington National Cemetery.

WILLIAM GIBBS McADOO

Senator, Presidential Candidate

(October 31, 1863–February 1, 1941)
Sec. 2, Lot 4969, Grid W–32/33

William Gibbs McAdoo served in Woodrow Wilson's Cabinet for more than five years but resigned to seek the Democratic nomination for President in 1920. Unsuccessful in his first attempt, he again sought the nomination in 1924, and was the clear favorite entering the convention. But McAdoo was again disappointed, losing the nomination after leading for more than one hundred ballots.

McAdoo was born in Marietta, Georgia where he attended rural schools. He received his degree from the University of Tennessee in Knoxville before studying law. Admitted to the bar in 1885, he commenced practice in Chattanooga, moving his practice to New York City in 1892. While in New York, McAdoo developed a system of train tunnels between New York and New Jersey beneath the Hudson River. From 1902 until 1913 he served as president of the company which constructed and operated those tunnels.

Following Woodrow Wilson's election as President in 1912, McAdoo was appointed Secretary of the Treasury and served in the Wilson Cabinet until 1918, when he resigned to begin his own campaign for the White House. There was no constitutional ban on a third term for presidents at that time, but it was widely known that President Wilson's health would not permit him to run for reelection. The party's nomination was, therefore, wide open.

When the party convened in San Francisco, McAdoo was a leading candidate but he lost the nomination to James M. Cox. In the presidential election that fall, Cox and his running mate, Franklin Roosevelt, were soundly defeated by Warren G. Harding and Calvin Coolidge.

McAdoo again sought the Presidency in 1924 and was clearly the front runner. At the convention he led on a record one hundred ballots before losing the nomination on the one hundred third ballot to John W. Davis.

In 1932 McAdoo, who had moved to Los Angeles ten years earlier, was elected to the Senate from California the same year that Franklin Roosevelt won the Presidency. He lost his bid for renomination in 1938 and returned to Los Angeles as chairman of the board of a steamship line. McAdoo died in 1941 while visiting Washington, D.C.

ANITA NEWCOMB McGEE

First Woman Army Surgeon

(November 4, 1864–October 5, 1940)
Sec. 1, Lot 526–B, KL–34/35

From an early age science played an integral part in the life of Anita Newcomb McGee. Her father, astronomer and mathematician **Simon Newcomb**, instilled in young Anita the desire to question and to more fully discover the world around her.

Born in Washington, D.C. while her father was stationed at the Naval Observatory, she spent her younger years questioning and discovering. She received her medical training at Columbian University (now George Washington University) and was awarded her M.D. in 1892.

Following her graduation, she practiced medicine in Washington, D.C. until 1896. In 1898 she was named director of the Daughters of the American Revolution Hospital Corps, which selected and trained nurses for Army and Navy service. Appointed acting Assistant Surgeon in the United States Army on August 29, 1898, she became the first woman ever named to that position. Her assignment in the Surgeon General's Office was as Superintendent of the Army Nurse Corps, which she organized. In 1900 the U.S. Congress approved her recommendation to make the Nurse Corps a permanent part of the Army. Then, having fulfilled her assignment, she resigned from the Army on December 13, 1900.

In 1904 McGee was named president of the Society of Spanish-American War Nurses. During that same year, she also gained recognition as a representative of the Philadelphia Red Cross Society when that Society entered into an agreement with the Japanese government to bring a party of trained former Army nurses to Japan for six months gratuitous service during the Russo-Japanese War.

Dr. McGee became a lecturer at the University of California in 1911, dedicating much of her time to scientific writing. She toured throughout the nation for a variety of magazines, lecturing widely on medical topics. Anita Newcomb McGee died on October 5, 1940 and is buried in her father's family plot at Arlington National Cemetery.

MONTGOMERY CUNNINGHAM MEIGS

Soldier, Engineer, Architect

(May 3, 1816–January 2, 1892)
Sec. 1, Lot 1, Grid N–32/33

Although Montgomery Meigs played a pivotal role in the creation of a national military cemetery on the grounds of the Arlington estate in 1864, he is better known for his architectural and engineering feats in and around Washington, D.C.

A native of Augusta, Georgia, Meigs attended the University of Pennsylvania and then transferred to the U.S. Military Academy where he graduated fifth in his class in 1836. Commissioned into the Artillery, Meigs held a degree in engineering and soon was transferred the Corps of Engineers. In 1837 he accompanied Robert E. Lee to St. Louis, Missouri to undertake navigational improvements of the Mississippi River.

During the 1850s Meigs initiated and completed several engineering projects in Washington, D.C., which greatly changed the city. He supervised the construction of the Washington Aqueduct that extended twelve miles from Great Falls on the Potomac River to a reservoir near Georgetown. The Cabin John Bridge, which he designed to carry Washington's main water supply and vehicular traffic, was, until this century, the longest single masonry arch in the world. Meigs also oversaw the construction of the wings and dome of the U.S. Capitol Building.

The best known architectural accomplishment of Meigs, however, is the Old Pension Building in Washington's Judiciary Square. That building was originally intended as a pension distribution center for Union soldiers. It is a large brick shell covering an interior space of 30,000 square feet; its exterior displays a terra cotta frieze depicting Union forces in battle. The Old Pension Building has been used for inaugural

Montgomery Meigs—the man responsible for recommending that the Arlington estate be used as a military cemetery—is buried in Section 1. A statue depicting Meigs' slain son, Lt. John Meigs, marks the young Meigs' grave next to his father.

balls and is officially classified a National Historic Monument. Indeed, in October 1985, it was rededicated as the National Building Museum.

Other buildings designed, at least in part, by Montgomery Meigs are the War Department Building, now called the Executive Office Building near the White House, and the National Museum Building, now known as the Centennial Building of the Smithsonian Institution.

It was in May 1861 that Montgomery Meigs was promoted to Brigadier General and named Quartermaster General. He was placed in charge of equipping all Union forces with every need, except ordnance; history has credited him with performing efficiently and with competence. Meigs has also been credited with holding a rather high opinion of himself and with possessing a violent, sometimes irrational, temper.

Although a Southerner by birth, Meigs considered the secessionists as revolutionaries and the soldiers who fought for the South as traitors. Among those he hated most were his former mentor, Jefferson Davis, his former commanding officer, Robert E. Lee, and his own brother, who fought for his family's native Georgia. It was his hatred of Lee that prompted him to recommend that Lee's home be made a military cemetery.

Meigs retired from the Army in 1882, but remained involved in Washington civic affairs. It was after his retirement that he designed the Old Pension Building. He also served as a regent at the Smithsonian Institution and was an early member of the National Academy of Sciences. Meigs died in Washington on January 2, 1892 and was buried at Arlington, the cemetery he had personally established. Interred here with him are his wife, and his son, Lt. **John Rodgers Meigs**. Lt. **Meigs'** grave is marked by a reclining bronze statue of young **Meigs** depicting the dramatic scene of his death during the Civil War on October 3, 1864.

Also buried near Montgomery Meigs is his father, **Josiah Meigs**, who had served as a commander of the General Land Office and who died on September 4, 1822 and was buried in Congressional Cemetery in Washington. He was later reintered at Arlington beside his son.

NELSON APPLETON MILES

Civil War Veteran, General in Chief of the Army

(August 8, 1839–May 15,1925)
Sec. 3, Lot 1873, Grid U–16

Nelson Appleton Miles entered the Army as a volunteer Captain during the Civil War and, despite his lack of formal military training, rose to the military's highest rank, General in Chief of the Army. Yet his record was tarnished when troops under his command undertook one of the most tragic massacres of Indians in American history.

Born near Westminster, Massachusetts in 1839, Miles was a twenty-one-year-old Captain in the Twenty-second Massachusetts Regiment when the Confederates fired on Fort Sumter to begin the Civil War. He was first wounded at Fair Oaks (Seven Pines) on May 31, 1862. Undaunted, he returned to combat at Antietam and, under fire, assumed command of his regiment, earning a promotion to Lt. Colonel. Just three months later at Fredericksburg, Miles was severely wounded when he was shot through the throat. In May of 1863, he was wounded a third time while fighting at Chancellorsville. For his continued bravery throughout the Civil War, Miles was belatedly awarded the Congressional Medal of Honor in 1892.

Controversy first touched his career immediately after the war while he was commanding Fortress Monroe, Virginia. He was entrusted with the custody of Jefferson Davis, the former President of the Confederacy. Under Miles' strict orders, Davis was denied any privileges and kept manacled in a dark, musty cell. Leaders of both the North and the South roundly criticized Miles for this harsh treatment of his prisoner.

Miles' career as a reputed Indian fighter began in 1869 when he was transferred to the Fifth Infantry on the western frontier. Following the defeat of Lt. Colonel George Armstrong Custer in 1876, Nelson Miles was given the command of one of the columns that forced the Sioux and Northern Cheyenne Indians either into Canada or onto existing reservations. His reputation preceded him to Arizona where he succeeded General **George Crook** and captured the elusive Apache leader, Geronimo, in 1886.

In 1890 Miles commanded federal troops responsible for keeping the peace with the Sioux Indians in South Dakota. The government became alarmed when a religious movement known as the "Ghost Dance" spread among the Sioux. Fearing an uprising, Indian police were sent to take the Sioux chief, Sitting Bull, into custody hoping to disarm the movement. Sitting Bull resisted and was killed. A large group of his followers fled and joined Chief Big Foot's band of Sioux on the Cheyenne River. There they were captured by Miles' troops and taken to a cavalry camp at Wounded Knee Creek. While disarming the Indians, a shot was fired and a bloody battle followed. Two hundred men, women, and children were massacred by the soldiers. Later, as a result of the controversy with the Sioux at Wounded Knee, Miles was reassigned to Chicago where he led the federal troops that suppressed the Pullman strike in 1894.

The following year, upon the retirement of **John McCallister Schofield**, Miles inherited the title of General in Chief of the Army, joining such other men as Ulysses S. Grant, William Tecumseh Sherman, and **Philip Henry Sheridan** who had held that position. Due to a reorganization of the Army, he was the last person ever to bear that title. When the war with Spain broke out in 1898, Miles expected to be named commander of all combat forces. However the Secretary of War, who had long been at odds with Miles, prevailed upon President William McKinley to deny Miles the position.

This 1930s photograph shows the mausoleum of Nelson A. Miles (at left) which is located on a cul-de-sac at the end of Miles Drive in Section 3. Also located atop this hill overlooking the old South Post of Fort Myer and the city of Washington are the graves of Vinnie Ream and Edmund Rice.

Unwilling to retire on his own, Miles was forced into retirement at the mandatory age of 64 in 1903 by President Theodore Roosevelt. Having finished his first autobiography in 1896, Miles wrote a second in 1911. As the Army's most senior officer, General Miles was honored as Grand Marshall of the parade which preceded the dedication of the Memorial Amphitheatre at Arlington in 1920. He died in 1925 at the age of 85 in Washington, D.C., and is buried in one of only two family mausoleums in Arlington National Cemetery. The other mausoleum belongs to the family of Brigadier General **Thomas Crook Sullivan**(Sec. 1, Lot 236, Grid MN–34).

MARC ANDREW MITSCHER

Commander, World War II's Task Force 58

(January 26, 1887–February 3, 1947)
Sec. 2, Lot 4942, Grid W–32/33

Although he was not a model plebe at the Naval Academy, Marc Andrew Mitscher became a model commander who contributed invaluable service in the Pacific Theatre during World War II, serving as commander of the inimitable Task Force 58.

Marc Mitscher moved from his hometown of Hillsboro, Wisconsin to Oklahoma City, Oklahoma when he was still a child. There his father was elected mayor and through the efforts of a friend in Congress, the elder Mitscher secured for his son an appointment to the Naval Academy. Never a serious academician, Marc Mitscher nevertheless graduated in 1910 and was assigned to the Pacific Fleet. In October of 1915 he reported for naval aviation training, becoming Naval Aviator No. 33 the following year when he received his wings. World War I saw Mitscher serving in three different stateside naval stations.

In 1919 Mitscher participated in man's first transatlantic flight when three NC-1 Flying Boats attempted the crossing. Piloting one of the planes, Mitscher was forced down short of the Azores,

but earned the Navy Cross for his efforts. In 1926 he was transferred to the U.S. Navy's first aircraft carrier, *Langley*. He was
later named to head the air department of another carrier, *Saratoga*,
and Mitscher himself landed the first plane on its deck in 1928.

When the new aircraft carrier, *Hornet* was commissioned in
October 1941, Mitscher was given that command and found himself
in the Atlantic when the Japanese attacked Pearl Harbor. Ordered
to the Pacific, Mitscher's carrier became the secret "Shangra La"
from which Colonel Jimmy Doolittle's famed B-25 Bombers made
their morale-boosting raids on Tokyo in April 1942. Later that year
he led the *Hornet* to the first important U.S. victory over Japan
at Midway Island where his planes sank four Japanese carriers.
In July 1941 he rose to the rank of Rear Admiral, directing all U.S.
aircraft during the bitter Solomon Islands campaign in 1943.

Mitscher's greatest achievements occurred, however, following
his appointment as commander of the legendary Fast Carrier Task
Force, Pacific Fleet, or Task Force Fifty-eight as it came to be
known around the world. From his flagship, *Yorktown* Mitscher
led air strikes from his fast carriers against the island of Truk in
the Carolinas in February 1944. That success was followed by
equally impressive performances in the Battle of the Philippine
Sea in June (during which Mitscher provided air support for
Douglas MacArthur's invasion of the Philippines); the Battle of
Leyte Gulf in October; and the capture of Iwo Jima and Okinawa
in early 1945. Also during this period, planes under Mitscher's
command struck the Japanese mainland and sank the super battleship, *Yamato*. Fighting deadly kamikazes, Mitscher was twice
forced to transfer his flagship when first the *Bunker Hill* and then
the *Enterprise* suffered damage. He ended up aboard the *Randolph*.

Mitscher returned to Washington, D.C. in July 1945, having
earned the respect and trust of his pilots. He took extraordinary
risks to save the lives of airmen, as, for example, on the evening
of June 20, 1944. During the Battle of the Philippine Sea, many
of Mitscher's pilots were returning after dark. Knowing that they
were inexperienced in night landings and that they would be low
on fuel, he ordered all the ship's lights turned on so that the pilots
could see the flight deck. This move, unheard of during war, en-
dangered all on board, including Mitscher himself, but his concern was first for his pilots' welfare. He himself was a pilot who

had survived three crashes and he would not let his own pilots down.

In 1946 Mitscher earned promotion to the Four-star rank of Admiral and was given command of the Atlantic Fleet. While still in active service, Mitscher died of a chronic heart ailment at Norfolk, Virginia in 1947. He is buried at Arlington near other great naval men of World War II.

AUDIE MURPHY

World War II's Most Decorated Soldier, Actor

(June 20, 1924–May 28, 1971)
Sec. 46, Lot 366-11, Grid O/P–22/23

He wanted to join the Marines, but he was too short. The Paratroopers wouldn't have him either. Reluctantly, he settled on the Infantry, enlisting to become nothing less than the most decorated hero of World War II. He was Audie Murphy, the baby-faced Texas farmboy who became an American legend.

Murphy grew up on a sharecropper's farm in Hunt County, Texas. Left at a very young age to help raise ten brothers and sisters when his father deserted their mother, Audie was only sixteen when his mother died. He watched as his brothers and sisters were doled out to an orphanage or to relatives. Seeking an escape from that life in 1942, he looked to the Marines.

War had just been declared and, like so many other young men, Murphy lied about his age in his attempt to enlist. But it was not his age that kept him out of the Marines; it was his size. Not tall enough to meet the minimum requirements, he tried to enlist in the Paratroopers, but again was denied entrance. Despondent, he chose the Infantry.

Following basic training Murphy was assigned to the Fifth Regiment, Third Infantry Division in North Africa preparing to invade Sicily. It was here in 1943 that he first saw combat, proving himself to be a proficient marksman and highly skilled soldier. Consistently his performance demonstrated how well he understood the techniques of small unit action. He landed at Salerno to fight in the Volturno River campaign and then at Anzio.to be part of the Allied force which fought its way to Rome. Throughout these campaigns, Murphy's unmatched skills earned him advancements in rank while many of his superior officers were being transferred, wounded, or killed. After the capture of Rome, Murphy won his first decoration for gallantry.

Shortly thereafter his unit was withdrawn from Italy to train for Operation Anvil-Dragoon, the invasion of southern France. During seven weeks of fighting in that successful campaign, Murphy's division suffered 4,500 casualties, and he became one of the most decorated men in his company. But his biggest test was yet to come.

Following the death of Audie Murphy in 1971, so many people visited his grave that a special walkway was built to accommodate the crowds. The government regulation headstone of Murphy—the most decorated soldier in World War II—is not large enough to display all of his commendations.

On January 26, 1945, near the village of Holtzwihr in eastern France, Lieutenant Murphy's forward positions came under fierce attack by the Germans. Against the onslaught of six Panzer tanks and 250 infantrymen, Murphy ordered his men to fall back to better their defenses. Alone, he mounted an abandoned burning tank destroyer and, with a single machine gun, contested the enemy's advance. Wounded in the leg during the heavy fire, Murphy remained there for nearly an hour, repelling the attack of German soldiers on three sides and single-handedly killing fifty of them. His courageous performance stalled the German advance and allowed him to lead his men in the counterattack which ultimately drove the enemy from Holtzwihr. For this Murphy was awarded the Congressional Medal of Honor, our nation's highest award for gallantry in action.

By the war's end, Murphy had become the nation's most

decorated soldier, earning an unparalleled twenty-eight medals, including three from France and one from Belgium. Murphy had been wounded three times during the war, yet, in May of 1945, when victory was declared in Europe, he had still not reached his twenty-first birthday.

Audie Murphy returned to a hero's welcome in the United States. His photograph appeared on the cover of *LIFE* magazine and he was persuaded by actor James Cagney to embark on an acting career. Still very shy and unassuming, Murphy arrived in Hollywood with only his good looks and — by his own account — "no talent." Nevertheless, he went on to make over forty films. His first part was just a small one in *Beyond Glory* in 1948. The following year he published his wartime memoirs, *To Hell and Back*, which received good reviews. Later he portrayed himself in the 1955 movie version of the book. Most film critics, however, believe his best performance was in *Red Badge of Courage*, Stephen Crane's Civil War epic.

After nearly twenty years he retired from acting and started a career in private business. But the venture was unsuccessful, eventually forcing him into bankruptcy in 1968. Murphy — who once said that he could only sleep with a loaded pistol under his pillow — was haunted by nightmares of his wartime experiences throughout his adult life. In 1971, at the age of 46, he died in the crash of a private plane near Roanoke, Virginia.

Audie Murphy lies buried in Arlington Cemetery just across Memorial Drive from the Memorial Amphitheatre. A special flagstone walkway has been constructed to accommodate the large number of people who stop to pay their respects to America's most decorated soldier. Located at the end of a row of graves, his tomb is marked by a simple, white, government-issue tombstone which lists only a few of his many military decorations. The stone is, as he was, too small.

SIMON NEWCOMB

Astronomer, Rear Admiral (Retired)

(March 12, 1835–July 11, 1909)
Sec. 1, Lot 527, Grid KL–34/35

Simon Newcomb was no ordinary seaman. The only courses he wanted to chart were those of the planets and the stars. He was a sailor who avoided the sea.

Simon Newcomb was born in Wallace, Nova Scotia and was educated by his father, an itinerant schoolteacher. By the age of five, young Simon was spending several hours a day calculating multiplication and division problems. At the age of sixteen he was apprenticed to an herb doctor in Salisbury, New Brunswick but he literally ran away from the 'doctor' when he realized that the man was a quack who never saw patients. Simon joined his father who had settled in Maryland. He took up teaching in rural Maryland schools, spending his free time in nearby Washington, D.C., where he studied mathematics and developed an interest in astronomy.

In January 1857 Newcomb applied for and received employment with "The American Ephemeris and Nautical Almanac" in Cambridge, Massachusetts. The Almanac was an annual handbook for astronomers, which included the predicted positions of the principal celestial bodies and other astronomical phenomena. While working there, Newcomb enrolled in Harvard's Lawrence Scientific School, graduating in 1858. In 1861 he was commissioned as a professor of mathematics in the United States Navy and was assigned to the Naval Observatory in Washington, D.C. His primary task was to find and to correct errors in published values for the positions and motions of various celestial objects. During this period Newcomb also negotiated the contract for the new twenty-six-inch telescope at the Naval Observatory which was built in 1873.

In 1877 Newcomb was promoted to Captain and named Senior

Mathematics Professor in the Navy as well as Superintendent of the American Nautical Almanac Office. It was in the latter position that Newcomb undertook his greatest work—the thorough revision of the motion theory and position tables for all major celestial bodies in the solar system. The result of his work, which took more than twenty years to complete, became a standard reference which was recognized throughout the world and which is still in use today. He also led several field expeditions, including one to the Cape of Good Hope to observe the Venus transit of 1882.

As contributing editor of the *American Journal of Mathematics*, Newcomb was named a professor of mathematics and astronomy at Baltimore's Johns Hopkins University in 1884. He led an international conference in Paris in 1896 which adopted a common system of ephemerides—the tables of computed places of celestial bodies over a period of time. Another such conference was held in 1950 which reaffirmed the validity of Newcomb's tables.

In 1897 Newcomb reached the age of mandatory retirement for Navy Captains but was allowed to continue his work under grants from the Carnegie Institute of Washington. In 1899 he founded the American Astronomical Society, serving as its president for six years. Then in 1906, after he had been retired for nine years, he was granted the extraordinary promotion to Rear Admiral. Throughout his lifetime Simon Newcomb was the recipient of numerous honorary degrees, and of foreign and domestic civilian commendations, also gaining election to the National Academy of Sciences. He died in Washington, D.C. on July 11, 1909.

ARTHUR D. NICHOLSON, JR.

Casualty of the Cold War

(June 7, 1947–March 24, 1985)
Sec. 7A, Lot 171, Grid U–23/24

Not all soldiers who sacrifice their lives for their country do so during great battles in great wars. Occasionally, a solitary soldier on a singularly important mission is forced to make that ultimate sacrifice without warning and without provocation. Such a soldier was Arthur Nicholson.

In 1947 the nations of the Warsaw Pact and of NATO entered into an agreement whereby they would exchange military delegations to prevent the escalation of tension in Europe. Major Arthur Nicholson was a member of the American Military Liaison Group established by that agreement and based in Potsdam, East Germany. On March 24, 1985 Major Nicholson, along with his driver, Jessie G. Schatz, was on a routine reconnaissance patrol near Ludwigslust, East Germany.

Nicholson and Schatz pulled to within three hundred yards of a restricted area which was used as a training camp by a Soviet tank regiment of the Second Guards Division. Dressed in camouflage fatigues and carrying a thirty-five millimeter camera and a pair of high-powered binoculars, Nicholson emerged from the jeep. Unarmed, he was attempting to photograph the interior of a shed containing Soviet military equipment. Suddenly, without warning, a shot was fired by a Soviet sentry hidden in nearby bushes. Schatz yelled to Nicholson, "Watch out! Come back!" Then a second bullet was fired from the Soviet's AK–47 assault rifle. This one flew past Schatz's ear. Still a third bullet was fired, tearing into Nicholson's chest. "I've been shot, Jess!" Nicholson yelled as he fell to the ground.

Schatz grabbed the first-aid kit and leaped from the vehicle, scrambling forward to assist Nicholson, but he was forced back into the jeep by Soviet soldiers who held him at gunpoint as

Nicholson lay bleeding to death. At least thirty minutes passed before Nicholson was examined by a Soviet soldier and pronounced dead, thereby becoming the first uniformed American soldier killed by Soviet gunfire in more than two decades.

The following day, Nicholson's body was received by a United States Army Honor Guard at the center of Berlin's Glienicker-Brucke Bridge which separates West Berlin from East Germany. This was the same location where Soviet Spy Rudolf Abel was exchanged in 1962 for downed American spy pilot, **Francis Gary Powers**.

The United States admitted that Nicholson had been stretching the limits of his privileges as a member of the Liaison Group, but contended that such conduct allowed the Soviets only the right to detain him, not to kill him.

The son of a retired Navy Commander, Nicholson had moved from McLean, Virginia to Redding, Connecticut where he graduated from high school in 1965. Shortly after he received his bachelor's degree from Transylvania University in Lexington, Kentucky in 1969, Nicholson entered the Army. He recognized the dangers connected with his work, volunteering for such duty because, in his own words, he wanted "to be on the cutting edge."

Major Arthur D. Nicholson, Jr. was buried with full military honors in Section 7A of Arlington National Cemetery. His regulation GI headstone acknowledges his service in East Germany as part of the U.S. Military Liaison Mission.

IGNACE JAN PADEREWSKI

President-in-exile of Poland, Composer

(November 18, 1860–June 29, 1941)
Sec. 24 [The Maine Memorial]

On September 1, 1939 World War II erupted when Adolph Hitler's troops invaded Poland. Within a few short weeks, that country fell to German domination, forcing the legitimate Polish government into exile. The Polish leaders who sought refuge in the United States selected seventy-nine-year-old Ignace Jan Paderewski as its President. Paderewski never saw Poland again, dying in exile in 1941. President Franklin Roosevelt authorized the "temporary" interment of the Polish patriot in the vault of the USS *Maine* Memorial at Arlington, specifying that his body was to remain here until Poland was again free and his body could be returned to his homeland. Nearly five decades later, Paderewski remains at Arlington.

Ignace Jan Paderwski was born in Podolia, in the Ukraine region of the Soviet Union. At a very early age he displayed extraordinary musical talent; at the age of twelve he entered the Warsaw Conservatory, achieving the remarkable distinction of being named a professor just six years later. In 1884 Paderewski became a pupil of the famed pianist Theodor Leschetizky in Vienna, and in 1887 he began his career as a concert pianist, a career that would flourish for more than fifty years. He toured throughout Europe, beginning a concert tour of the United States in 1891 during which he gave 117 recitals in ninety days. Yet his greatest love was not music; it was his homeland, Poland.

During World War I he gave concerts to raise relief funds for Polish refugees and to help inspire men to enlist in the Polish army. It was Paderewski who represented Poland at the Versailles Peace Conference where he convinced President Woodrow Wilson to include the cause of Polish independence in his Fourteen Points. He served as both Prime Minister and Foreign Minister of the Polish Republic.

During the 1920s Paderewski resumed his musical career, publishing his memoirs in 1938. When Germany invaded Poland, he dedicated himself to raising thousands of dollars for the relief of Poles throughout the world. He was named President of the

Polish National Council, the government in exile. He died in New York City in 1941, leaving behind a grand legacy of music. His compositions include "Manru," "Sonata in A Minor for Violin and Piano," "Polish Fantasy," and his last composition, "Symphony in B Minor," a musical picture of Poland's tragic history.

It was to this country that Ignace Jan Paderewski fled in search of freedom during World War II. Upon his death, the people of the United States honored this Polish native son with interment in our nation's most important military cemetery; here he shall remain until his homeland is once again free. His tomb is marked by several plaques dedicated to his memory including one placed by the American Legion and another by the Polish Legion of American Veterans and Auxiliary.

JAMES PARKS

Former Arlington Estate Slave

(?, 1843–August 21, 1929)
Sec. 15, Lot 2, Grid G–26

Only one person buried in Arlington National Cemetery was also born on this property. That person is James Parks, born to slave parents living on the Arlington estate at the time it was owned by **George Washington Parke Custis**. The exact date of Parks' birth remains uncertain, though he is believed to have been born in 1843. An interesting note: Neither Washington Custis nor his wife, Mary Lee Fitzhugh Custis, were born at Arlington. Custis moved here when he built the first wing of Arlington House in 1802; his wife joined him after their marriage in 1804.

Under the terms of George Washington Parke Custis' will, all of his slaves were to be trained and freed by 1862, five years after his death. When the Civil War erupted, Robert E. Lee, as executor of Parke Custis' will, was making provisions for the training and manumission of Parks and the other slaves on the Arlington estate. In April and May of 1861, Lee and his family left the estate. Parks, then about eighteen years old, remained behind attaching himself to the military unit that occupied the premises.

When Secretary of War Edwin M. Stanton designated Arlington as a national military burial ground in 1864, Parks was still living on the property. He became a grave digger and maintenance man for the cemetery, continuing in that work until his death in 1929. When Parks died, the Secretary of War, in recognition of Parks' lifelong service to Arlington and in full awareness that Parks did not meet the formal burial qualifications, granted special permission to inter Parks' body in Arlington. James Parks died in Arlington County on August 21, 1929. He was believed to be about eighty-six years old at the time of his death. His grave in Section 15 is marked with a special commemorative headstone.

ROBERT EDWIN PEARY

Explorer

(May 6, 1856–February 20, 1920)
Sec. 8, Lot S–15, Grid X–8/9

Engraved on the tombstone of Robert Edwin Peary is the Latin phrase: "*Inveniam Viam Aut Facium*," meaning "I shall find a way or make one." These words describe the lifelong quest of Admiral Peary to become the first person ever to reach the North Pole. Enduring unimaginable hardship, Peary—accompanied by his longtime friend and assistant, Matthew Henson, and four Eskimo aides—did indeed "find a way" across the Arctic icecap, and on April 6, 1909 they stood together on top of the world.

Peary and his mother moved from Pennsylvania to South Portland, Maine after his father died. As a child he lived the outdoors life. He graduated with Phi Beta Kappa honors from Bowdoin College in 1877, receiving a degree in civil engineering. Then, after working a short time with the United States Coastal and

Geodetic Survey, Peary joined the U.S. Navy Civil Engineering Corps in 1881 as a Lieutenant.

It was in 1886 that Peary discovered his true vocation on an exploratory trip into the unknown interior of Greenland. That trip whetted his appetite for other expeditions to explore the uncharted Arctic regions. Over the next eleven years Peary made four more trips to Greenland, some of them lasting for more than a year. These expeditions earned him great fame as an explorer and a scientist. He proved that Greenland was, in fact, an island, and he returned from his 1893 expedition with three gigantic meteorites, among them the largest the world has ever seen. It weighs a full ninety tons and remains on permanent display at the Hayden Planetarium in New York City.

As an explorer Peary pioneered new methods of travel in the Arctic. He traveled with minimal equipment, foregoing the traditional heavy tents and sleeping bags. Instead, he built igloos along the way and wore thick fur suits day and night. He also restricted the size of his parties so that he could move quickly over long distances. However, his feats of exploration did not come without a physical cost.

In an area where the temperature rarely climbs above $-50°F$ and where high winds whip across frozen seas, frostbite was a constant threat. In the course of one treacherous search for a route to the North Pole during which the temperature registered $-60°F$, Peary noted in his journal, "a suspicious 'wooden' feeling in the right foot...and I found, to my annoyance, that both feet were frosted." Shortly thereafter, Peary's toes were amputated. His physical hardships, however, did not halt his explorations.

In 1897, granted a leave of absence from the Navy, Peary announced his intention to reach the Pole. One year later, his ship *Windward* set out on a voyage of discovery, but that voyage—which lasted four years—was unsuccessful. Not deterred, Peary again set sail in 1905 aboard the *Roosevelt*, an icebreaker built to his specifications. His exploration party left the ship on the north coast of Ellesmere Island and pushed northward on sledges over the icebound Arctic Ocean. At 87 degrees, 6 minutes, Peary set a new "farthest north" record, just 175 miles short of the Pole, but he and his crew were forced to turn back when supplies ran so dangerously low that they nearly starved to death.

A bronze star marks the North Pole on this globe erected by the National Geographic Society in honor of Arctic explorer Robert Peary. The monument was dedicated on this site in 1922 as shown in this old photograph. Peary's grave was later moved nearer to Jesup Drive.

Still undaunted by the failures and physical hardships, Peary courageously set out in July 1908 on what he knew would be his last chance to reach his elusive goal—the North Pole. In February 1909 Peary and six sledge teams left Cape Columbia on the northern coast of Ellesmere Island. His plan was simple. Each team would take turns breaking the trail, then they would leave supplies and fall back. Peary, Henson (America's famous black explorer), and four Eskimos comprised the last team. On February 28 severe temperatures, driving snow, and physical exhaustion once again threatened the lives of the explorers. But they would not give up. They inched their way northward until, on April 6, Peary, Henson, and their Eskimo companions stood where no persons had ever stood before—the North Pole.

Expecting a hero's welcome upon his return to the United States, Peary found instead a former assistant of his, Dr. Frederick Cook, claiming that he had reached the Pole nearly a year earlier. Peary's reaction: "Cook has simply handed the public a gold brick." Charges and countercharges followed until testimony of Cook's companions (that during their expedition they never lost sight of land) showed that Cook had perpetrated a malicious hoax.

In 1911 the United States Congress officially recognized Peary's achievement and voted him their thanks. In March of that year he was granted the rank of Rear Admiral, Retired. The recipient of numerous medals, awards, and honorary degrees, Peary continued a heavy schedule of speaking engagements throughout his life, also serving as president of the American Geographical Society.

When Peary died on February 26, 1920 in Washington, D.C.,

he was buried at Arlington. On April 6, 1922 exactly sixteen years following his discovery of the North Pole, a memorial erected by the National Geographic Society was dedicated on his gravesite. President Warren G. Harding presided over the ceremonies, which were attended by a large crowd including **William Howard Taft**, Chief Justice of the Supreme Court and President of the United States at the time of Peary's discovery. The memorial depicts a large globe of the world with the North Pole vividly marked by a bronze star. Engraved in Latin on the monument is Peary's motto: *Inveniam Viam Aut Facium* (I shall find a way or make one).

Buried with Peary is his wife, **Josephine Diebitsch Peary**, who was the first woman to spend a winter in the Arctic when she accompanied her husband there in 1891.

JOHN J. ("BLACK JACK") PERSHING

General of the Armies, Pulitzer Prize-winning Author

(September 13, 1860–July 15, 1948)
Sec. 34, Lot S–19, Grid U–12

The United States Congress conferred upon John J. Pershing the highest rank ever awarded an American, that of General of the Armies. Only one other person in our history was permitted that rank: the *first* General of the Armies, George Washington. Such was the esteem in which General Pershing was held following the Allies' victory in Europe in World War I. Yet, when this great general died, his last request was that he be buried with the men he had fought beside, and that his grave be marked with the same white regulation tombstone marking their graves.

General of the Armies Pershing began his life in modest surroundings. He was born in Laclede, Missouri, the son of a railroad switchman. At age seventeen, Pershing taught in a rural school for black children to earn enough money to pay for his college education at Kirksville Normal School (now Northeast Missouri

State University). In 1881, answering an advertisement for the Military Academy's entrance exam, Pershing sat for the exam and won entry to West Point in 1882. Graduating in 1886 as president of his class and Captain of Cadets, he was commissioned in the Cavalry.

After getting his commission, Pershing was ordered to the western frontier where he earned his first combat citation. From 1891 until 1895 he served as a professor of military science at the University of Nebraska, earning a law degree there in his spare time. From Nebraska, Pershing returned to West Point as a tactical officer.

In 1898 at the outbreak of the Spanish-American War, Pershing was sent to the Philippines where he earned a Silver Star. In 1904 he was assigned as Military Attache of the American Embassy in Tokyo after the Russo-Japanese War broke out. Returning to the United States the following year, Pershing married Helen Frances Warren, the daughter of Senator Francis E. Warren of Wyoming.

Although John Pershing's military prowess stands unquestioned, his promotion to Brigadier General in 1906, in which he leapfrogged 862 other officers, prompted a great deal of professional resentment. The promotion raised rumors of favoritism and political dealing, fueled by the fact that his father-in-law was Chairman of the Senate Military Affairs Committee. Nevertheless, Pershing continued to serve with great distinction—returning to the Philippines as Military Commander and remaining there until 1913.

In 1914 Pershing returned to the U.S. where President Woodrow Wilson assigned him to "pursue and disperse" the band of Mexican guerrillas under Pancho Villa that was terrorizing the Southwestern United States. Leaving his family in San Francisco, Pershing went to El Paso, Texas to coordinate his campaign. But just prior to his incursion into Mexico, he received the tragic news that a fire had swept through his family's quarters, killing his wife and three daughters. Only his six-year-old son had survived. Despite this tragic personal loss, Pershing pressed on with his assignment and effectively thwarted Villa's terrorism. During this campaign Pershing was promoted to Major General.

Upon the heels of Pershing's return to Washington in 1917,

President Wilson named him to command the American Expeditionary Forces being sent to France after America's declaration of war against Germany. The Army he was ordered to command did not yet exist; his task was to create it. No one knew better than Pershing how long and arduous a fight this would be. He recommended an army of 1,000,000 men by 1918, to expand to 3,000,000 men by the following year.

One of Pershing's first actions upon arriving in France was to pay respects at the Tomb of the Marquis de Lafayette, the French general who had provided invaluable assistance to American forces under General George Washington during the American Revolution. Lafayette became a close friend and confidant of Washington. As Pershing laid a wreath on the French soldier's grave, his aide announced, "Lafayette, We are here!" This gesture signified to the French people that the United States was ready to assist them as Lafayette had assisted the struggling young American republic in 1776.

Once engaged in Europe, Pershing fought diligently to maintain the integrity of his American forces. He did not, and would not, concur with the plan to use American forces only as replacements for depleted French and British units. Indeed, it was Pershing and his American troops who defeated the Germans in the St. Mihiel Salient in September of  1918. Then in October, the Americans fought bravely and bitterly against the Germans along the seemingly impenetrable Hindenburg Line during the Meuse-Argonne Offensive until, at last, the German ranks were ruptured and the Allies marched toward the Armistice on November 11, 1918.

Upon his return to the United States Pershing received a hero's welcome. Congress conferred upon him the rank of General of the Armies, a rank which had been created by Congress in 1799 explicitly for George Washington. Interestingly, it was later learned that Washington had never accepted the rank, so the Congress conferred it upon General Washington posthumously in 1976, maintaining Washington's place as the senior ranking officer on the U.S. Army roster. Therefore, only two men in American history have ever received this highest rank.

Pershing served as Army Chief of Staff from 1921 until his retirement in 1924. He went on to chair the American Battle Monuments Commission and to write his two-volume memoirs. Published in 1931, *My Experiences in the World War*, earned him a Pulitzer Prize. Although retired and living at Walter Reed Hospital in Washington, D.C., Pershing was called upon during World War II for advice and counsel by the Army Chief of Staff, General **George C. Marshall**. It was during World War I in France that Pershing met **Marshall** as a young logistics officer. **Marshall** became an aide to Pershing for the duration of the war and remained on the General's staff until Pershing's retirement.

Throughout his career, John J. Pershing was known as "Black Jack." It was a nickname given to him early in his career, when he commanded an all-black outfit. But it came to symbolize the strict discipline and military toughness of this great general. When he died in Washington in 1948, his funeral cortege was led by the President of the United States, Harry S Truman, himself a veteran "doughboy" from World War I. After the funeral service in the Memorial Amphitheatre at Arlington, Pershing was buried on top of a grassy knoll near the other veterans of The Great War; and as he had requested, his grave was marked by a simple white stone. Buried beside him is his grandson, **Richard W. Pershing**, killed in Vietnam in 1968.

DAVID DIXON PORTER

Rear Admiral of the Navy, Civil War Hero

(June 8, 1813–February 13, 1891)
Sec. 2, Lot S-5, Grid S/T–35

David Dixon Porter's life as a seaman seemed preordained. Even as a child in Chester, Pennsylvania, Porter lived a life that many young boys only dream about. The son of a naval hero from the War of 1812, young Porter accompanied his famous father on a mission to fight pirates in the West Indies at the age of eleven. By the time he was thirteen, and while his father was serving as Commander-in-Chief of the Mexican Navy, Porter was appointed a midshipman in the United States Navy. As a young teenager, he served on the warship *Congress*, which sailed in both Mediterranean and Brazilian waters.

David Porter, at the age of thirty-three, played a diplomatic role in 1846 when he was dispatched to the Dominican Republic on an observation mission for the State Department. In 1847, as First Lieutenant, he sailed on the war steamer, *Spitfire*, and led the landing party that captured the main fort at Tabasco, Mexico. For his heroics, Porter was given command of the *Spitfire*. He then left the Navy for a short time to captain civilian vessels, but rejoined the Navy in 1855 to command the steamship, *Supply*. Among his exotic exploits was sailing to North Africa to undertake transporting camels to the American Southwest for experimentation by the U.S Army. But it was his conduct during the Civil War that earned him a place of distinction in American history.

At the outbreak of that war, Porter served under another famous American Admiral, David Glasgow Farragut, who was none other than Porter's adopted brother. Porter's father had adopted the homeless Farragut child and had raised both future naval heroes side-by-side, the same way they fought during the Civil War. Porter commanded Union gunboats on the Mississippi and succeeded in breaking through the crucial Confederate blockade of the river at Vicksburg, a task at which so many other commanders had failed. He eventually commanded the largest fleet of the war — sixty vessels — in the blockade of the Confederate Atlantic coast, and led the assault on Fort Fisher, North Carolina.

After the war Porter became only the second U.S. Naval officer in our nation's history to attain the rank of Admiral. His adopted brother, Admiral David Farragut, was the first. Porter later served as Superintendent of the Naval Academy and wrote several books on naval history, including a biography of his father.

He died in Washington, D.C. on February 13, 1891 and was buried on the hillside below Arlington House. Although his tombstone bears the inscription "temporarily erected," that same marker has sufficed for nearly one hundred years.

JOHN WESLEY POWELL

Explorer, Geologist, Native American Linguist

(March 24, 1834–September 23, 1902)
Sec. 1, Lot 408, Grid L–35

Adventure was the hallmark of John Wesley Powell's life. From his early childhood in Mount Morris, New York, he traveled widely with his minister father, cultivating a desire to explore and discover, a desire which inspired him throughout his life. It was this adventuresome spirit that led Powell to undertake his dangerous exploration of the Colorado River.

Powell's father, a Methodist minister, travelled with his young son throughout the Midwest spreading the gospel. Young John was educated in schools in Ohio, Wisconsin, and Illinois. After attending Oberlin College in Ohio and Wheaton College in Illinois, Powell graduated from Illinois Wesleyan University which was named — as was Powell himself — for the founder of Methodism, John Wesley.

With the outbreak of the Civil War, Powell joined the Second

Illinois Artillery in 1861, climbing to the rank of Major. However, Powell did not survive that war without injury. During the bloody Battle of Shiloh in 1862, he lost the lower part of his right arm.

Following the war, Powell returned to Illinois Wesleyan to teach geology. It was there in Bloomington, Illinois that he began planning his exploration of the Colorado River and its canyons. By 1869 much of America's western frontier had been explored and charted, but the Colorado River remained unexplored. It was still the subject of mysterious folk tales filled with uncharted dangers. For Powell it also represented an untapped source of geological treasures. The river, which carves its way through the Grand Canyon, had never been navigated, nor had anyone studied the canyon's unique geological formations. Powell was eager to undertake the challenge.

On May 24, 1869 Powell and his companions launched their boats into the Green River in Wyoming to begin a thousand mile journey over the uncharted, rapid white water of the Green and Colorado Rivers. That journey did not end until August 30 when Powell and six members of his crew arrived at the junction of the Colorado River and Lake Mead in southern Nevada. The survivors were sunburned and nearly starved. However, the expedition brought recognition to Powell and kindled in him the hopes of another, more scientific journey. The one-armed adventurer did attempt another expedition down the river, but impassable high water forced him to terminate the trip prematurely.

From 1871 until 1879 Powell directed a government-sponsored geological and geographical survey of public lands in the western United States. It was also during this time that Powell undertook a study of Native American languages, publishing *An Introduction to the Study of Indian Languages*. Then, when the U.S. Bureau of Ethnology of the Smithsonian Institution was established in 1879, Powell was named its first director. He also served as director of the U.S. Geological Survey from 1881 until 1892.

Although Powell retired in 1894, he remained active in the National Geographic Society, of which he was a founding member. He died in 1902 in Haven, Maine.

FRANCIS GARY POWERS

Spy Pilot

(August 17, 1929–August 1, 1977)
Sec. 11, Lot 685–2, Grid OP–15/16

Just as the long Cold War between the United States and the Soviet Union began to thaw in 1960, the Soviet Union shot down a U–2 reconnaissance plane deep within its borders. The Soviets charged it was an American spy plane. The United States claimed it was just a NASA weather plane which had strayed off course. The incident not only severely strained relations between the two superpowers, forcing the cancellation of a scheduled summit meeting between President Eisenhower and Soviet Party Chief Nikita Khrushchev, but it also changed the life of Francis Gary Powers forever.

Powers was the only boy among the six children of a Kentucky coal miner. Born in Jenkins, Kentucky he graduated from nearby Pikeville College, joined the Air Force as a private, and went into flight training. After two years he was commissioned his wings and stayed in the Air Force until 1956, at which time he went to work as a civilian pilot for Lockheed Aircraft Corporation, the company that developed the U–2 plane. In actuality, however, Powers was working for the CIA.

Eventually, Powers joined a group of pilots who were CIA operatives stationed at a base in Adana, Turkey. From there the pilots flew surveillance missions into the heart of the Soviet Union photographing Soviet long-range ballistic missile installations. Both the CIA and the pilots believed that at an altitude of 60,000 feet they were beyond the range of Soviet missiles. They were wrong. On May 1, 1960 a Soviet missile found its intended target, a U–2 plane piloted by Powers near the city of Sverdlovsk.

In the heated exchange between the governments following the downing of the plane, the Eisenhower administration maintained that the plane had been on a routine weather reconnaissance flight and strongly denied that the flight had been a spy mission. To rebut the American claim, the Soviets not only produced the American pilot at a highly publicized press conference, but they also displayed the extensive photographic and surveillance equipment found on board the American plane. Ultimately, our government acknowledged the mission's true purpose, but stated that the surveillance flights had been undertaken to monitor Soviet missile advances that threatened world security.

Powers was publicly tried for espionage in Moscow. He appeared as a quiet man who didn't quite understand the full ramifications of his actions. Convicted and sentenced to ten years in a Soviet prison, he served less than two years, gaining his freedom as part of a dramatic exchange for a convicted Soviet spy being held by the United States. Colonel Rudolf Abel, an alleged member of the Soviet KGB, was convicted in New York City in 1957 for espionage activities against the U.S. He was given a thirty-year sentence which was commuted in 1962 by President **John F. Kennedy** in order to arrange the swap for Powers. On February 10, 1962, in a theatrical ceremony staged in the center of the Glienicker-Brucke Bridge between West Berlin and East Germany, Abel and Powers were exchanged.

Powers returned to the United States and was received, not as a hero, but rather as a mercenary. He was criticized by some Americans for having not committed suicide upon being captured. In 1970 Powers wrote *Operation Overflight*, his account of the incident in which he defended his behavior. He stated that the CIA had never advised suicide and criticized the agency for implying that it had.

The rest of Powers' career was spent first working for Lockheed, then for a Los Angeles radio station as a traffic reporter pilot. Briefly, he left to work for an aircraft communications manufacturer, but returned to broadcasting with station KNBC in Los Angeles as a reporter using his helicopter to achieve special vantage points. On August 1, 1977, after videotaping scenes of a brush fire, Powers and his cameraman were heading back to their base when their helicopter crashed in Encino, California. The cause of the crash was believed to be a lack of fuel. Powers died in the wreckage.

Francis Gary Powers is buried in Arlington Cemetery near

the graves of other Americans whose deaths were flight-related—
military aviation pioneer Lt. **Thomas Selfridge** and astronauts
Virgil Grissom and **Roger Chaffee**.

MARY RANDOLPH

Author, First Burial at Arlington

(August 9, 1762–January 28, 1828)
Sec. 45, Special lot near the Custis Walk, T–36

Just below Arlington
House, along Custis Walk, is a
solitary grave surrounded by a
red brick wall. This is the final
resting place of Mary Randolph;
it is also the oldest grave on the
Arlington estate.

Mary Randolph was a de-
scendant of one of the oldest and
most distinguished families in
Virginia. A direct descendant of
Pocahontas, she was a cousin to
Mary Lee Fitzhugh Custis, the wife of the builder of Arlington
House, and to Robert E. Lee. Mary Randolph also claimed among
her many cousins Thomas Jefferson, whose daughter was married to Mary Randolph's brother, Thomas Mann Randolph, a
former Governor of Virginia. Mary Randolph is believed to be
the godmother of Mary Anna Custis Lee, the wife of Robert E.
Lee. She was married to David Mead Randolph.

She was considered the quintessential mistress of the plantation, publishing a book entitled *The Virginia Housewife*, a domestic
guide which included recipes, instruction on candlemaking, her-
bal cures, and even how to dress a turtle. The book, a best seller
in its time, is still in print today.

The beautiful stone which graces Mary Randolph's tomb was provided by her youngest son, Burwell Starke Randolph, who had been a midshipman in the United States Navy when he fell from a mast and suffered severe permanent injuries. He believed that his mother's death was hastened by her tireless caring for him and his needs. The stone reads:

> Sacred to the memory of Mrs. Mary Randolph. Her intrinsic worth needs no eulogium. The deceased was born the Ninth of August 1762 at Ampthill near Richmond Virginia and died the 23rd of January, 1828 in Washington City. A victim of maternal love and duty. As a tribute of filial gratitude this monument is dedicated to her exulted virtues by her youngest son. Requiescat in pace.

When Mary Randolph died in 1828, Washington Custis allowed her burial on the Arlington estate because of her special ties to his wife and daughter and because of her affection for the estate.

VINNIE REAM (HOXIE)

Sculptor of Lincoln

(September 25, 1847–November 20, 1914)
Sec. 3, Lot 1876, Grid T–16

President Abraham Lincoln was accustomed to hearing special requests from Senators and Congressmen, so when Senator James Rollins of Missouri approached him in 1864 indicating that he had a request, Lincoln was not surprised. Yet Rollins' request was truly extraordinary. A member of the Senator's constituency wanted permission to have the benefit of personal sittings by the President to make sketches for a statue of Lincoln... and the constituent was a seventeen-year-old girl. President Lincoln quickly dismissed the idea. There was a war on, and besides, "Why should anyone want a picture of a man so homely?" he asked. Rollins pressed the point. The young lady was very talented and she would be heartbroken if she lost the chance, he said. Lincoln didn't budge. Finally Rollins pointed out that the young girl came from a very poor background. The President began to stir. "She is poor, is she?" the President asked. "Well, that is nothing against her. I will sit for the model," Lincoln said with a nod. With that nod, Vinnie Ream began her sessions with Abraham Lincoln. They continued almost daily until she saw him for the last time on April 14, 1865, the day he was shot.

Vinnie Ream was born in Madison, Wisconsin in 1847. Soon after her birth her family moved to Columbia, Missouri where she met Senator Rollins. Then they moved again, this time to Washington, D.C., where her father worked as a surveyor for the Land Office while Vinnie took a job at the Post Office sorting mail to and from the front.

Vinnie's interest in sculpting began when Senator Rollins introduced her to Clark Mills, a well-known sculptor who had designed and cast the figure of Freedom which adorns the top of the United States Capitol. Impressed with her natural ability, Mills offered Vinnie free instruction. Soon she was making likenesses of many famous clients, including George Armstrong Custer, Thaddeus Stevens, and Horace Greeley.

The sittings with Lincoln took place at the White House, usually during lunch. Ream recounted later that the President brooded much during this time and talked little. When he did speak, it was about his young son, Willie, who had died at the age of eleven in February 1863. Sometimes he wept. This was the man Vinnie Ream captured in her sketches.

Following President Lincoln's death, Congress authorized a competition for a sculpture of Lincoln to be placed in the rotunda of the Capitol. In July 1866, after much ado, Vinnie Ream was awarded the commission and $10,000. She was the first woman ever awarded a government commission but she was not without her critics. Several members of Congress even suggested that she had compromised her morals to secure the commission. About her detractors, Vinnie indignantly replied, "These people know nothing of art."

The statue was completed in 1870 and was unveiled amidst great excitement and expectation on January 7, 1871. As the drape fell from the sculpture, the crowded rotunda erupted into tumultuous applause. Vinnie Ream had captured the essence of Abraham Lincoln, the man. Today her statue still stands proudly in the Capitol rotunda.

Vinnie Ream's career flourished after she finished the sculpture of Lincoln. Other works of hers that can be seen around Washington include the statue of Admiral David Farragut in Farragut Square and the Native American Sequoia, also located in the Capitol. In 1878 Vinnie married Lt. **Richard Hoxie**, an army engineer who often helped her with her work. Ream saw herself as a pioneer for women sculptors and encouraged them at every opportunity. When she died in 1914, as a military spouse, she was buried in Arlington National Cemetery. Her grave, which is shared with her husband, is marked by a pedestal bearing a bas-relief of herself on its side and a bronze reproduction of her work, Sappho, the poetess, on its top.

WALTER REED

Pioneer Bacteriologist

(September 13, 1851–November 22, 1902)
Sec. 3, Lot 1864, Grid TU–16/17

Walter Reed dedicated his life to the study and prevention of disease and is credited with the discovery of a cure for yellow fever; but his own life was tragically cut short by another one-time widespread killer: appendicitis.

Like many children living in the South during the Civil War, Walter Reed was forced to delay his education until the end of the war. Ultimately, however, he left his home in Belroi, Virginia and entered the University of Virginia where in 1869 he earned his medical degree. After graduation he moved to New York City and earned a second medical degree from Bellevue Hospital Medical College in 1870. For the next five years he served as an intern at Kings County Hospital.

In 1875 Reed enlisted in the Army Medical Corps and was commissioned a First Lieutenant, Assistant Surgeon. After serving at various posts for the next fourteen years, including the Arizona Territory, he continued his studies in bacteriology and pathology in 1890 at Johns Hopkins University in Baltimore. In 1893 he was transferred to Washington, D.C. to accept the post of curator of the U.S. Army Medical Museum while also serving as professor of bacteriology and clinical microscopy at the newly organized Army Medical School. By 1895 he had been selected as Chairman of the Department of Bacteriology and Pathology at Columbian (now George Washington University) Medical School.

After the war with Spain erupted in 1898, many American soldiers contracted yellow fever while serving in tropical zones. Dr. Reed was named by Surgeon General **George M. Sternberg** to chair a commission to investigate the causes and transmission of that dreaded disease. Reed advanced the theory that the fever was transmitted by the stegomyia mosquito, rather than simply by contaminated water. He established an experimental station near Havana, Cuba and after seven months of study—which included exposing himself and others to the disease—Reed and his commission members conclusively proved his mosquito theory. Yellow fever cases were reduced from 1,400 in the year 1900 to only 37 in 1901 and there was not a single case in 1902.

Reed returned to resume his work at the Army Medical School in 1901. A sudden attack of appendicitis on November 22, 1902 claimed his life at the age of fifty-one. General **Leonard Wood**, the Military Governor of Cuba, said of Walter Reed, "I know of no other man on this side of the world who has done so much for humanity as Dr. Reed. His discovery resulted in saving more lives than were lost in the Cuban War." The Army Medical Center in Washington D.C. is named in Walter Reed's honor.

REVOLUTIONARY WAR VETERANS

Although the American Revolution ended nearly eighty years before Arlington National Cemetery was established, eleven veterans of that war have been reinterred at Arlington. This makes Arlington the only national cemetery to claim veterans buried within its walls from every war in American history. Many of these men had been deceased more than a century when requests were made to allow their burial at Arlington. Nine of them are buried in Section 1 between Arlington House and the Fort Myer Gate. **Pierre Charles L'Enfant** and **Hugh Auld** are buried in Section 2. What follows is a brief remark about each of these men who fought, not to defend our nation, but to create it. The lives of two of these veterans, **Pierre Charles L'Enfant** and **James McCubbin Lingan**, are discussed in separate profiles.

HUGH AULD

(1745–1813)
Sec. 2, Lot 4801 Grid U–31

Hugh Auld served as a Lieutenant in the Talbot County Militia in 1780. He died at Deep Water Point Farm, near Clairborne, Maryland and was buried in a family plot there. He was reinterred in Arlington on April 11, 1935. Buried next to Auld is his son and namesake who was a veteran of the War of 1812 and died on November 2, 1820.

WILLIAM WARD BURROWS

(1758–1805)
Sec. 1, Lot 301–B, Grid NO–33/34

William Ward Burrows is the oldest member of the United States Marine Corps buried at Arlington National Cemetery. The epitaph on his tombstone states:

> His death and such, Oh reader, with thy own,
> Has free from terrors and without a groan,
> His spirit to Himself, the almighty drew,
> Mild as a [illegible] exhales the [illegible] dew.

JOSEPH CARLETON

(1754–1812)
Sec. 1, Lot 299, Grid MN–33/34

Joseph Carleton was born in Longmanthby, Cumberland County, England. He came to the colonies and served as a Paymaster in the American Army during the Revolution. After the war he worked as a merchant and lived in Georgetown, now a part of Washington, D.C. When he died in 1812, he was buried in the Presbyterian Cemetery in Georgetown and was reinterred at Arlington on November 13, 1907.

JOHN FOLLIN

(1761–1841)
Sec. 1, Lot 295, Grid MN–33/34

John Follin, a native of Fairfax County, Virginia, joined the American Navy in 1778. He was captured by the British while at sea and was held for three years as a prisoner of war. He was exchanged at the close of the Revolution.

JOHN GREEN

(1730–1793)
Sec. 1, Lot 503, Grid KL–34/35

John Green's monument proudly boasts that Green was born and died at his family home, Liberty Hall, in Culpepper County, Virginia and that he commanded one of the first companies of Minutemen of that county. He rose to the rank of Colonel of the Tenth Virginia Volunteers and was a founding member of the Society of the Cincinnati. His tombstone also  indicates that he was directed to be presented a sword by the Continental Congress for meritorious service. He was originally interred at Liberty Hall and was reinterred at Arlington on April 23, 1931. John Green has been deceased longer than any other person buried at Arlington National Cemetery.

JAMES HOUSE

(1761–1834)
Sec. 1, Lot 297–A, Grid MN–33/34

House enlisted in the Continental Army on March 14, 1777 at the age of fifteen and served as a matross (artillery gunner) in Captain Drury Ragsdale's Company of Artillery assigned to the State of Virginia. Originally buried in the Old Presbyterian Cemetery in Georgetown (now a part of Washington, D.C.), General House was reinterred at Arlington on May 12, 1892.

THOMAS MEASON

(1726–1813)
Sec. 1, Lot 297–B, Grid MN–33/34

General Meason was born in Uniontown, Pennsylvania, the birthplace of another great American General, **George C. Marshall**. He was a resident of Georgetown, in the District of Columbia when he died on March 10, 1813. He was buried in the Old Presbyterian Cemetery there before he was reinterred at Arlington on May 12, 1892. Thomas Meason was born before any other person buried in Arlington National Cemetery, making him the oldest person buried here.

WILLIAM RUSSELL

(1735–1793)
Sec. 1, Lot 314–A, Grid MN–34/35

Commissioned a Colonel on December 19, 1776, Russell became a Brigadier General of the Thirteenth, Tenth, Fifth and Eleventh Virginia Regiments. During the winter of 1777–78, he was stationed at Valley Forge. Following the fall of Charleston, he was taken prisoner and held from January 1, 1783 until May of that year. Following the Revolutionary War, he resided in Fincastle County, Virginia and served in the Virginia State Senate. He died while visiting his son in Front Royal, Virginia and was buried in a homemade walnut coffin on their family plot. He was reinterred at Arlington on July 7, 1943.

CALEB SWAN

(Died November 29, 1809)
Sec. 1, Lot 301–C, Grid MN–33/34

Originally from Massachusetts, Swan served as an ensign in the Third and Eighth Massachusetts Regiments. He rose to the rank of Paymaster General of the Army and was given a land grant for his service. Originally buried in the Old Presbyterian Cemetery in Georgetown in the District of Columbia, Swan was reinterred at Arlington on May 12, 1892.

FRANK REYNOLDS

Television Newscaster

(November 29, 1923–July 20, 1983)
Sec. 7A, Lot 180, Grid TU–23/24

Few of the millions of Americans who watched his national news broadcasts knew much about Frank Reynolds. Of course he was seen as a competent, compassionate journalist, but very few people knew of his many awards for excellence in broadcast journalism, his devotion to his family, and his distinguished military record.

Frank Reynolds was born in East Chicago, Indiana and attended Wabash College in downstate Crawfordsville, dropping out after his first year of studies to enlist in the United States Army during World War II. In that war, he rose to the rank of Staff Sergeant and was wounded, for which he was awarded a Purple Heart.

Reynolds' career in broadcast journalism began in 1947 when he joined station WJOB in Hammond, Indiana. Later, he worked for the CBS affiliate in Chicago (WBBM) and then for the ABC affiliate (WBKB, now WLS). After fourteen years in Chicago, Reynolds was promoted in 1965 to the network news division of ABC and served as that network's White House correspondent. He later coanchored the national evening news with Howard K. Smith, but lost the anchor job when Harry Reasoner joined the ABC news team. In 1978 Reynolds returned to the anchor's desk as chief anchor on the "World News Tonight" program and held that post until his death in 1983.

Reynolds was an innovative broadcast journalist. He anchored the forerunner to ABC's "Nightline" program, which evolved from special late night coverage of the crisis in Iran in 1979 when fifty-three Americans were held hostage. From 1965 until his death he covered each of the national political conventions and each of the manned space flights for ABC television. In 1979 he was awarded the coveted George Foster Peabody Award for excellence in broadcast journalism, and in 1980 Reynolds was again honored by his peers with an Emmy award for his coverage of that year's national election.

Illness forced Reynolds from his anchor desk in April of 1983. He never recovered from his illness, dying in his suburban Washington, D.C. home on July 20 of that year.

Reynolds was eulogized by his friend, President Ronald Reagan, as a "very decent man, not only in the way he lived, but in the way he did his job." A measure of the worldwide impact of Frank Reynolds' death was evident in a letter sent from the Vatican which was read at his funeral. Sentiments from that letter are immortalized on his tombstone. The inscription reads:

a man who cared
Beloved Husband and Father
Dedicated Journalist

EDMUND RICE

Medal of Honor Winner, Weapons Inventor

(1842–July 20, 1906)
Sec. 3, Lot 1875, Grid T–16

Many tombstones in Arlington attempt to tell the story of the person buried there, but no stone does it better than that marking the grave of Edmund Rice. Cited for "conspicuous bravery on the third day of the battle of Gettysburg," Rice was granted our nation's highest award, the Congressional Medal of Honor. A simple granite rock proudly displays, in beautiful detail, a bronze replica of that medal which once graced the uniform of this Civil War hero.

Rice enlisted in the Union Army in his hometown of Cambridge, Massachusetts during the early days of the Civil War. In July 1861 he was appointed Captain of the Nineteenth Massachusetts Infantry. It was at Gettysburg in 1863 that he displayed his uncommon courage. Under attack by General George Edward Pickett's troops, Rice led his division in a countercharge against overwhelming odds. When the battle dust settled, Rice found himself severely wounded behind enemy lines, but his counterattack had been successful.

Rice mustered out of the Army as a Colonel on June 30, 1865. Unhappy with civilian life, he reenlisted the following year and remained a soldier until 1903, when he retired with the rank of Brigadier General. Rice is well known for his invention of several military weapons including the trowel bayonet, stacking swivel, and the knife-intrenching bayonet.

His simple but descriptive grave is located among several unusual tombstones in the area around the cul-de-sac at the end of **Miles** Drive in the southwest section of Arlington.

HYMAN G. RICKOVER

Admiral, "Father of the Nuclear Navy"

(January 27, 1900–July 8, 1986)
Sec. 5, Lot 7000, Grid VW–36

Hyman Rickover's Naval career spanned more than sixty years, during which time he became one of the U.S. Navy's most important scientists and administrators. Rickover's tenacious and farsighted viewpoints inspired both plebes and Presidents. Yet it was that same tenacity which resulted in his forced retirement at the age of eighty-two.

Born to Jewish parents in the Czarist Russian village of Makow about fifty miles north of Warsaw, Hyman Rickover immigrated to the United States when he was just six years old. Raised in Chicago, Rickover earned an appointment to the U.S. Naval Academy in 1918, graduating in 1922, 106th in a class of 539. His first assignment was aboard a battleship *Nevada* where he served for five years. That tour of duty was followed by postgraduate study at Annapolis and at Columbia University in New York City.

The only sea command of Rickover's long career came in 1937 when he was named Captain of a mine sweeper *Finch* which was stationed in China. During World War II Captain Rickover directed the electrical section of the Navy's Bureau of Ships. Although he spent most of the war ashore, he did manage a ship repair base on Okinawa toward the end of the war. Perhaps the most important assignment in Rickover's career came in 1946 when he was named to a special team of scientists to study the feasibility of a nuclear propulsion system for the Navy. This work resulted in the development of the world's first nuclear powered submarine, the *Nautilus*, which was launched in 1954.

The success of the *Nautilus* revolutionized the U.S. military's sea power. With a nuclear propulsion system a vessel could travel tens of thousands of miles without the necessity of refueling. In 1957 the *Nautilus* cruised for 62,500 miles on its first load of nuclear fuel. In 1958, on a voyage from Hawaii to Great Britain, it became the first submarine to pass under the North Pole's icecap.

While Hyman Rickover was pivotal in bringing nuclear power to the Navy's submarine and surface fleet, his achievements did not result in his advancement in rank. It was not until 1958 – and only after a Congressional investigation – that Rickover was promoted to flag officer rank as a Vice Admiral. He was named a full Admiral in 1973 at the age of seventy-three. But despite his age Rickover had no intention of retiring. He was able to remain on active duty well beyond the normal retirement age, in part because of the considerable influence he wielded on Capitol Hill. However, by 1982 his influence had diminished and – now eighty-two years old – Rickover was forced into retirement.

Admiral Rickover considered himself a maverick and nearly everyone he worked with agreed. During one interview in 1984 Rickover recounted that he never kept a copy of the Navy regulations in his office. "One time some guy brought it in," Rickover confessed, "and I told him to get the hell out and burn it." A brilliant scientist, Rickover was unrelenting in his demands upon his subordinates. Yet he was able to instill in those who worked with him a desire for excellence. President Jimmy Carter recalled that, next to his parents, Admiral Rickover had influenced his life more than anyone else.

The great esteem in which Admiral Rickover was held was evidenced during his retirement dinner in 1982 when three former Presidents – Jimmy Carter, Gerald Ford, and Richard Nixon – appeared at the dinner to show their respect for the Admiral. In July 1985 Hyman Rickover suffered a stroke and remained in ill health until his death on July 8, 1986 at his home in Arlington, Viriginia. He was buried with simple military honors at Arlington National Cemetery. A memorial service was later held at Washington's National Cathedral.

MARY ROBERTS RINEHART

Mystery Writer, Playwright, War Correspondent

(August 12, 1876–September 22, 1958)
Sec. 3, Lot 4269, Grid X–17/18

Mary Roberts Rinehart had studied nursing, married a doctor, and expected to spend her life caring for the sick when she wrote a few stories in 1906 to try to earn some money. The result: she quickly became America's premier mystery writer. And when World War I broke out in Europe, she landed a position as this country's first female war correspondent.

Mary Roberts, born in Pittsburgh, Pennsylvania in 1876, was the recipient of a typical Victorian upbringing. A nursing student, she married a doctor, **Stanley Marshall Rinehart**, just four days after her graduation from nursing school. It seemed that she would spend her life attending her husband's patients, but in actuality, it was he who retired from his medical practice to attend to her writing career.

A family financial squeeze in 1903 prompted Mary to try her hand at writing, an almost unheard of action for a woman in 1903. Fortunately, her work proved highly popular. Her first story, "The Man in Lower Ten," was serialized by *The Saturday Evening Post* in 1907. It was her first novel, however, that brought her national attention. *The Circular Staircase*, published in 1908, was heralded as a breakthrough in crime fiction for its innovative melding of humor and horror.

It was also *The Saturday Evening Post* that approached Rinehart about being their correspondent to cover the war in Europe. After what Rinehart herself called "grave consultations" with her husband, she finally agreed to undertake the assignment. Undaunted at being the only woman correspondent, she fearlessly covered the action, imbuing her war stories with the same flare and excitement that had been the hallmarks of her novels.

Following the war Mary Rinehart returned to the United States and successfully tried her hand as a playwright. Collaborating with Avery Hopwood, she produced *The Bat*, a stage hit in 1920. By 1921 the Rineharts had moved to Washington, D.C. and her husband forsook his own medical career to manage his wife's thriving business affairs. Roughly ten years later, in 1932, Dr. **Rinehart** died and Mary moved to New York where she continued to bask in the limelight as America's best mystery writer, still writing baffling whodunits into her seventies.

Mary Roberts Rinehart died in 1958 at the age of eighty-two in New York City. She is buried in Arlington with her husband, who had attained the rank of Major in the United States Army.

THE RODGERS FAMILY

A Naval Dynasty

Sec. 1, Lot 130, Grid O–32/33

Since the United States Navy was founded in 1798, the Rodgers family has produced many outstanding naval officers. The first was Commodore John Rodgers (1773–1838) who was the highest ranking naval officer during the War of 1812. Although he himself is not buried at Arlington, two of his grandsons and his great-grandson are buried together in Section 1 of the cemetery: **John Augustus Rodgers, Thomas Slidell Rodgers** and **John Rodgers**.

JOHN AUGUSTUS RODGERS

(July 26, 1848–March 2, 1933)

John Augustus Rodgers was born in Havre-de-Grace, Maryland, the brother of Rear Admiral Frederick Rodgers. He was appointed to the Naval Academy, class of 1868, and saw action during the Civil War on the ironclad *Marion* in its pursuit of the Confederate steamers *Florida* and *Tallahassee* in the summer of 1864. From 1868 until 1880 Rodgers served in the Pacific Squadron, then was stationed at the Washington Navy Yard. During the Spanish-American War, he took part in the famous battle against the Spanish Admiral Cervera at Santiago, Cuba, serving under **William T. Sampson** and **Winfield Scott Schley**. For "eminent and conspicuous conduct" in that battle, he was advanced five numbers in rank. Upon his retirement on July 26, 1910 he had attained the rank of Rear Admiral. John Augustus Rodgers returned to his home in Havre-de-Grace where he died on March 2, 1933 at the age of eighty-five.

THOMAS SLIDELL RODGERS

(August 18, 1858–February 28, 1931)

Born in Morristown, New Jersey, Thomas Slidell Rodgers graduated from Annapolis in 1878. During the Spanish-American War he served on the *Bennington* and *Monterey* and was commissioned Executive Officer on board the new *Maine* from 1902 until 1905. Rodgers was named Chief of Naval Intelligence between 1912 and 1913, and Director of the Naval War College from 1915 through 1916. On June 13, 1916 he was promoted to the rank of Rear Admiral and given command of Division Seven Battleship Force, Atlantic Fleet. Thomas Slidell Rodgers retired from active duty on July 19, 1916 and died fifteen years later, on February 28, 1931.

JOHN RODGERS

(January 15, 1881–August 27, 1926)

John Rodgers, the son of **John Augustus Rodgers** and nephew of **Thomas Slidell Rodgers**, is the youngest of the Rodgers family buried at Arlington. Also counted among his ancestors is Commodore Matthew C. Perry, naval hero of the War of 1812.

John Rodgers, born in Washington, D.C., attended and graduated from the U.S. Naval Academy in 1903. As a Lieutenant he served aboard the *Nebraska* in 1908 and turned his dreams from ships to planes in 1911 when he was assigned to the flying school operated by the Wright brothers. Rodgers became only the second Naval officer in history to qualify as a pilot and helped to organize the Naval Air Station at San Diego, California. During the early days of World War I, Rodgers commanded the Submarine Division One of the Atlantic Fleet and earned a Distinguished Service Medal for dangerous minesweeping activities in the Atlantic. Later named commanding officer of the Submarine Base at New London, Connecticut, Rodgers was promoted to Commander and placed in charge of the Naval Air Station at Pearl Harbor.

Perhaps Rodgers' greatest adventure came when he was chosen to command one of two experimental Navy seaplanes to fly nonstop from San Francisco to Hawaii. He took off in the PN–9 biplane from California on August 31, 1925 with a crew of four. The companion plane ditched about 300 miles after takeoff, but Rodgers was determined that his plane would continue the mission alone. Flying all night, his craft ran out of fuel just four hundred miles short of Hawaii and Rodgers was forced to ditch in the Pacific. For nine days he and his crew drifted on the open sea, uncertain of their fate. Rodgers fashioned a makeshift sail from the canvas of the wing and was able to sail toward Hawaii. Fatigued and sunburned, he and his crew were finally picked up by a submarine just fifteen miles off shore. Although he did not complete the flight, he still set the distance record for seaplane navigation.

Rodgers later served as Chief of the Bureau of Aeronautics, then commanded an experimental seaplane squadron. On August 27, 1926 he was on board an inspection flight from Washington, D.C. to Philadelphia, Pennsylvania when his plane went down in the shallow waters of the Delaware River; the impact of the crash pinning Rodgers in the cockpit. He suffered severe injuries, and died of his wounds. It is significant to note that from 1798 until his death in 1926, a member of his family with the name "John

Rodgers" had been actively serving in the United States Navy. John Rodgers now rests beside his father and uncle in Section 1 at Arlington.

WILLIAM STARKE ROSECRANS

Civil War General, Congressman

(September 6, 1819–March 11, 1898)
Sec. 3, Lot 1862, Grid T–16/17

If there had not been a sinister interception of a telegram to President Lincoln from General William Starke Rosecrans, there is little doubt that Rosecrans would have been the seventeenth President of the United States.

During the 1864 presidential campaign many Republicans were encouraging Rosecrans to oppose President Lincoln for their party's nomination for president. With the Union far from victory over the Confederacy, members of the Republican Party felt that perhaps a new candidate was needed to head their ticket. Rosecrans chose not to oppose the President and Lincoln, seeking to gain support both within the ranks of his party and among the general public, decided to ask Rosecrans to be his running mate.

The President wired the request to General Rosecrans, who was with his troops in the field, and Rosecrans responded favorably. However, control of the telegraph lines in wartime fell under the jurisdiction of the Secretary of War, Edwin M. Stanton, a man considered by many to be the second most important and clearly the most ambitious person in Washington. Stanton did not want Rosecrans on the ticket and so did not convey the General's response to Lincoln. Failing to receive that reply, the President assumed that Rosecrans did not want the position, offering it instead to Andrew Johnson. The rest is recorded in history. Vice-President Johnson assumed the presidency less than a year later when Lincoln died in April 1865. Had it not been for Edwin Stanton's interception of Rosecrans' acceptance of Lincoln's offer, Rosecrans would have become the Vice-President and our nation's seventeenth President.

William Starke Rosecrans, a native of Kingston Township, Ohio, graduated from West Point in 1841 ranked fifth in his class despite having received only sporadic education prior to his entry into the military academy. During the Civil War he showed great promise as an officer, gaining promotion to Brigadier General in May 1861.

During 1862 he served under General Ulysses S. Grant, but failed to carry out Grant's plan to trap retreating Confederate soldiers at Iuka, Mississippi. This failure resulted in a rift between Grant and Rosecrans that lasted the remainder of their lives. Rosecrans resigned from the army in 1867 to serve as Minister to Mexico, a position he lost when Grant became president.

Turning his attention to mining and railroad interests in California, he served in Congress from 1881 until 1885, becoming chairman of the House Committee on Military Affairs. In that position, he was one of the few people who opposed restoring Grant to the rank of General after he had suffered severe financial losses and even after it was disclosed that Grant was dying of cancer. William Starke Rosecrans died in Los Angeles, California in 1898 and was buried in Section 3 of Arlington National Cemetery.

WILLIAM THOMAS SAMPSON

Naval Hero of the Spanish-American War

(February 9, 1840–May 6, 1902)
Sec. 21, Lot S–9, Grid MN–20/21

William T. Sampson produced one of the greatest naval victories in American history, or did he? When American naval forces completely destroyed the Spanish fleet under the command of Pascual Cervera y Topeta at Santiago, Cuba during the Spanish-

American War, it sounded a death knell for Spain's war effort. Sampson was commander of those forces, but during the actual battle, he was away from the fighting, conferring with the commander of the land forces. By the time he returned to the scene, Cervera's fleet had been completely disarmed by the American naval vessels under the immediate command of **Winfield Scott Schley**. A national controversy arose as to whether **Schley**, who was in command during the battle, or Sampson, who had outlined the general battle plans, should be credited with the victory. That question threw the United States Navy, the American press, and the American people into an often-heated debate.

The press appeared to take the side of **Schley** but the special Navy Inquiry Board headed by the revered naval hero, Admiral George Dewey, found that Sampson had acted properly and should, therefore, as Commander in Chief of the forces, be credited with the victory. Even **Schley** acknowledged that as commanding officer Sampson was entitled to the victory. That did not end the controversy, however. As a result, the Navy promoted both Sampson and **Schley** to the rank of Rear Admiral in 1899.

Sampson, a native of Palmyra, New York, entered the Naval Academy in 1857. Ranked first in his class, he graduated in 1861. During the Civil War, he served in and around the Washington, D.C. area, seeing action aboard the *Potomac* in the Gulf of Mexico. In 1862 he served as an instructor at the Naval Academy which had been temporarily moved to Newport, Rhode Island. In 1864 he was Executive Officer aboard the new ironclad, *Patapsco*, as part of the South Atlantic Blockading Squadron when it was sunk by a Confederate torpedo.

Following the war Sampson held various posts on land and at sea. He headed the Department of Physics and Chemistry at the Naval Academy, served aboard frigates, and was Superintendent of the Naval Observatory in Washington, D.C. Later, while assigned to the torpedo station at Newport, Sampson urged the creation of a Naval War College, returning to the Naval Academy to serve as Superintendent. He also was Chief of the Bureau of Ordnance from 1893 until 1897. In 1897 he was given command of the new battleship, *Iowa* and was promoted to Commander in Chief of the North Atlantic Squadron.

When the Spanish-American War began in April 1898, Sampson moved his squadron toward a blockade of Cuba. Although **Winfield Scott Schley**, who headed the Flying Squadron at that time, technically outranked Sampson, he was placed under Sampson's command. Sampson ordered **Schley** into a blockade position of Santiago Harbor, hoping to keep the Spanish Admiral Cervera from entering the harbor while Sampson returned to Key West to convoy Army troops. **Schley** did not move directly to the blockade position, allowing Cervera to sail his fleet into the safety of the harbor.

Sampson joined **Schley** on June 1 and, as commander, Sampson established the blockade – which included searchlights trained on the narrow harbor entrance at night – to keep Cervera from escaping. Sampson also launched reconnaissance operations to obtain more information regarding Cervera's intentions. On July 3, Sampson was aboard the *New York* seven miles east of the harbor to meet with General William Rufus Shafter to coordinate land forces. It was at this moment that Cervera chose to attempt his escape from the harbor. He was met by the guns of the American fleet under the direct command of **Schley** aboard the *Brooklyn*. In less than four hours the entire Spanish fleet was sunk or run ashore while the Americans suffered only minimal casualties. Sampson did not arrive on the scene until near the end of the battle.

Following the war, Sampson's health began to decline, though he did retain command of the North Atlantic fleet for another year. In 1899 he was named Commandant of the Boston Navy Yard but retired soon thereafter. He died in Washington, D.C. on May 6, 1902.

WINFIELD SCOTT SCHLEY

Naval Hero

(October 9, 1839–October 2, 1909)
Sec. 2, Lot 1207, Grid TU–31/32

Winfield Scott Schley took part in some of the greatest American naval exploits of the nineteenth century. Yet his greatest battle took place not on the high seas but in the arena of public opinion. That public battle resulted from the overwhelming defeat of the Spanish fleet at Santiago Harbor, Cuba during the Spanish-American War.

Schley was commander of the Flying Squadron in 1898 when he was ordered to join the naval forces under the command of **William T. Sampson**, an officer technically ranked below Schley. **Sampson**, who was searching for the Spanish fleet under Admiral Pascual Cervera y Torpeta, had ordered Schley to commence a blockade of Santiago Harbor while **Sampson** convoyed Army troops from Key West. Slow to respond, Schley's squadron allowed Cervera's forces to gain the security of the harbor before Schley established the blockade. On June 1 **Sampson** joined Schley on the scene and kept the Spanish vessels trapped within the harbor for over a month. Under **Sampson's** direction, searchlights were fixed on the narrow harbor entrance and reconnaissance operations were undertaken.

Finally, on July 3, Cervera made his move. **Sampson**, however, was on board the *New York* at that moment, seven miles east of the harbor entrance, meeting with General William Rufus Shafter to coordinate the land force operations. The American naval vessels were under the direct command of Schley, who greeted Cervera with a barrage of cannon fire. Within four hours, the entire Spanish fleet had been sunk or run aground. **Sampson** arrived on the scene just as the battle ended. News of the American victory erupted on the front pages of every newspaper in the U.S., igniting a heated debate over who deserved the credit for the spectacular American victory. Was it Schley, who was in command during the battle? Or **Sampson**, who had outlined the general battle plans?

The controversy grew to such a fever pitch that a special Naval Inquiry Board was impanelled with the venerable Admiral George Dewey as its chairman. Although the press appeared to favor Schley, the Board ruled that **Sampson** was proper in his command and, as such, should be given credit for the military operation. Even Schley himself acknowledged **Sampson's** right to claim the victory, but the controversy was still slow to die. Finally the Navy resolved the debate by promoting both men to the rank of Rear Admiral in 1899.

Long before the Spanish-American War erupted in 1898, Schley's career had been filled with adventure. A namesake of the famous Mexican War general, Winfield Scott, Schley was born in Frederick County, Maryland and graduated from the U.S. Naval Academy with the class of 1860. He served along the Atlantic seaboard during the Civil War and was given his first command when he sailed the captured Confederate vessel, *General Parkhill*, to the Admiralty Court in Philadelphia.

Following the Civil War, he served as a professor of modern languages at the Naval Academy from 1867 through 1869. Fifteen years later, Schley gained national attention when he undertook the hazardous command of the *Thetis* on a daring rescue mission to the Arctic. In 1881 Army Lieutenant **Adolphus Washington Greely** had begun an expedition to north of Greenland with a crew of twenty-four. By 1883 there had been no communication from them, so Schley sailed into the treacherous frozen seas of the North Atlantic. There, on June 23, 1884, at Cape Sabine in northern Greenland, Schley found **Greely** and six other survivors near death, rescuing them and bringing them safely back to America. Schley returned to the United States a hero, earned promotion to Commander, and was named Chief of Equipment and Recruiting.

In 1891 Schley was involved in another incident that became the focus of international attention. A liberty party from his ship, the *Baltimore*, which was docked in Valparaiso, Chile, was attacked by a mob; two of his sailors were killed. This ignited an international incident between the United States and Chile.

Following the Spanish-American War, Schley was named

Commander in Chief of the South Atlantic Station where he remained until reaching the mandatory retirement age of sixty-two on October 9, 1901. After his retirement Schley travelled widely, enjoying fame as a popular hero. Just seven days before his seventieth birthday, Schley died in 1909.

JOHN McALLISTER SCHOFIELD

Secretary of War, General in Chief of the Army

(September 29, 1831–March 4, 1906)
Sec. 2, Lot 1108, Grid T–31

John McAllister Schofield was a physics professor when the Civil War erupted and like so many other Americans, his life was never the same. Schofield left the classroom to become a Union Brigadier General, Secretary of War, and finally to achieve the highest position in the United States Army.

John Schofield's life took many unexpected turns. Growing up in Freeport, Illinois Schofield hoped for a military career. He entered the U.S. Military Academy, graduating in 1853. His first assignment was in Florida but he contracted malaria there and returned to West Point. At this point, his career changed direction for the first time when he was named to the Military Academy's faculty in the Department of Philosophy. Shortly thereafter, recognizing his own penchant for teaching, Schofield took his career in yet another direction, this time away from the Army, accepting a professorship in physics at Washington University in St. Louis, Missouri.

Schofield was teaching in St. Louis when hostilities broke out between the North and South in 1861. He received a commission as a Brigadier General and spent most of the war involved in the Missouri-Kansas military theatre. Ultimately Schofield was granted field command of the Army of the Ohio and accompanied General William Tecumseh Sherman in his drive through Georgia. From there he turned North again and continued to pressure the Southern troops all the way to Appomattox.

After the Civil War Schofield's career veered toward diplomacy when the State Department enlisted his services. Sent as an envoy to Paris, Schofield assisted in the mediation of a dispute between the United States and France over France's intrusion into Mexican affairs. He returned to the United States and resumed active Army duty in August 1866, assuming command of the Department of the Potomac and becoming Military Governor of Virginia during the volatile early days of Reconstruction. In 1868 President Andrew Johnson, who had just narrowly survived an impeachment trial by Congressional Radical Republicans and who was searching for a Secretary of War acceptable to his tempestuous critics in Congress, called upon Schofield as a compromise nominee to serve in that post. Schofield remained in public administration only through the end of President Johnson's term in 1869.

Upon the inauguration of Ulysses S. Grant as President of the United States, Schofield once again returned to active duty, was promoted to Major General, and for nineteen years held departmental and division commands which included a five-year stint as Commandant of West Point from 1876–1881. During his command of the Division of the Pacific in 1872, Schofield founded the naval base at Pearl Harbor. The Schofield Barracks at Pearl Harbor are named in his honor. Upon the death of General **Philip Henry Sheridan** in 1888, Schofield ascended to the highest ranking position in the military, General in Chief of the Army. He remained in that post until his retirement in 1895.

During a peaceful tenure as General in Chief, Schofield set military precedent when he placed himself under the authority of the Secretary of War. This was the first time in American history that the competition for authority between the country's ranking military officer and the Cabinet Secretary became clearly defined. Having served in both positions, Schofield is credited with recognizing the necessity for civilian control of the military. The precedent he set remains in effect today.

During the Spanish-American War, the retired General Schofield served as a personal military advisor to President William McKinley. John McAllister Schofield died in St. Augustine, Florida on March 4, 1906 and was buried with full military honors at Arlington.

THOMAS E. SELFRIDGE

First Military Aviation Fatality

(February 8,1882–September 17, 1908)
Sec. 3, Lot 2158, Grid QR–13/14

Just five years after the Wright brothers' first successful flight at Kitty Hawk, the United States Army invited them to Fort Myer, Virginia to demonstrate their new "flying device" for possible military applications. The U.S. Army was interested in a craft that could carry two people a distance of 125 miles at a speed of forty miles per hour, and the Wrights were confident that their airplane could meet the specifications.

Daily test flights began on September 3, 1908 from the Fort Myer parade ground immediately adjacent to Arlington National Cemetery. The spectacle of men flying in heavier-than-air machines attracted crowds of spectators from nearby Washington, D.C., so the Army planned a special Labor Day program of aerial displays. Among those attending the program were Secretary of War **William Howard Taft** and inventor Alexander Graham Bell.

On September 17, following two weeks of successful flight demonstrations, Orville Wright suggested that an Army observer be allowed to accompany him on one of the flights. Quick to volunteer for the duty was twenty-six-year-old Army Lieutenant Thomas Selfridge. Permission granted, Selfridge was strapped into the open seat next to Wright and they began their ascent. For three minutes Selfridge enjoyed a flawless flight. Then suddenly, while soaring at an altitude of 110 feet, the plane began to shake violently, causing Wright to lose control of the aircraft. The crowd of 2,500 spectators watched in horror as the propeller broke from the plane. Scrambling to regain some maneuverability as they fell toward the earth, Wright turned off the engine as a last hope to glide the plane toward a controlled landing. Within a minute, however, the plane crashed out of control onto the parade ground severely injuring Wright and requiring the immediate evacuation

In these never-before-published photographs Lt. Thomas E. Selfridge is shown sitting to the left of aviation pioneer Orville Wright just prior to their takeoff from the parade grounds of Fort Myer, adjacent to Arlington National Cemetery. Minutes later, Selfridge is pictured being carried from the wreckage of the plane which fell out of control from a height of more than one hundred feet, seriously injuring Wright and killing Selfridge.

of Selfridge to Walter Reed Hospital. He was pronounced dead three hours later.

Thomas Selfridge—the nephew and namesake of Rear Admiral Thomas O. Selfridge—was born in San Francisco, California in 1882. Young Selfridge attended the United States Military Academy at West Point, graduating with the class of 1903. It was soon clear to Army officials that Selfridge displayed a great interest in flying, which prompted one Army official to call Selfridge the "most enthusiastic aeronautical expert" in the Army. Selfridge worked with several well-known aviators and inventors, including balloonist **Thomas Scott Baldwin** of Quincy, Illinois and Alexander Graham Bell. Selfridge worked with Bell on the "June Bug" project which was the first attempt by the U.S. Army to put a man aloft by use of a kite.

Lt. Selfridge was buried with military honors in Section 3 of Arlington National Cemetery, just a few hundred yards from the site of the airplane crash which cost him his life and cost the U.S. military its first aviation fatality. Since Selfridge's death, other pioneers of flight have been interred at Arlington. Buried near his grave are two of the three Apollo One astronauts—**Virgil Grissom** and **Roger Chaffee**—who were killed on January 27, 1967 while performing a simulated launch for their space flight. In May 1986 two more astronauts—Captain **Michael Smith** and Commander **Francis (Dick) Scobee**—were buried at Arlington National Cemetery. They were among the seven Shuttle Challenger astronauts killed on January 28, 1986 when their spacecraft exploded just after launch from Cape Canaveral, Florida. Another pilot, **Francis Gary Powers**, is also buried in Section 3. He was the American reconnaissance airman shot down over the Soviet Union in 1960 and later convicted as an American spy.

PHILIP HENRY SHERIDAN

Civil War General, General in Chief of the Army

(March 6, 1831–August 5, 1888)
Sec. 2, Lot S-1, Grid ST–33/34

Arlington National Cemetery was established as a result of the Civil War in 1864. Many of those buried here are fallen heroes of that war, including generals from both the North and the South. Prominent among these historic graves is that of Philip Henry Sheridan, generally considered to be the third most important Union General, ranking only behind Ulysses S. Grant and William Tecumseh Sherman.

The son of Irish immigrants and one of six children, Sheridan was born in Albany, New York. He attended the U.S. Military Academy, but his record there was less than sterling. Only after the original appointee failed to qualify was Sheridan accepted for admission and even then he was suspended for a year after lunging at an upperclassman with a bayonetted rifle. He finally graduated with the class of 1853 and spent his early years on the western frontier.

When the Civil War began, Sheridan was a relatively unknown thirty-year-old Lieutenant of Infantry serving in Oregon. His involvement in the war as a troop commander did not commence until April of 1862 when he was named Quartermaster of the Staff of Henry Wager Halleck, Supreme Commander of the Western Theatre. With Halleck, Sheridan took part in the campaign against Corinth, Mississippi, was soon promoted to Colonel and given command of a cavalry brigade which he led on a successful raid against Booneville, Mississippi. Further successes at Perryville, Kentucky and Stone's River, Tennessee earned him a rapid and steady rise in rank and in command. By September 1863, "Little Phil," a nickname that fit his 5′ 5″ frame had attracted the attention of General **William Starke Rosecrans** and he was promoted to Brigadier General. Although suffering defeat with **Rosecrans** at Chickamauga, Sheridan later rallied his forces to record a major victory at Missionary Ridge. Impressed with Sheridan's performance, General Grant promoted him to Commander of the Cavalry of the Army of the Potomac.

In 1864 Sheridan led a raid on Richmond, Virginia which resulted in the death of General J.E.B. Stuart, one of the South's great cavalry leaders. Sheridan's best-known victory occurred shortly after he was given command of the Army of the Shenandoah in August 1864. It occurred at Cedar Creek, Virginia and has been immortalized in the poem, "Sheridan's Ride," by Thomas Buchanan Read.

Sheridan's army was camped at Cedar Creek, but the General was about fifteen miles north in Winchester on his way back from Washington, D.C. Awakened before dawn to the sounds of distant gunfire, Sheridan rode quickly out of Winchester and was greeted by the sight of his own army fleeing the battle site. Though a short man, Sheridan cut a very authoritarian figure when mounted on his stallion. He commanded his troops to regroup and counterattack, and they obeyed his orders, eventually routing the Confederate troops from the Shenandoah Valley. For this Sheridan was promoted to Major General and received the express gratitude of the U.S. Congress.

For Sheridan the rest of the war must have seemed like a mopping up exercise. He kept constant pressure on General Robert E. Lee's forces in Virginia, and on April 1, 1865 won a key victory at Five Forks, blocking Lee's retreat to the South. On April 9, 1865 Sheridan himself was present to witness Lee's surrender at Appomattox Court House.

After the Civil War Sheridan was given command of the Division of the Gulf which pressured the army of Napoleon III to end its occupation of Mexico and which hastened the fall of his puppet emperor, Maximilian, in 1867. President Andrew Johnson named Sheridan military commander of Louisiana and Texas during

Reconstruction, but the President soon removed him because of Sheridan's harsh administration. He was returned to the western frontier, promoted to Lieutenant General in 1869, and given command of the Division of the Missouri.

In 1884, after the death of William Tecumseh Sherman, Sheridan was named General in Chief of the Army, the highest ranking position in the American Armed Forces. Then, in 1888, Sheridan was promoted to full General. He never retired from the Army, dying in 1888 while still on active duty. He finished his autobiography, the two volume *Personal Memoirs of P.H. Sheridan*, just before he died.

Philip Henry Sheridan is buried at Arlington just south and east of Arlington House, but his tomb is not easily recognized because it is surrounded by several trees and cannot be read from the walkway above the grave. His marker bears a large bas-relief of the General. Only the word "Sheridan" is written on the stone. Sheridan's wife and several of his children are buried near him.

THE SHUTTLE CHALLENGER ASTRONAUTS

FRANCIS R. (DICK) SCOBEE

(May 19, 1939–January 28, 1986)
Sec. 46, Lot 1129-4, Grid O–23/24

MICHAEL J. SMITH

(April 30, 1945–January 28, 1986)
Sec. 7A, Lot 208-1, Grid TU–23/24

Across the country the scenes were reminiscent of the 1960s— schoolchildren huddled around television sets, watching a rocket carry Americans into space. But it was not the 1960s, it was the 1980s when reusable manned orbiters were launched into space and returned to earth with regularity. For most Americans, space flight had become commonplace. To the millions of schoolchildren watching this launch, however, there was nothing commonplace about it. This mission had generated a great deal of publicity because included among its crew was America's first "ordinary citizen in space," schoolteacher Christa McAuliffe. In the months preceding the launch, Christa McAuliffe had rekindled an interest in space exploration, not only among the nation's schoolchildren, but among all its citizens. She personified the belief that any American could accomplish anything if he or she just put their minds to it. So it was McAuliffe's presence among the seven crew members of the Space Shuttle *Challenger* that brought millions of Americans to their television screens on January 28, 1986.

At 11:38 A.M. EST, the *Challenger* lifted off from Pad 39–B of the Kennedy Space Center at Cape Canaveral, Florida. Slowly but steadily the shuttle cleared the tower, heading for its mission among the stars. Suddenly, seventy-three seconds and nine miles into the flight, as millions of American schoolchildren watched in horror, the orbiter exploded into a vast, billowing white cloud, pierced by red and orange flames. As thousands of pieces of debris fell into the Atlantic Ocean, two booster rockets trailed away from the explosion sight, leaving many spectators believing that the Shuttle had been able to clear the explosion, and was heading for the emergency landing strip nearby. But soon that proved not to be the case. The valiant crew of the Space Shuttle *Challenger* lost their lives as a result of that explosion. Along with Christa McAuliffe, the crew included shuttle commander Francis R. (Dick) Scobee, pilot Michael J. Smith, mission specialists Ellison S. Onizuka, Judith A. Resnik, and Ronald E. McNair, and payload specialist Gregory B. Jarvis.

It was several agonizing weeks after the explosion before the remains of the shuttle crew were finally located and identified. On April 29, 1986 those remains were released to the families of the astronauts for private burial services. Unfortunately, not all of the recovered remains could be positively identified. Therefore, in a private ceremony on May 20, 1986, those unidentified remains were placed in a single, common grave at Arlington, dedicated to the memory of all seven shuttle astronauts. Two crew members whose remains were identified—mission commander Dick Scobee and shuttle pilot Mike Smith—are buried at Arlington Cemetery.

Shuttle *Challenger* astronauts Michael J. Smith and Francis (Dick) Scobee were buried at Arlington in May 1986.

Francis Richard Scobee was born in the little Washington town of Cle Elum (a Native American name meaning "swift water"). The son of a railroad engineer, he graduated from nearby Auburn High School in 1957. Following graduation, Scobee went to work for the giant aircraft manufacturer, Boeing, which had been the principal employer in the area since World War II. But Scobee left Boeing in October of that year, enlisting in the United States Air Force.

Stationed at Kelly Air Force Base in San Antonio, Texas, Scobee was trained as an aircraft mechanic. It was while he was in San Antonio that he met June Kent whom he married the following year; he was twenty, she was sixteen. Dick Scobee juggled his Air Force duties to find the time to join his wife as a night student at nearby San Antonio College. By 1963 Dick had earned two years credit toward his degree when he first learned of the Air Force's Airman's Education and Commissioning Program, aimed at making officers out of enlisted men. He was quickly accepted and was enrolled at the University of Arizona where he received a degree in aerospace engineering in 1965. In September of that same year he was commissioned a Lieutenant and entered pilot training school at Moody Air Force Base in Georgia.

During the mid-1960s American military involvement in

Southeast Asia escalated sharply, increasing the need for trained pilots. Scobee left for Vietnam in November 1967, assigned to the 535th Tactical Airlift Squadron. During his tour of duty in Vietnam, Scobee earned many military decorations, including the Distinguished Service Cross and the Air Medal.

In July 1971 Dick Scobee made his first contact with America's space program when he entered the Aerospace Research Pilot School at Edwards Air Force Base in California. Following 700 hours of study on the ground and 150 hours in the air, Captain Scobee was awarded his test pilot's wings in June 1972. It seemed only natural to Scobee that he would then apply for astronaut training, which he did in 1977. The following year, when NASA was selecting a new group of astronauts to fly the space shuttles, Dick Scobee was among them. After twenty-two years he retired as a Major from the Air Force, moving his family to Houston, Texas to concentrate on his NASA duties. While there, June Scobee received her Ph.D. from Texas A & M University and was named a visiting assistant professor at the University of Houston.

In April 1984 Dick Scobee made his first journey into space as second in command of one of NASA's most successful flights. As pilot of the *Challenger*, he maneuvered the spacecraft so that his fellow crew members could retrieve the broken Solar Max satellite. After it was repaired on board the shuttle, the satellite was returned to its correct orbit. Scobee and the other members of the crew later appeared at an in-flight press conference sporting T-shirts which read Ace Satellite Repair Co.

Dick Scobee was chosen to command Mission 51-L, the twenty-fifth space shuttle flight scheduled for January 20, 1986. The mission assumed celebrity status when it was announced that included among its crew would be schoolteacher Christa McAuliffe. On January 28, 1986, after five delayed launches, the rocket's main engines roared into action at 11:38 A.M. Seventy-three seconds later, nine miles above the Atlantic Ocean, the mission ended in a fiery explosion.

On May 19, 1986 Dick Scobee would have celebrated his forty-seventh birthday. Instead, he was buried at Arlington National Cemetery during a brief, solemn ceremony. His grave is marked by a regulation headstone, bearing the Air Force's astronauts' insignia. Immediately adjacent to his grave are the graves of three airmen killed in 1980 during an aborted attempt to rescue American hostages held in Iran.

Michael J. Smith grew up on a small farm outside Beaufort, a small fishing village on the North Carolina coast. The family farm was located near the Beaufort-Morehead City airport, providing Mike with a vantage point from which to watch the planes taking off and landing. He began taking flying lessons before most people learn to drive. On April 30, 1961 he made his first solo flight; it was his sixteenth birthday.

Mike Smith graduated from Beaufort High School in 1963, gaining an appointment to the United States Naval Academy at Annapolis. In 1967 he graduated 108th in his Academy class of 893 students. Ten days later he married Jane Jarrell, a young girl from Charlotte, North Carolina whom he had met several years earlier. The next stop for Smith was the U.S. Naval Postgraduate School in Monterey, California. He had been one of twelve students chosen to study aeronautical engineering in a newly formed accelerated program.

Following the completion of his graduate studies in March 1968, Smith began an extended period of flight training followed by a tour of duty aboard the USS *Kitty Hawk* during the Vietnam War. After his arrival in Vietnam in 1972, Smith flew 225 combat missions and was awarded, among other decorations, the Navy Distinguished Flying Cross, the Vietnamese Cross of Gallantry with Silver Star, and thirteen Strike Flight Air Medals. In 1973 Smith returned to the United States, entering the U.S. Navy Test Pilot School at Patuxent River, Maryland. Finally, five years later, he applied for the position he had always hoped for—astronaut. But he was not accepted. Smith applied again. This time his dream was realized when he was asked to enter the astronaut class of 1980.

Mike Smith acclimated quickly to NASA and the space program. In 1985 his familiarity with the program led to his assignment to assist civilian astronaut Senator Jake Garn during Garn's preparation for a 1985 Shuttle flight. The Senator affectionately referred to Smith as "my mother hen." For Mike Smith his first mission was Flight 51–L aboard the Shuttle *Challenger*. Although it had been scheduled to liftoff on January 20, 1986, it was delayed five times before given the go-ahead on January 28.

As pilot of the *Challenger*, Smith and Commander Dick Scobee were busy on the flight deck reviewing checklists and monitoring computers, readying themselves for the mission that would carry the first ordinary citizen into space, schoolteacher Christa McAuliffe. As the *Challenger* left Pad 39-B, the external fuel tank ruptured and highly-flammable rocket fuel began leaking. One minute and twelve seconds into the flight that fuel ignited, causing the explosion that destroyed *Challenger* and killed its crew.

Michael J. Smith was granted a posthumous promotion to Captain and was buried with full military honors at Arlington National Cemetery on May 3, 1986. The Navy astronaut insignia—depicting Navy pilot wings and a shooting star—adorns his black marble headstone.

Following the explosion of the *Challenger*, President Ronald Reagan immediately appointed a blue-ribbon commission headed by former Attorney General and Secretary of State William P. Rogers to investigate the Shuttle explosion. On June 9, 1986 the Rogers Commission made their report public. The cause of the *Challenger* accident was determined to be the failure of O-rings on the right-hand booster rocket. A joint in that rocket had failed to contain the pressure of hot gases produced by burning rocket fuel. Flames burned through the booster rocket's wall, causing the booster rocket to tear away from the external fuel tank which ruptured, spilling highly flammable liquid hydrogen and liquid oxygen. When ignited, these liquid fuels caused the massive explosion which destroyed the *Challenger* and killed its crew.

A memorial to the seven Shuttle Challenger astronauts marks the common grave that contains remains of the astronauts which were recovered but could not be identified. Dedicated March 21, 1987, the memorial is located in Section 46 next to the grave of Shuttle Commander Dick Scobee. Grid 0-23/24.

WALTER BEDELL SMITH

General, Ambassador, CIA Director

(October 5, 1895–August 9, 1961)
Sec. 7, Lot 8197–A, Grid VW–24

The administrative and diplomatic abilities of Walter Bedell Smith received great recognition both during and after World War II. Despite an investigation regarding his handling of intelligence material related to a possible attack on Pearl Harbor, Smith continued to serve in vital U.S. government posts, including positions as Ambassador to the Soviet Union, Director of the CIA, and Under Secretary of State.

Walter Bedell Smith first entered military service in 1913 when he joined the National Guard in his home town of Indianapolis. He had studied at Butler University in Indianapolis but was forced to withdraw when his father became seriously ill. During World War I Smith was commissioned a 2nd Lieutenant in the Army Reserve. Called to action in France, Smith took part in the battle of the Marne and was later wounded during the battle of Aisne.

In 1920 Smith joined the regular Army and was assigned to the new Bureau of Military Intelligence. Throughout that decade Smith worked for the military Bureau of the Budget and later commanded native troops in the Philippines, earning promotion to Captain. During the 1930s Smith acquired most of his formal military training. He completed the courses of study at the Infantry School at Fort Benning, Georgia, the Command and General Staff School at Fort Leavenworth, Kansas and the Army War College in Washington, D.C. While at Fort Benning, Smith became acquainted with then Colonel **George C. Marshall**. This proved to be a lifelong friendship.

When **Marshall** was named Army Chief of Staff in 1939, he brought Smith with him to Washington. Smith assumed the duties of Secretary to the General Staff and subsequently served as Secretary to the Anglo-American Joint Chiefs of Staff after the

United States entered World War II.

Smith's career was threatened briefly in 1941 following the Japanese attack on Pearl Harbor. On Saturday, December 6, 1941, the day before the infamous attack, Smith decided not to deliver a routine intelligence pouch to Chief of Staff General **Marshall** who was spending the weekend outside of Washington. He took it upon himself to hold the material until the following Monday. Smith stated that he was led to believe the pouch contained only a partially decoded Japanese cable and that the cable was not urgent. It was later shown to contain information about an impending attack. Smith, however, was exonerated by President Franklin Roosevelt, General **Marshall**, and the Congress following a thorough investigation.

Promoted to Brigadier General in 1942, he was named Chief of Staff for General Dwight Eisenhower in North Africa. Smith negotiated the surrender of Italy in 1943 and signed the formal surrender papers on behalf of the United States. Following his success in North Africa, Smith was named Chief of Staff for the Supreme Headquarters of the Allied Expeditionary Forces (SHAEF). As Eisenhower's emissary, he participated in the Malta Conference and was a member of the Allied group that accepted Germany's formal surrender.

After the war President Harry Truman appointed Smith to succeed W. Averell Harriman as U.S. Ambassador to the Soviet Union in the early years of the Cold War. It was during his tenure in Moscow that the Berlin Crisis occurred. As Ambassador, Smith also served as an official delegate to the Paris Peace Conference in 1946, and to all the Foreign Ministers' Conferences until 1949.

Having gained special permission from Congress to retain his military status while serving in a diplomatic post, Smith returned to the U.S. in 1949 to assume command of the First Army. That command was short-lived, however, because President Truman named Smith as the second Director of the CIA, mandating him to reorganize the agency. While Director, Smith was promoted to General.

Unlike most officials of the Truman administration, Smith did not leave the government when Dwight Eisenhower assumed the presidency. Rather, he was named by President Eisenhower to be Under Secretary of State, under **John Foster Dulles**. This time

Smith resigned his military commission to take the diplomatic position. Then in 1954 he resigned from government service to enter the private sector.

As a civilian Smith served on the Boards of Directors for several major companies including NBC, RCA, United Fruit Company, and Corning Glass Works. During his illustrious career he not only received the Distinguished Service Medal from this country, but also was decorated by thirteen other countries, including Great Britain, France, and the Soviet Union. Walter Bedell Smith died in Washington D.C. in 1961 and is buried in Arlington near his mentor and close friend, **George C. Marshall**.

GEORGE M. STERNBERG

U.S. Army Surgeon General

(June 8, 1838–November 3, 1915)
Sec. 2, Lot 994, Grid S–32/33

George Sternberg's medical career in the United States Army took him from front line care of the wounded in the Civil War, during which he himself was wounded, to the highest ranking medical officer in the United States Army.

Sternberg was the eldest of ten children of a Lutheran clergyman whose ancestors immigrated from Germany. He was educated at Hardwick Seminary in New York where his maternal grandfather was a professor of theology. At age sixteen he started teaching school in Germantown, New Jersey and at nineteen he began studying medicine in a private doctor's office. Subsequently, he graduated from the College of Physicians and Surgeons in New York City in 1860.

In 1861, when hostilities began between the North and the South, Sternberg passed the exam for admission to the Army Medical Corps and was appointed Assistant Surgeon on May 28, 1861. Assigned to the infantry, Sternberg cared for the wounded under heavy fire at Gaines Mill and Malvern Hill. He was also involved in the first Battle of Bull Run, where he was wounded and captured by Confederate soldiers. Held at Fairfax Court House, Sternberg managed to escape and returned to his regiment. He was promoted to the rank of Major, and was known for often disregarding his own safety while tending to the sick and wounded. Before the end of the war, he contracted typhoid fever.

Doctor Sternberg was promoted to Lt. Colonel following an encounter with Indians at Clearwater, Idaho in 1877. He carried out various assignments on the western frontier before first returning to New York and then to Florida to set up hospitals to cope with the widespread epidemic of yellow fever. Between the Civil War and the Spanish-American War in 1898, Sternberg was credited with establishing more than a dozen new hospitals throughout the country.

In 1890 Sternberg was named Surgeon General of the Army, becoming the highest ranking medical officer in the Armed Forces. During his tenure, he founded two hospital ships and aided Dr. **Anita Newcomb McGee** in organizing the female nurse corps and the Corps of Dental Surgeons. It was Sternberg who appointed Dr. **Walter Reed** to head the Yellow Fever Commission in 1900, the commission which ultimately discovered the source of the deadly disease. However, Dr. Sternberg considered his greatest achievement to be the establishment of the Army Medical School in Washington, D.C. In 1902 Sternberg retired from the Army and died at his home in Washington on November 3, 1915.

ROBERT DEAN STETHEM

"Young American Hero"

(November 21, 1961–June 15, 1985)
Sec. 59, Lot 430, Grid EE–25

Robert Stethem was a twenty-three-year-old steelworker Second Class in the United States Navy assigned to the Navy's underwater construction team. He enjoyed his work because it gave him a chance to travel, as it did in early June 1985 when Seaman Stethem joined an inspection and repair project on a U.S. military facility in Nea Makri, Greece. It had been a routine assignment and after completing it, Stethem boarded TWA Flight 847 in Athens to fly back home to America.

Shortly after takeoff a group of fanatic Shiite Muslims commandeered the plane, triggering a tragic drama which resulted in the brutal beating and murder of young Stethem. Soon after taking over the plane, the Arab hijackers realized that Stethem was a U.S. serviceman and made him the target of their hatred of the United States. Yet, even when his very life was threatened, Stethem never denied his American military status. Courageously, Robert Stethem withstood the brutal attack which the air pirates directed at him. The other passengers, after their eventual release, recounted Stethem's bravery, marvelling at his ability to maintain his dignity, never forgetting that as a Seaman he represented the United States of America. Frustrated by their inability to destroy Stethem's proud spirit, the hijackers shot the young sailor at point blank range, and as the world watched in horror, threw his body from the plane onto the tarmac at Beirut Airport.

The hostage drama continued for two weeks after the killing of Robert Stethem, but thankfully all the other passengers and the crew members were freed. Robert Stethem's body was returned to the United States and he was buried with full military honors at Arlington National Cemetery. This young man from Waldorf, Maryland was recalled by one neighbor as "just the kind of kid you'd like to have as your own son." Polite and athletic, Stethem had played defensive back on the varsity football team at Thomas Stone High School, where he graduated in 1980. The son of two career Navy parents, Robert enlisted in the Navy within six months of his high school graduation.

President Ronald Reagan, speaking on behalf of all Americans, called Robert Stethem a "young American hero." Stethem's bravery and ultimate sacrifice for his country were further recognized when his parents, Richard and Patricia Stethem, accepted the Purple Heart on their son's behalf. On April 25, 1986 Robert Stethem was posthumously awarded the Bronze Star. He is buried in Section 59 of Arlington amid the graves of the twenty-two Marines who were also the victims of terrorism when their barracks in Beirut were bombed by Arab extremists in October 1983.

POTTER STEWART

Supreme Court Justice

(January 23, 1915–December 7, 1985)
Sec. 5, Lot 40–2, Grid W–36

It was a most unusual decision for a Supreme Court Justice in good health to retire at the age of sixty-six. Appointed for life, many justices serve into their seventies and beyond. Yet Potter Stewart knew the constant demands of time and energy made by our nation's highest court on its justices, and, after twenty-three years on the Supreme Court, he decided to more fully devote himself to his family. With that decision, he graciously ended a highly respected career.

Born in Jackson, Michigan Stewart grew up in Cincinnati where he became a lifelong Reds baseball fan. Even after he moved to Washington in 1958, he continued to consider the Cincinnati Reds as "invincible." Still, even as a child, the law was his greatest love. His father, James Garfield Stewart, was a justice on the Ohio Supreme Court.

Following his cum laude graduation from Yale University in 1937, he studied for a year at Cambridge University in England as a Henry Fellow. Then he returned to Yale to receive his law degree in 1941. Stewart saw active sea duty with the Navy in the Atlantic, Caribbean, and Mediterranean theatres during World War II. He retired as a Lieutenant in 1945. After the war he practiced law in New York City, later returning to his home in Cincinnati where he served on the City Council from 1950 to 1953 and as Vice-Mayor in 1952 and 1953.

Vice-President George Bush and members of the Supreme Court headed by Chief Justice Warren Burger (at left) attend the graveside services for former Justice Potter Stewart in December 1985.

In 1954, at age thirty-nine, he was appointed by President Eisenhower to the United States Court of Appeals for the Sixth Circuit, becoming the youngest federal judge serving at that time. In 1958 he was again appointed by President Eisenhower, this time to the United States Supreme Court, replacing another Ohio native, Justice Harold H. Burton. Forty-three years old, Stewart became the fifth youngest justice ever to serve on our nation's highest court.

Justice Stewart rendered some of the most important decisions in the Court's history, especially those rulings related to the First Amendment, to criminal law, and to capital punishment in America.

He served under two Chief Justices, **Earl Warren** and Warren Burger. When he retired in 1981 he was succeeded by the first woman ever appointed to the Court, Sandra Day O'Connor.

Justice Stewart remained active after he left the Court. He served on many commissions, visited numerous law schools, and read law books for Recording for the Blind. He is the sixth Supreme Court Justice to be buried at Arlington, joining **Oliver Wendell Holmes**, **William Howard Taft**, **Earl Warren**, **Hugo Black**, and **William O. Douglas**.

WILLIAM HOWARD TAFT

President, Chief Justice of the United States

(September 15, 1857–March 8, 1930)
Sec. 30, Grave S–14, Grid YZ–39/40

William Howard Taft's career spanned fifty years, included a term as President of the United States and nearly a decade as Chief Justice of the Supreme Court, making him the only person in American history to serve in both positions.

When William Taft was born in Cincinnati in 1857, he became part of a family whose name has become synonymous with public service in Ohio. His father, Alphonso Taft, became Attorney General of the United States in 1876 during the administration of Ulysses S. Grant. William distinguished himself as a student, graduating second in his undergraduate class at Yale in 1878 and first in his law school class at the University of Cincinnati in 1880.

He began his long and remarkable public service career as an assistant prosecuting attorney for Hamilton County, Ohio in 1881. His first position on the bench was as an Ohio Superior Court judge in 1887, a post he held for three years until he was appointed Solicitor General of the United States by President Benjamin Harrison. As Solicitor General, his chief responsibility was to represent the United States in all cases before the Supreme Court. He resumed his judicial career as a U.S. Circuit Judge for the Sixth Circuit in 1892, simultaneously serving as Dean of the Law Department of the University of Cincinnati until 1900.

On March 12, 1900 President William McKinley appointed Taft President of the Philippine Commission, charged with governing the islands acquired as a result of the recent war with Spain. Subsequently, Taft was named the first civilian governor of the Philippines and served in that position until 1904. As governor, Taft introduced many needed reforms and programs to the islands, including modern roads, schools, sanitation systems, and land reform. It was during his term as governor that Taft made one of the most difficult decisions of his career. In 1902 President Theodore Roosevelt wanted to appoint Taft to fill a vacancy on the Supreme Court, a position Taft had coveted all his life. Yet Taft felt obligated to finish the work he had started in the Philippines, so he reluctantly declined Roosevelt's offer certain that he would never sit on the High Court. Instead, Roosevelt appointed a jurist from Massachusetts, **Oliver Wendell Holmes, Jr.**, who remained on the court for nearly thirty years. Taft completed his term as governor, then accepted an appointment to Roosevelt's Cabinet as Secretary of War in 1904, a post that Taft's father had held twenty-five years earlier.

President Roosevelt, choosing not to seek reelection in 1908, turned to Taft as the man to succeed him in the Oval Office. Taft publicly declared that he did not want to be President, but bowed to the pressure of his wife, **Helen Herron Taft**, President Roosevelt, and other members of his own family. After winning the Republican Party's nomination, he faced perennial Democratic nominee, **William Jennings Bryan** in the general election. Taft won a sweeping victory and settled into the White House, a place he later described as "the lonesomest place in the world."

Taft's presidency was not known for innovative policies, but rather for its *laissez faire* approach to government. Unfortunately, he also managed to incur the wrath of his predecessor and patron, Theodore Roosevelt. In fact, Roosevelt was so unhappy with Taft's performance that he himself ran against Taft for the Republican nomination in 1912. At the party's Chicago convention, the Republicans witnessed a real donnybrook. Going into the convention, Roosevelt had won the most votes during the primaries and separate state conventions. Taft, however, had gathered a majority of the delegates' support and won the nomination on the first ballot. Never a man to be outdone, Roosevelt formed his own third party, The Bull Moose Party, and challenged both Taft and the Democratic nominee, Woodrow Wilson, in the national election. With the Republican ranks deeply divided, Wilson won an easy victory, receiving 435 electoral votes to Roosevelt's 88 and Taft's meager 8.

Taft, whose six-foot, more-than-three-hundred pound, frame made him the largest man ever to serve as this nation's President, was an avid sportsman and included golf among his favorite pastimes. His term as President may not be known for its great international or domestic policies, but several noteworthy events did occur during his tenure. He was the first President to throw out the first baseball of the season, in a game between the Philadelphia Athletics and the Washington Senators in 1910, thus starting a yearly tradition. Also during his presidency, both the North and South Poles were reached by manned expeditions for

A large marble monument marks the graves of William Howard Taft and Helen Herron Taft. William Howard Taft is the only person in American history to serve both as President and as Chief Justice of the Supreme Court. Helen Herron Taft is the only First Lady buried at Arlington.

the first time, and the famous cherry trees were planted in Washington.

After Taft vacated the Oval Office, he joined the faculty of Yale Law School and served as president of the American Bar Association, but in 1921 his greatest dream came true when President Warren G. Harding appointed the former president Chief Justice of the United States Supreme Court. Taft led the Court with distinction, gaining special recognition as a skilled administrator. It was under his guidance and direction that the present Supreme Court Building was designed and constructed. So important did Taft consider his service as Chief Justice that he once said, "The truth is that in my life I don't ever remember that I was President."

He retired from the High Court on February 3, 1930 due to ill health and died five weeks later. He was both the first American President and first Supreme Court Chief Justice to be buried at Arlington. His grave is marked by a Stoney Creek Granite monument which rises fourteen and a half feet. Commissioned by Taft's widow and sculpted by James Earl Frazer, it is in the Greek Stele form, surmounted by a carved ornamental device in the acroteria motif.

President Taft's wife, **Helen Herron Taft** died in 1943 at the age of 82 and is buried beside her husband. It was Mrs. **Taft** who succeeded in bringing the cherry trees to Washington's Tidal Basin. She is the only former First Lady interred in Arlington National Cemetery.

HOYT SANFORD VANDENBERG

Air Force Chief of Staff

(January 24, 1899–April 2, 1954)
Sec. 30, Lot 719, Grid WX–38/39

Hoyt Sanford Vandenberg was born in Milwaukee, Wisconsin just before the turn of the twentieth century and graduated from

West Point in 1923. His early career was primarily spent becoming a crack pilot; by 1929 he had achieved command of the Sixth Pursuit Squadron at Schofield Barracks in Hawaii. Ten years later Vandenberg completed instruction at the Army Command and General Staff School as well as at the Army War College. Assigned to the Plans Section of the Air Corps Headquarters, he worked daily with General **Hap Arnold** to draft contingency plans in case the United States entered the war then raging in Europe. Vandenberg rose to the rank of Colonel on January 27, 1942; in August of that year he was named Chief of Staff of General James Doolittle's Twelfth Air Force in England.

Later involved in the North African campaign and the invasion of Sicily and Italy, Vandenberg received special recognition from General Dwight Eisenhower and was promoted to Brigadier General. In August of 1943 he was appointed Deputy Chief of the Army Air Force Headquarters Staff in North Africa. Vandenberg took part in the early planning of the invasion of Europe, and following his promotion to Major General in March 1944, he joined General Eisenhower's staff.

His contributions to the American war effort continued. In July 1944 Vandenberg was selected by General **George C. Marshall** to command the Ninth Air Force which was ultimately the largest Air Force in Europe. As commander, he orchestrated the air support for General **Omar Bradley's** Twelfth Army Group in its drive across Europe. For his spectacular performance, General Eisenhower promoted him once again, this time to Lt. General.

Following the war President Harry Truman named Vandenberg as Director of the Central Intelligence Group, the forerunner to the CIA. Then, in April 1947, he left the Intelligence Group and returned to Air Force duty, soon taking the post of Deputy Commander in Chief of the Air Staff. In October of that year he was promoted to full General and became the first Vice Chief of Staff in the newly organized United States Air Force. Six months later, upon the retirement of General Carl Spaatz, Vandenberg was elevated to Chief of Staff of the U.S. Air Force.

During his tenure as Air Force Chief of Staff, **Vandenberg** conducted the Berlin Airlift and the new Air Force was first tested in combat—during the Korean War. Vandenberg retired a highly decorated airman in June 1953 and died of cancer the following year in Washington, D.C., at the age of fifty-five. After his death, the sprawling Air Force base in Southern California was renamed as a lasting tribute to General Vandenberg.

JONATHAN MAYHEW WAINWRIGHT

General, World War II POW

(August 23, 1881–September 2, 1953)
Sec. 1, Lot 358–B, Grid L/M–35/36

When General Jonathan Mayhew Wainwright was taken prisoner by the Japanese in May of 1942 he was the highest ranking POW in the Pacific Theatre. He had been forced to abandon his defense of the Bataan Peninsula in the Philippines when he ran out of food and equipment and his position was overrun by a much larger Japanese force. For three years in POW camps in the Philippines, on Taiwan, and in Manchuria, Wainwright suffered from the belief that he had disgraced himself and his country by his surrender. He was beaten by his captors and suffered merciless humiliation in front of his fellow prisoners. However he refused to be broken, maintaining his dignity as a commander and as a man until Soviet troops liberated him in August of 1945. He returned to the United States, to receive not only a hero's welcome from the American public, but also the Congressional Medal of Honor from President Harry Truman.

Wainwright was the product of a family that had produced military heroes for generations. His grandfather was a Union naval officer killed in action in Galveston Harbor during the Civil War; his uncle was killed while fighting pirates off the coast of Mexico in 1870; and his father, a veteran of the American Indian frontier and Spanish-American War, died on active duty in Manila in 1902. Born in Walla Walla, Washington, Wainwright attended West Point as had his father before him. He graduated in 1906 and made his first tour of duty in the Philippines in 1908.

During World War I, Wainwright participated in the St. Mihiel and the Meuse-Argonne Offensives in France. He returned to the United States in 1920, spending much of the period between the world wars learning the textbook side of professional soldiering. He graduated with honors from the Command and General Staff School in 1928 and was recommended for advance command training. In 1934 he completed study at the Army War College and by 1940 he had risen to the rank of Major General and was on his way back to Manila, this time to assume command of the Philippine Division.

After the Japanese attack on Pearl Harbor, he became field commander of U.S. and Filipino forces under Douglas MacArthur. When MacArthur left for Australia, Wainwright was ordered to defend the Bataan Peninsula where he and his men earned the name "the battling bastards of Bataan." Against overwhelming odds, Wainwright's forces fought gallantly until they were forced to surrender to General Tomobumi Yamashita on Corregidor Island. Although he waited three years to be rescued, his liberation came in time for him to be airlifted to the deck of the USS *Missouri* in Tokyo Bay to witness the surrender of General Yamashita on September 2, 1945.

Following the war, Jonathan Mayhew Wainwright was given command of the Fourth Army at Fort Sam Houston, Texas. In 1946 he published his autobiography, *General Wainwright's Story*, then retired from the Army the following year. Out of uniform, Wainwright became an insurance company executive. On September 2, 1953, exactly eight years after the surrender of Japan, he died of a massive stroke in San Antonio, Texas. In recognition of his outstanding military record, he was granted the extraordinary posthumous honor of lying in state in the vaulted chapel of the Memorial Amphitheatre at Arlington. General Wainwright is now buried in Arlington near another hero: his father, **Robert Powell Wainwright**.

EARL WARREN

Governor, Vice-Presidential Candidate, Chief Justice

(March 19, 1891–July 9, 1974)
Sec. 21, Lot S–32, Grid M–20/21

Earl Warren's public career spanned nearly half a century, from 1920 until 1969. During that time he held elective offices on the local and state levels, ran for Vice-President, and sought his party's nomination for President. After more than thirty years in elected office, Warren undertook his most important task, that of Chief Justice of the United States Supreme Court.

Earl Warren's father was an immigrant from Norway; his mother a native of Sweden. Born in Los Angeles, Earl worked at odd jobs in order to pay his tuition at the University of California. After spending time as a railroad call boy, a freight hustler, and a truck driver, Warren graduated from college in 1912. Two years later, he earned his law degree and entered private practice. Warren enlisted in the Army during World War I, attaining the rank of First Lieutenant. He returned to his private practice, but left it in 1920 to become a deputy assistant city attorney for the City of Oakland, California. He never again engaged in the private practice of law.

In 1925 Warren was appointed District Attorney of Alameda County, California and was reelected to that position in 1926, 1930, and 1934. During his tenure as District Attorney, he gained a reputation as an effective crime fighter, sending a city manager and several city councilmen to jail on graft charges. In 1938 Earl Warren undertook his first campaign for statewide office, seeking election as Attorney General. Although he was a Republican, Warren took advantage of a California law allowing candidates to cross-file under several party labels. In that primary election, he also ran on the Democratic Party and Progressive Party tickets. Warren won all three primaries, and went on to win the November general election. But during his campaign, Warren suffered a devastating personal tragedy—the murder of his father.

Early on a Saturday evening, his father was sitting home alone in his chair, reading the paper. It was a warm evening and apparently his father fell asleep, leaving the doors and windows open. The evidence later showed that someone had come into the house, struck his father on the head with a short piece of pipe, crushing his skull. His father's body had been dragged into the bedroom, where the killer had left him on the bed to die. It was the next morning before the crime was discovered. No one was ever arrested for the murder. While many theories were advanced, Earl Warren subscribed to the belief that a vagrant traveling on the trains which passed near his father's house had seen his father alone, entered the house, killed him, and stole his father's wallet. The wallet was found a short distance from the house. It had been the only thing missing.

Warren served one term as California's Attorney General, then set his sights on the Governor's mansion. Winning the Republican primary, he was pitted against a strong Democratic incumbent. Despite being rated the underdog, Warren won the election with 57% of the vote. He stood for reelection in 1946, again winning easily. As Governor of California, he was viewed as a political conservative because he denounced "communistic radicals" and supported the wartime internment of all persons of Japanese ancestry. However, following the war, he developed a progressive image, proposing a state program of prepaid medical insurance accompanied by liberal welfare and pension benefits.

In 1948 the Republican nominee for President, Governor Thomas Dewey of New York, chose Warren to be his running mate. Although the polls predicted an easy win for the Dewey-Warren ticket, and though some newspapers even printed headlines proclaiming a Dewey win, President Harry Truman won another term, sending Warren back to the statehouse in California. That election was the only one Earl Warren ever lost during his thirty years in elective office.

Warren ran for a third term as Governor in 1950, this time facing a formidable opponent, James Roosevelt, son of the late President Franklin Roosevelt. Nonetheless, Warren won by a two-to-one margin. Two years later in 1952, a Presidential election year, Warren indicated that he was interested in the Republican Party's nomination for President. By the time the nominating convention began, it was clear to Warren that the race was between former General Dwight Eisenhower and Ohio Senator Robert Taft. Waiting until just the right moment, Warren threw his support behind Eisenhower, a move that helped the former General win the nomination. Eisenhower was in Warren's political debt and it didn't take long after his election for President Eisenhower to repay his colleague.

On September 8, 1953 U.S. Supreme Court Chief Justice Fred Vinson died in office. President Eisenhower considered a successor to Vinson, first offering the position to **John Foster Dulles**, but **Dulles** preferred to remain in his post as Secretary of State. Eisenhower then offered the position to New York Governor Thomas Dewey, but Dewey also declined, citing his desire to retire from public life. Only then did the President offer the position to Earl Warren. Warren was sworn in as the fourteenth Chief Justice on October 5, 1953.

Earl Warren's service on the United States Supreme Court continued for nearly sixteen years, during which time the Court undertook numerous landmark cases dealing with racial equality, discrimination, voting rights, housing, prisoners' rights, defendants' rights and reapportionment. Chief Justice Warren delivered many of those decisions, often disappointing conservatives who had expected a far less progressive attitude from the Chief Justice. Not the least vocal among his critics was the man who appointed him, Dwight Eisenhower. Asked about his nomination of Warren after he left the White House, Eisenhower characterized it as "the biggest damn fool mistake I ever made."

It was during Warren's tenure as Chief Justice that President **John F. Kennedy** was assassinated in Dallas in 1963. President Lyndon Johnson, shortly after he was sworn in to succeed the slain President, appointed Earl Warren to chair a special commission to investigate the **Kennedy** assassination. The Warren Commission, as it came to be called, found that Lee Harvey Oswald had acted as a lone assassin when he shot President **Kennedy** and that Jack Ruby had also acted alone when he killed Oswald. That commission came under strong criticism for not probing more deeply into the possibility of a conspiracy.

In June 1968 Chief Justice Warren decided to retire. However he did not leave office immediately because a Senate filibuster prevented a vote on President Johnson's nominee to succeed him, Associate Justice Abe Fortas. When that nomination was finally withdrawn, Warren agreed to stay on the bench until the end of the summer term of 1969. His successor, Warren Burger, was sworn in on June 23, 1969.

Earl Warren died on July 9, 1974, ending a distinguished public service career. He was buried with military honors at Arlington National Cemetery.

JOHN WINGATE WEEKS

Senator, Secretary of War

(April 11, 1860–July 12, 1926)
Sec. 5, Lot 7064, Grid W–35/36

Near the tomb of John F. Kennedy is a large granite monument that marks the grave of one of the most influential men of the early twentieth century, John Wingate Weeks.

Born in Lancaster, New Hampshire, Weeks graduated from the United States Naval Academy in Annapolis in 1881. Following his military service, Weeks moved to Boston and joined his family's prestigious banking and brokerage firm, Horn-blower and Weeks. He was elected to Congress in 1904 and re-mained in the House as one of Massachusetts' representatives until 1913 when he was elected to the U.S. Senate.

Weeks sought the Republican nomination for President at the Chicago convention in 1916, but was defeated by Charles Evans Hughes who ultimately lost the general election to Woodrow Wilson. John Wingate Weeks served as Secretary of War in the administrations of Warren G. Harding and Calvin Coolidge. He died at the age of sixty-six in Washington, D.C.

GEORGE WESTINGHOUSE

Inventor, Manufacturer

(October 6, 1846–March 12,1914)
Sec. 2, Grave 3418, Grid U–29/30

George Westinghouse was born in Central Bridge, New York, and by the time he died sixty-eight years later he had patented literally hundreds of inventions, organized over fifty companies, and was president of thirty corporations, including Westinghouse Electric.

Young George developed his great interest in machines while working in his father's shop as a boy. His insatiable curiosity and his powerful creative drive resulted in his development of a rotary engine when he was only fifteen years old. At age sixteen he join-ed thousands of other boys who enlisted in the Army at the out-break of the Civil War to save the Union. During that war, he served in both the Army and Navy. Within a year of the war's end, Westinghouse was again busy inventing.

Many of his inventions were directed toward the burgeoning railroad industry. By 1866 he had already perfected two impor-tant devices for the railroads. The first was a device to replace derailed railroad cars. Still a relatively young industry, railroads suffered regularly from train derailments which would block tracks for days. The second invention, known as a "railroad frog," helped modernize the rail industry. The "frog" allowed trains to switch from one track to another, enabling trains to pass each other.

Perhaps his most important railroad invention was his perfection of the air brake. Not only did this provide for a more efficient way to stop trains, but it improved the safety of them as well. His air brake proved so successful that he organized a company to manufacture it. Following the enactment by the U.S. Congress of the Railroad Safety Appliance Act of 1893, Westinghouse standardized the air brake, allowing equipment from different lines to work together.

Among other significant Westinghouse inventions was a system to safely pipe natural gas into homes and the gas meter which allows the utility company to record a household's natural gas consumption. Finally, among his other hundreds of inventions was his introduction of alternating current (AC) for electric power transmission. It was this interest in electricity that lead him to develop one of the nation's largest corporations, Westinghouse Electric Company. He lost control of the corporation during a financial panic in 1907, and within four years, he severed all ties with the company.

George Westinghouse's health failed soon after his divestiture in Westinghouse Electric. He died in New York City on March 12, 1914 and was buried a few days later in Arlington National Cemetery.

EARLE GILMORE WHEELER

Chairman, Joint Chiefs of Staff

(January 13, 1908–December 18, 1975)
Sec. 30, Lot 434–1, Grid AA–39

Earle Wheeler's last assignment was his toughest: he was named Chairman of the Joint Chiefs of Staff during the Vietnam

War. However, he was not troubled by the public skepticism with America's involvement in that war, a skepticism that troubled so many other officers at that time. But if Wheeler did not fully appreciate the depth of the nation's disillusionment during his tenure in Vietnam, he was forced to personally confront it three years after his retirement when he was questioned by a Congressional committee about his involvement in secret bombing raids into Cambodia.

Earle Gilmore Wheeler was born in Washington, D.C. in 1908, the son of a dentist. He attended the United States Military Academy at West Point, New York, graduating in 1932. Commissioned into the Infantry, his first assignment was at Fort Benning, Georgia where he graduated from the Infantry School in 1937.

Wheeler spent a year in Tientsin, China, returning to America in 1938. He became an instructor at West Point in 1940, ultimately completed the course of study at the General Staff and Command School, and attained the rank of Colonel in November 1943. In 1944 in the midst of World War II, Wheeler was sent to Europe as Chief of Staff of the Sixty-third Infantry Division which landed at Marseilles, France and joined the Seventh Army under General Alexander Patch. After the war Wheeler remained in Europe, spending two years with the U.S. Constabulary in occupied Germany.

After completing the course of study at the National War College in Washington, D.C., Wheeler returned to southern Europe where he was assigned to NATO forces. In 1952 he was promoted to Brigadier General and remained with NATO until 1955 when he was recalled to work with the General Staff at the Pentagon in Washington.

In April 1960 Wheeler gained promotion to Brigadier General and was named director of the staff of the Joint Chiefs of Staff. In March 1962 he was promoted to full General and again returned to Europe as deputy commander of all U.S. military forces under General Lauris Norstad. President **John F. Kennedy** named Wheeler Chief of Staff of the Army in 1962, and in 1964 Wheeler succeeded General **Maxwell Taylor** as Chairman of the Joint Chiefs, holding that post throughout the escalation of American involvement in Vietnam. He retired in 1970.

In 1973, after three years of retirement, Wheeler was called to testify on Capitol Hill at the confirmation hearing for General **George Brown** to become Chairman of the Joint Chiefs. At that time he disclosed that in 1969 he personally had been ordered by President Richard Nixon to order General **Brown** to conduct secret bombing raids into Cambodia. When questioned more closely about the propriety of keeping those secret raids from the American public, Wheeler justified his actions by stating that no one with a "need to know" was deceived.

After his retirement Wheeler lived in West Virginia. On December 18, 1975, having suffered a heart attack, he was en route by ambulance from his home in West Virginia to Washington, D.C. when his condition worsened. His ambulance was forced to stop at a hospital in Frederick, Maryland. Wheeler died there at the age of sixty-seven. He now rests in Arlington near the graves of other American Generals, including **Omar Bradley** and **Nathan Twining**.

JOSEPH WHEELER

Confederate General, Congressman, U.S. Army General

(September 10, 1836–January 25, 1906)
Sec. 2, Lot 1089, Grid ST–32/33

Although a well-known General in the Confederate Army, Joseph Wheeler came to symbolize the move by former Confederate soldiers to reunite the nation after the Civil War. He served eight terms in the United States Congress representing the state of Alabama and becoming chairman of the powerful Ways and Means Committee.

The grandson of General William Hall of Revolutionary War fame, Joseph Wheeler was born and raised in Augusta, Georgia. He graduated from the U.S. Military Academy in 1859 then attended the Cavalry School at Carlisle Barracks, Pennsylvania. By 1860 he was promoted to Lieutenant and assigned to the Regiment of Mounted Riflemen at Fort Craig in the New Mexico Territory. Immediately after Georgia voted to secede from the Union in 1861, Wheeler resigned his commission and accepted a position in the forces of his native state.

Only twenty-four years old, standing 5'5" tall and weighing just 125 pounds, Wheeler was promoted to Colonel and named commander of the Nineteenth Alabama Infantry under General Braxton Bragg. In February 1862 Wheeler's units were part of the Confederate forces concentrated near Corinth, Mississippi. He led his men into combat at Shiloh and was widely praised for successfully covering the Confederate withdrawal. In July of the same year, the cavalry of the Army of the Mississippi was placed in Wheeler's charge. Following his successes at Perryville, he was promoted to Brigadier General and named to head the cavalry in the new Army of the Tennessee. Before the war's end, Wheeler had risen to the rank of Lt. General, had been wounded three times in battle, and had survived sixteen horses which had been shot out from under him.

In May 1865 — soon after Lee's surrender at Appomattox Courthouse but before all hostilities had ceased — Wheeler was captured by Union soldiers as he attempted to prevent the capture of Jefferson Davis, President of the Confederacy. For his actions, Wheeler spent two months in a federal prison before being paroled.

After the war Wheeler worked for a time in the hardware business in New Orleans, but spent his spare time studying law, eventually being admitted to the Louisiana state bar. He moved to Alabama where, persuaded to run for the United States House of Representatives in 1883, he won a seat in the Forty-seventh Congress. During his eight terms in Congress, among his other legislative accomplishments, Wheeler served on the Military Affairs Committee with his former military nemesis, Union General **William Starke Rosecrans**. He came to represent many of the viewpoints of postwar Southerners: favoring a paternal attitude towards blacks but opposing civil rights, encouraging whites to forget the divisions brought about by the war, and concentrating on the industrialization of the South.

Many of the sectional wounds produced by the Civil War still existed, however, when war with Spain was declared on April 25, 1898. Recognizing the opportunity to again demonstrate his desire for reconciliation between North and South, Wheeler, then sixty-one years old, resigned his seat in Congress and volunteered for military service. Sharing his hope for unity, President William McKinley commissioned Wheeler a Major General in the U.S. Army and gave him command of volunteer forces in the invasion of Cuba. Showing daring and independence, Wheeler's forces launched a successful attack against the Spanish at Las Guasimas that cleared the way for an American advance on Santiago. Only illness kept Wheeler from taking part in the renowned march up San Juan Hill.

After the Spanish-American War, Wheeler was unable to regain his seat in Congress but was promoted to Brigadier General and assigned to the Philippines. He later was recalled to serve in the United States, retiring from the Army in September 1900. Joseph Wheeler died in New York City in 1906. Apparently determined to carry on his crusade for reconciliation between North and South even posthumously, General Wheeler chose not to be buried among the Confederate soldiers at Arlington; rather his grave is near such famous Union soldiers as **Philip Henry Sheridan**, **John Lincoln Clem**, **John McAllister Schofield**, and **George Crook**. Also of note is that Joseph Wheeler represents the State of Alabama in the Capitol's Statuary Hall.

CHARLES WILKES

Explorer, Civil War Naval Commander

(April 3, 1798–February 8, 1877)
Sec. 2, Lot 1164, Grid TU–32

Having achieved great fame for leading an expedition resulting in the discovery that Antarctica is a separate continent, Charles Wilkes nearly single-handedly brought Great Britain into the United States Civil War against the Union by provoking the *Trent* affair.

Born in New York City, Charles Wilkes graduated from the

United States Naval Academy in 1822. Sixteen years later, in 1838, he was placed in charge of the first scientific expedition ever outfitted by the United States government. Only a Lieutenant, Wilkes commanded a five-year voyage which surveyed 280 islands in the southern seas, 800 miles of Pacific Northwest coastline, and 1,500 miles of unexplored Antarctic coastline. Finally, on January 30, 1840, his expedition determined that Antarctica was a separate continent and not just a massive ice field.

It was during the Civil War that Wilkes caused a serious international incident. In November of 1861 the *Trent* affair nearly allied the South and Great Britain, which could have destroyed the Union. Wilkes had been granted the command of the *San Jacinto* whose mission was to assist in the Union blockade of Southern ports. Two agents of the Confederacy, James Mason and John Slidell, attempted to avoid the Union blockade by boarding a British vessel, the *Trent*, in Havana Harbor. Mason and Slidell were on their way to Great Britain where they hoped to persuade the British government to support the Southern cause. Wilkes uncovered the purpose of the voyage and, without orders, stopped the *Trent*, took the Confederates prisoner, and transported them to Boston. As a neutral nation, Britain was entitled to the unencumbered use of the high seas. Yet Wilkes' actions clearly violated that principle. In response Britain mobilized 8,000 troops into Canada, demanded an apology from the United States and also demanded the immediate release of Mason and Slidell. President Lincoln, who realized Wilkes' serious error, released the prisoners and made a formal apology to Britain. Following their release, Mason and Slidell continued their mission to Europe, but in spite of the actions of Charles Wilkes, that mission failed.

In 1862 Commodore Wilkes was placed in command of a squadron sent to the West Indies to protect United States commerce in the region. However, Wilkes' actions spurred protests from several foreign powers alleging neutrality violations. In 1864 he was court-martialled for insubordination and suspended from duty. However, on July 25, 1866 Wilkes received the commission of Rear Admiral, Retired. He died in 1877 in Washington, D.C. and was buried with full military honors at Arlington National Cemetery.

LEONARD WOOD

Rough Rider, Colonial Governor, Presidential Candidate

(October 9, 1860–August 7, 1927)
Sec. 21, Lot S–10, Grid N–20

Planning to follow in his father's footsteps, Leonard Wood left his Winchester, New Hampshire home to enter Harvard Medical School in 1880. Following his graduation in 1883, Wood began his private practice only to find it too mundane a lifestyle to fit his ambitions. On a whim he accepted a commission as a medical officer in the U.S. Army in 1885, hoping to fulfill his desire for more adventure. He was not disappointed. His military career not only took him around the world, but also elevated him to the highest post in the United States Army and fueled his run for the presidency.

Leonard Wood's first assignment was to the Arizona Territory where he served under General **George Crook** and assisted in the capture of Apache Chief Geronimo in 1886. He was awarded the Congressional Medal of Honor for his role in that historic action though some controversy erupted over whether he played a major enough role to warrant his award.

In 1895 Wood became White House physician to President Grover Cleveland and later held the same post under President William McKinley. It was while he was serving in Washington that Wood developed a close friendship with the young Assistant Secretary of the Navy, Theodore Roosevelt, a friendship that would serve Wood well when the war with Spain broke out in 1898. At that time, through Roosevelt's help, Wood was given command of the First Volunteer Cavalry, better known as the Rough Riders. Contrary to widespread popular belief, Roosevelt never commanded the Rough Riders, although he was with them when they fought up San Juan Hill near Santiago de Cuba.

Following the armistice with Spain, Wood was named Governor of Cuba and began a career as a colonial administrator. As

Governor from 1899 to 1902, he prepared the island for independence, building roads and schools and assisting Dr. **Walter Reed** in stamping out yellow fever by clearing vast swamps and marshes. On May 20, 1902 Wood relinquished his authority as the Military Governor to the popularly elected civilian President, Tomas Estrada Palma.

By the time Wood relinquished his role as Cuban governor, he had become a Brigadier General and his friend Teddy Roosevelt was President. In 1904 Roosevelt appointed Wood Governor of the Moro Province in the Philippine Islands. There, Wood quelled the combative Moros, gained promotion to Major General, and was named Commander of the Philippine Division. In 1910 President **William Howard Taft**, who himself had served as Philippine Governor in 1904, named Wood as Army Chief of Staff, thereby completing Wood's meteoric rise in rank. In less than a decade Wood had advanced from a Captain in the Medical Staff to the highest post in the Armed Forces.

Wood resigned as Chief of Staff in 1914. When World War I erupted in Europe during that same year, Wood became a vocal advocate for peacetime preparedness, often differing publicly with President Woodrow Wilson over the conduct of the war. Then in 1920 Leonard Wood sought the Republican nomination for President. Facing Warren G. Harding, Wood entered the nominating convention as the leading candidate. After ten ballots, however, Harding was named the winner. Wood, offered the presidency of the University of Pennsylvania in 1921, turned it down in hopes of an appointment as Secretary of War in President Harding's Cabinet. That appointment never came. Instead, Wood reluctantly accepted the position as colonial governor of the Philippines.

In 1927, at the age of sixty-seven, Wood returned from Manila to New York to seek surgical treatment of a tumor which had resulted from an earlier head injury. Sadly, he died on the operating table. Leonard Wood is buried near the monument to the Rough Riders and near the gravesites of many of the soldiers with whom he fought side-by-side in the Spanish-American War. Also, an army base in southern Missouri bears his name in tribute to his distinguished service to our country.

HORATIO GOUVENEUR WRIGHT

Chief of Army Engineers

(March 6, 1820–July 2, 1899)
Sec. 45, Lot S–4, Grid ST–34/35

The grave of Horatio Wright is prominently situated on the lawn in front of Arlington House overlooking the grave of **John F. Kennedy**. It is marked with a tall obelisk and commands a panoramic view of Washington's skyline which is punctuated by a more famous obelisk—the Washington Monument—the completion of which Wright supervised as Army Chief of Engineers in 1884. At that time the Washington Monument was the tallest structure in the world.

Born in Clinton, Connecticut Wright attended the United States Military Academy at West Point, graduating in 1841. He remained as an instructor at the academy for one year, then began a ten-year assignment in the Florida Keys where he undertook numerous engineering projects. At the outbreak of the Civil War Wright was stationed at the Norfolk (Virginia) Navy Yard. When it became clear that Confederate troops would overrun the base, he was ordered to destroy the dry dock on April 20, 1861. But during Wright's daring raid on the dry dock, he was captured by the advancing Southern troops and held as a prisoner. He was released within a short period and was then ordered by the Army to go to Washington D.C. to assist in fortifying the city. By August 1861 he was promoted to Major, and in November of that same year distinguished himself as commander of the landing force which occupied Fort Walker near Hilton Head, South Carolina.

Wright returned to Washington later in the year, helping to repulse the attack by Jubal Early's forces in July of 1864. Then in October 1864, it was Horatio Wright who was in command of Union forces at Cedar Creek when General Early's Confederate troops attacked. The ensuing battle forced Union soldiers into retreat. General **Philip Sheridan's** recoupment of his scattered troops became the subject of T. Buchanan Read's famous poem "Sheridan's Ride."

After the war Wright was named Military Commander of Texas until 1866, when he turned his attention to civil engineering. Included among his many engineering feats are the East River Bridge in New York City and the Sutro Tunnel in Nevada. Yet, his best known undertaking remains the completion of the Washington Monument. Its construction had stopped in-progress because of the Civil War and a lack of funding. Under Wright's direction, construction was resumed in 1880 and was completed in 1884, the very year he retired from the Army with the rank of Brigadier General.

The obelisk marking Horatio Wright's grave was erected as a memorial to him by the survivors of the Sixth Army Corps, Army of the Potomac, which he commanded from the Battle of Spotsylvania in May 1864 until the end of the Civil War.

OTHER NOTABLE PERSONS
BURIED AT ARLINGTON

Bernt Balchen (1899-1973) Aviator Who Flew with Byrd, Sec. 2, Lot 4969-2 (WX 32/33)

Thomas Scott Baldwin (1856-1923) Pioneer Balloonist, Sec. 1, Lot 1284 (LM-33)

Alan B. Banister (1905-1963) WWII Submarine Commander, Sec. 34, Lot 158-11 (VW-12/13)

Floyd Bennett (1890-1928) Arctic Explorer Who Accompanied Peary, Sec. 3, Lot 1852-B (S-16/17)

Anthony Drexel Biddle (1897-1961) Ambassador to Poland and Spain, Sec. 30, Lot 1172 (S-37)

Hiram Bingham (1875-1956) US Senator and Governor of Connecticut, Sec. 1, Lot 357 (LM-35/36)

D.L. Brainard (1856-1946) Member, Greely Arctic Expedition (1881), Sec. 2, Lot 955 (RS-31/32)

Omar Bundy (1861-1940) Decorated WWI General, Sec. 3, Lot 2521 (PQ-15/16)

Bennett Champ Clark (1890-1954) US Senator from Missouri, Sec. 2, Lot 3435 (UV-29/30)

J. Lawton Collins (1896-1987) WWII General, Ambassador to Vietnam, Sec. 30, Lot 422 (ZAA-38)

Dwight F. Davis (1879-1945) Sec'y of War, Founded Tennis' Davis Cup, Sec. 2, Lot 4962 (WX-32/33)

Edward P. Doherty (1840-1897) Captured John Wilkes Booth, Sec. 1, Lot 690 (J-33)

Robert Fechner (1876-1939) Dir., Civilian Conservation Corps, Sec. 22, Lot 15540 (L-22/23)

Walter Flowers (1933-1984) Congressman, Watergate Committee Member, Sec. 7A, Lot 182 (TU-23)

Ruth M. Gardiner (1914-1943) First Army Nurse Killed in WWII, Sec. 21, Lot 197 (M-19/20)

Francis M. Gibson (1847-1919) Commander of Custer Relief Party, Sec. 1, Lot A-107 (J-32/33)

George Graham (1757-1830) Secretary of War under Madison and Monroe, Sec. 3, Lot 1989 (RS-14/15)

Robert Guggenheim (1885-1959) Ambassador to Portugal, Sec. 2, Lot 4732-2 (V-33)

Marguerite Higgins (Hall) (1920-1961) Prize-Winning War Correspondent, Sec. 2, Lot 4705 (UV-32/33)

John Hinkel (1906-1986) Arlington Cemetery Historian and Author, Sec. 7A, Lot 153 (U-24)

Donald Holleder (1934-1967) West Point All-American Football Player, Sec. 1, Lot 168 (N-33/34)

John B. Hutson (1890-1964) Ass't Sec'y General of the United Nations, Sec. 15, Lot 33A (J-25)

Edward Jones (1757-1829) Treasury Official under George Washington, Sec. 1, Lot 298 (NO-33/34)

Louis Vaughn Jones (1895-1965) Concert Violinist, Howard Univ. Professor, Sec. 43, Lot 511 (W-44)

Kenneth Keating (1900-1975) US Senator from NY, Ambassador to Israel, Sec.5, Lot 141 (W-36/37)

Otto Kerner (1908-1976) Governor of Illinois, US Court of Appeals Judge, Sec. 3, Lot 2547 (P-16/17)

Harley Kilgore (1893-1956) US Senator from West Virginia, Sec. 30, Lot 536 (Y-38)

Iven C. Kincheloe (1928-1958) Korean War Air Force Ace Pilot, Sec. 2, Lot 4872-1 (V-32/33)

Jeff King (1860-1964) Army Cavalry Scout, Oldest Person at Arlington, Sec. 35, Lot 1566 (OP-20/21)

Peter Lisagor (1915-1976) Newspaper Columnist, Sec. 2, Lot 4968-B (W-32/33)

Allard Lowenstein (1929-1980) Assassinated Congressman, Sec. 30, Lot 2005-1 (TU-35/36)

Lee Marvin (1924-1987) Actor, Purple Heart Recipient, Sec. 7A, Lot 176 (U-24)

Paul V. McNutt (1891-1964), Governor of IN, Ambassador to Philippines, Sec. 2, Lot 4969-B (W-33)

William Miller (1914-1983) NY Congressman, 1964 Vice-Presidential Candidate, Sec. 5, Lot 93 (W-36)

Michael Musmanno (1897-1968) Nuremberg Judge; PA Chief Justice, Sec. 2, Lot 4735-E (UV-33/34)

Alured Bayard (A.B.) Nettleton (1838-1911) Secretary of Treasury, Sec. 1, Lot 127-B (O-32/33)

William O'Dwyer (1890-1964) Mayor of New York, Ambassador to Mexico, Sec. 2, Lot 889 (R-31/32)

Robert Patterson (1891-1952) Secretary of War during WWII, Sec. 30, Lot 612 (X-39/40)

Lemuel Penn (1915-1964) Prominent Educator, Sec. 3, Lot 1377 (LM-19)

Spotswood Poles (1887-1962) Negro League All-Star Baseball Player, Sec. 42, Lot 2324 (U-46)

John A. Rawlins (1831-1869), Sec. of War under Andrew Johnson, Sec. 2, Lot 1007 (S-32/33)

Henry M. Robert (1837-1923) Created "Robert's Rules of Order", Sec. 3, Lot 3945 (V-16)

Daniel Sickles (1825-1914) Flamboyant Congressman Acquitted of Murder, Sec. 3, Lot 1906 (ST-16)

William H. Standley (1872-1963) Ambassador to the USSR during WWII, Sec. 2, Lot 1188-2 (T-31)

Maxwell Taylor (1901-1987) Chairman Joint Chiefs, Ambassador to S. Vietnam, Sec. 7A, Lot 20 (U-24)

Keith Ware (1915-1968) Vietnam War Medal of Honor Winner, Sec. 30, Lot 258-3 (YZ-40)

Orde Wingate (1903-1944) British Army WWII General, Zionist Commando, Sec. 12, Lot 288 (XY24/25)

Some of the information on this page was discovered in the outstanding history of Arlington National Cemetery written by Col. **John V. Hinkel** entitled **Arlington: Monument to Heroes**, Prentice-Hall, 1970.

ARLINGTON'S MAJOR MONUMENTS AND MEMORIALS

Since its founding in 1864 Arlington National Cemetery has evolved from a paupers' cemetery — hastily established to satisfy the overwhelming demand for burial space during the Civil War — into our country's most important national shrine. The placement at Arlington of many of America's most cherished memorials has contributed to the cemetery's honored status. Described below are thirty-five of the major monuments that can be seen in Arlington. Each has been dedicated to the memory of a particular cause or event in American history or to a special group of individuals.

ARGONNE CROSS

Sec. 18, Grid K–12/13

The Argonne Forest region in northeast France near the Belgian border was the scene of some of the fiercest fighting during the last days of World War I. The American Expeditionary Force lost thousands of its men and women in the Argonne region. Many of the American casualties were not returned home but instead were buried in France. Following the war, the remains of many of those Americans were disinterred and were reburied either in military cemeteries in Europe or were returned to the United States. Over two thousand of the men who gave their lives in France for the defense of freedom are now buried in Arlington National

Cemetery, primarily in Section 18. In a corner of that large section with its many rows of simple white headstones rises the simple white rood known as the Argonne Cross.

A grove of nineteen pine trees forms an emerald grotto which surrounds the thirteen-foot marble cross. These trees represent the trees of the Argonne Forest where so many lost their lives.

On November 17, 1921 Secretary of War **John Wingate Weeks** approved the idea of a memorial to all those who died in France, regardless of where they are presently buried. Through the efforts of the Argonne Unit American Women's Legion, that stately cross now stands with an eagle and wreath engraved on its face.

Planted nearby is a memorial tree dedicated on April 28, 1985 by the Prelacy of the Armenian Apostolic Church on behalf of Armenian survivors of World War I.

CANADIAN CROSS (CROSS OF SACRIFICE)

Sec. 46, Grid O–24/25

Few countries enjoy the bonds of goodwill and friendship that the United States and Canada share. Our common border remains the longest unguarded frontier on earth, and our nations have shared triumphs and tragedies throughout history. It was in this spirit that, in 1925, Canadian Prime Minister MacKenzie King first proposed a memorial to the large number of United States citizens who enlisted in the Canadian Armed Forces and lost their lives during World War I. Because the Canadians entered the war long before the United States, many Americans enlisted in Canada to join the fighting in Europe.

On June 12, 1925 President Calvin Coolidge approved the request, and on Armistice Day 1927 the monument near the Memorial Amphitheatre was dedicated. Designed by Canadian architect Sir Reginald Bloomfield, the monument consists of a bronze sword adorning a twenty-four-foot gray granite cross.

The inscription on the cross reaffirms the sentiment expressed by Prime Minister King regarding Americans who served in the Canadian Armed Forces. Following World War II and the Korean War, similar inscriptions on other faces of the monument were dedicated to the Americans who served in those conflicts.

CHAPLAINS' HILL

Sec. 2, Grid X–28

Tall oak trees rise majestically above the area of Arlington known as Chaplains' Hill, so named because chaplains from five wars rest here. These chaplains, representing many different faiths, brought spiritual – and often physical – aid and comfort to American servicemen stationed throughout the world.

The keystone to this special area of Arlington is the Chaplains' Monument, dedicated to the twenty-three chaplains who lost their lives in World War I. Although it stands only five-and-a-half feet tall, its purpose is immeasurable for it recognizes the invaluable services rendered by men of faith in all wars. Erected by chaplains who served in the Great War, it was dedicated on May 5, 1926.

Among the men who went into battle unarmed and who are now buried on this grassy hill are Colonel **John T. Axton**, the Army's first Chief of Chaplains; and World War II's Chief of Chaplains, **William A. Arnold**, the first chaplain to attain General's rank. He later served as a Catholic Auxiliary Bishop of New York.

Representative of the chaplains who served during the Vietnam War is Major **Charles Joseph Watters** (Sec. 2E, Lot 186-A, Grid VW-29/30) who was posthumously awarded the Congressional Medal of Honor for his actions on November 19, 1967. With complete disregard for his own safety during an assault on Hill 875 near Dak To, Chaplain Watters, unarmed, was rendering aid to his fallen comrades when he was killed by a nearby bomb explosion.

Inscribed on the face of the Chaplains' Monument is the quote from the Bible (John 15:13): "Greater love hath no man than this, that a man lay down his life for his friends."

CONFEDERATE MONUMENT

Sec. 16, Grid I-23

The history of Arlington National Cemetery is steeped in the Civil War, for it was this great national struggle that necessitated the establishment of this cemetery to bury its many dead. For many years following the war, the bitter feelings between North and South remained, and although hundreds of Confederate soldiers were buried at Arlington, it was considered a Union cemetery. Family members of Confederate soldiers were denied permission to decorate their loved ones' graves and in extreme cases were even denied entrance to the cemetery.

These ill feelings were slow to die but over time they did begin to fade. Many historians believe it was the national call to arms during the Spanish-American War that brought Northerners and Southerners together at last. In that war numerous Confederate veterans volunteered their services and joined their Northern brothers on the battlefield in the common defense of our nation. In

The solemn figure of a woman representing the South extends a laurel wreath toward her fallen sons. The peaked headstones which mark the graves of Confederate soldiers surround the Confederate Monument in Jackson Circle.

June of 1900, in this spirit of national reconciliation, the United States Congress authorized that a section of Arlington National Cemetery be set aside for the burial of Confederate dead. By the end of 1901 all the Confederate soldiers buried in the national cemeteries at Alexandria, Virginia and at the Soldiers' Home in Washington were brought together with the soldiers buried at Arlington and reinterred in the Confederate section. Among the 482 persons buried there are 46 officers, 351 enlisted men, 58 wives, 15 Southern civilians, and 12 unknowns. They are buried in concentric circles around the Confederate Monument, and their graves are marked with headstones that are distinct for their pointed tops. Legend attributes these pointed-top tombstones to a Confederate belief that the points would "keep Yankees from sitting on them."

To further honor these citizens of the South, the United Daughters of the Confederacy petitioned to erect a major monument to the Confederate dead. On March 4, 1906 Secretary of War **William Howard Taft** granted their request. The cornerstone was laid on November 12, 1912 at a ceremony featuring speakers **William Jennings Bryan** and **James A. Tanner**, a former Union corporal who lost both legs at the second Battle of Bull Run. He was commander in chief of the Union veterans group, The Grand Army of the Republic. That same evening, **President William Howard Taft** addressed the United Daughters of the Confederacy at a reception held in the Daughters of the American Revolution's Centennial Hall.

Chosen to design the memorial was the world-renowned sculptor, **Moses Ezekiel**. **Ezekiel** brought more than just his artistic talents to this project for he was also a Confederate veteran who knew firsthand the horrors of the Civil War. He is now buried at the base of the famous monument which he created.

The Confederate Monument was unveiled before a large crowd of Northerners and Southerners on June 4, 1914, the 106th anniversary of the birthday of the President of the Confederacy, Jefferson Davis. President Woodrow Wilson delivered an address and veterans of both the Union and Confederacy placed wreaths on the graves of their former foes, symbolizing the reconciliation between the North and the South that is this memorial's central theme.

Former Confederate and Union officers join President Woodrow Wilson (at left) at the dedication ceremonies for the Confederate Monument in 1914.

Ezekiel created a monument rich in symbols. Standing atop the thirty-two-foot monument is a larger-than-life figure of a woman representing the South. Her head is crowned with olive leaves, her left hand extends a laurel wreath toward the South, acknowledging the sacrifice of her fallen sons. Her right hand holds a pruning hook resting on a plow stock. These symbols bring to life the biblical passage inscribed at her feet: "And they shall beat their swords into plow shares and their spears into pruning hooks."

The plinth on which she stands is embossed with four cinerary urns symbolizing the four years of the Civil War. Supporting the plinth is a frieze of fourteen inclined shields, each shield depicts the coat of arms of one of the thirteen Confederate states and Maryland, which did not join the Confederacy, but supported the South in the war.

Below the plinth is another frieze of life-sized figures depicting mythical gods and Southern soldiers. At the front of the monument, the panoplied figure of Minerva, Goddess of War and Wisdom, attempts to hold up the figure of a fallen woman ("The South") who is resting upon her shield, "The Constitution." Behind "The South," the Spirits of War are trumpeting in every direction calling the sons and daughters of the South to aid their falling mother. On either side of the fallen woman are figures depicting those sons and daughters who came to her aid and who represent each branch of the Confederate service: Soldier, Sailor, Sapper, and Miner.

Completing the frieze are six vignettes illustrating the effect of the war on Southerners of all races. The vignettes include a faithful black slave following his young master; an officer kissing his infant child in the arms of her mammy; a blacksmith leaving his bellows and workshop as his sorrowful wife looks on; a robed clergyman bidding farewell to his wife and young son; a young lady binding the sword and sash on her beau; and a young officer standing alone.

The base of the memorial features several inscriptions. On its front face are the seal of the Confederacy and a tribute by the United Daughters of the Confederacy, followed by the Latin phrase: *"Victrix Causa Diis Placuit Sed Victa Caton."* Translated this phrase means: "The Victorious Cause was Pleasing to the Gods, But the Lost Cause to Cato." On the rear of the monument is an inscription attributed to the Reverend Randolph Harrison McKim, who was a Confederate chaplain and who served as Pastor of the Epiphany Church in Washington for thirty-two years. It reads:

> Not for fame or reward
> Not for place or for rank
> Not lured by ambition
> Or goaded by necessity
> But in simple
> Obedience to duty
> As they understood it
> These men suffered all
> Sacrificed all
> Dared all-and died

In addition to **Moses Ezekiel**, three other Confederate soldiers are buried at the base of the monument. They are Lt. **Harry C. Marmaduke** who served in the Confederate Navy, Captain **John M. Hickey** of the Second Missouri Infantry and Brigadier General **Marcus J. Wright** who commanded brigades at Shiloh and Chickamauga.

THE HIKER

United Spanish War Veterans Memorial
Memorial Drive, Grid LL–40

Approaching Arlington National Cemetery along Memorial Drive, the first monument on the left is the United Spanish War Veterans Memorial, known as the Hiker. The solitary figure is an American veteran dressed in the uniform worn by the Army during the Spanish-American War. Displayed on its front face are the dates of that conflict, 1898–1902. Mounted on the base of the memorial is a bronze cross bearing the names of the four theatres of service for the war: Cuba, Puerto Rico, the United States, and the Philippine Islands. This memorial was erected by the United Spanish War Veterans, and was dedicated at a special ceremony on July 24, 1965.

LIVING MEMORIALS

Tree Dedications at Arlington

For many years trees have been planted on the grounds of Arlington National Cemetery as living memorials to a special group of people or an event.

508th PARACHUTE INFANTRY REGIMENT

Three blue spruce trees were planted on the south lawn of the Memorial Amphitheatre on October 20, 1982 to honor the memory of all members of the 508th who served in the European Theatre of Operations during World War II.

MEMORIAL TO THE SERVICEMEN KILLED IN BEIRUT, 1983

See separate listing below.

MIA/POW MEMORIAL

On October 9, 1983 the group known as No Greater Love planted a tree on the north side of the Memorial Amphitheatre in honor of persons who have fought in any war and who are listed as "Missing In Action" or as a "Prisoner of War."

MOTHERS' TREE

The American Legion Auxiliary planted a tree on a site north of the Memorial Amphitheatre on May 8, 1932 to pay tribute to all mothers who had suffered the loss of a child during active military service.

PEARL HARBOR SURVIVORS MEMORIAL

On December 7, 1984, the forty-third anniversary of the Japanese attack on Pearl Harbor, the Pearl Harbor Survivors Association planted a tree on the north side of the Memorial Amphitheatre in memory of all persons who survived that attack but who have since died.

POLISH LEGION OF AMERICAN VETERANS AND AUXILIARY

See **Ignace Jan Paderewski**

PRELACY OF THE ARMENIAN APOSTOLIC CHURCH MEMORIAL

See Argonne Cross

PURPLE HEART MEMORIAL

The Purple Heart was the first military decoration established by General George Washington during the Revolutionary War. Revised by President Herbert Hoover in 1932, its award was made retroactive to service during World War I. On May 30, 1984 The Military Order of the Purple Heart, a congressionally chartered organization, planted a tree and placed a plaque on the south side of the Memorial Amphitheatre, declaring the area an Historic Site of the Order.

SECOND SCHWEINFURT MEMORIAL

A maple tree and a plaque have been placed on the south side of the Memorial Amphitheatre by the Second Schweinfurt Memorial Association and have been dedicated to the memory of the airmen of the U.S. Army Eighth Air Force who attacked and destroyed a ball bearing factory in Schweinfurt, Germany on October 14, 1943.

VIETNAM VETERANS MEMORIAL

On March 6, 1979 the Veterans of Foreign Wars Auxiliary planted a tree and placed a plaque in honor of all service personnel who served during the Vietnam War. The site is located just north of the Memorial Amphitheatre.

McCLELLAN ARCH

Grid CC–27/28

Following the establishment of Arlington National Cemetery in 1864, the grounds were enclosed. Several gates provided pedestrian and vehicular access. The main entrance to the cemetery was located where the McClellan Arch currently stands and was constructed as the cemetery's principal gate.

The arch was designed by Mr. Lot Flannery and was constructed during the 1870s as a tribute to the Civil War General, George B. McClellan, whose wartime headquarters were located at Arlington House. It was a tribute to General McClellan rather than a memorial since he did not die until October 29, 1885 and he is not buried at Arlington.

Made of Seneca sandstone, the structure towers more than thirty feet above the roadway. Atop the arch facing east, the word "McClellan" is inscribed in gold. Below that is the phrase:

> "On fame's eternal camping ground
> their silent tents are spread,
> And glory guards with solemn round,
> the bivouac of the dead."

The west face of the arch is inscribed with the words:

> "Rest on embalmed and sainted dead,
> dear as the blood ye gave,
> no impious footsteps here shall tread
> on the herbage of your grave."

MEMORIAL AMPHITHEATRE

Grid Q–23

By the turn of the twentieth century Arlington National Cemetery had won its place in the hearts of Americans as a special site for honoring the valiant men and women who have served our country. It was no longer considered just a pauper's cemetery, a graveyard for people who had nowhere else to go. By 1900 many of the great soldiers of the Civil War—generals and privates alike—chose Arlington as their final resting place. Veterans of the Spanish-American War, including 229 crewmen from the USS *Maine*, had been buried here. Since 1868 it had become a gathering place each Memorial Day for solemn ceremonies honoring the nation's dead. And in 1914, with the dedication of the Confederate Monument, Arlington had truly become a national cemetery.

The Old Amphitheatre near Arlington House had provided a rostrum for speakers for forty years, but it could no longer accommodate the size of the crowds that were coming to attend the larger memorial ceremonies at Arlington. Therefore, in 1908 a movement was launched by the Grand Army of the Republic (GAR) to construct a larger, permanent facility. With a membership still in excess of 300,000 surviving members, the GAR, a Civil War veterans group, approached Congress and expressed their sentiment that Arlington National Cemetery had become a national shrine for all time. Judge **Ivory G. Kimball** (Sec. 3, Lot 1538), a GAR officer, stated in a hearing before Congress, "Arlington is not for today; it is not for the Grand Army of the Republic alone; it is not for the Spanish War veterans alone, but during all time as long as this nation lasts Arlington will be unique and will be the burial place for our soldiers."

On May 30, 1908 a commission was authorized by an Act of Congress to oversee the planning and construction of the Arlington Memorial Amphitheatre. The necessary appropriations were not made, however, until five years later on March 4, 1913, and bids were finally let on February 11, 1915. Such great importance was attributed to this structure that President Woodrow Wilson laid the cornerstone on October 13, 1915, in the presence of thousands of spectators, including veterans from the Civil War and the Spanish-American War.

Even before its completion, the Amphitheatre became a place of assembly. Memorial Day services were held in the unfinished amphitheatre in 1919 almost a year before it was dedicated on May 15, 1920. A memorable day of festivities accompanied that dedication. Grand Marshall for the event was the eighty-year-old former General in Chief of the Army, **Nelson Appleton Miles**. President Woodrow Wilson, unable to attend the dedication because of his ill health, was represented by Secretary of War Newton D. Baker.

The Memorial Amphitheatre remains today much as it was on the day it was dedicated in 1920. Frederick D. Owens, of the New York architectural firm of Carrere and Hastings and chief architect of the structure, endeavored to "obtain a classic and serious character in order to express the dignity of the [amphitheatre's] purpose." Such classic structures as the Theatre of Dionysus at Athens and the Roman Theatre at Orange were studied with the desire to meld classic design with the colonial character of the other buildings in Washington, such as the White House and the U.S. Capitol.

Made of white marble from Danby, Vermont the central feature of the structure is the large amphitheatre formed by a 152-by-200-foot ellipse which seats approximately 5,000 people. Forty-two special seating boxes are provided around the inside Doric marble colonnade that encircles the Amphitheatre. There are entrances at the four principal axes, with the main entrance from the east leading onto a stage large enough to accommodate between 250 and 300 people.

Inscriptions of quotations from Presidents Washington and Lincoln, as well as the names of prominent military figures and battlesites, adorn both the interior and exterior walls of the Amphitheatre. On the apse is carved the quote from George Washington's statement to the Provincial Congress in New York on June 26, 1775: "When We Assumed The Soldier We Did Not Lay Aside The Citizen."

The arch above the stage bears the inscription from Abraham Lincoln's Gettysburg Address: "We Here Highly Resolve That

A rare aerial view of the Memorial Amphitheatre during its final stages of construction in 1919. Also shown is the USS *Maine* Memorial (above and to the right of the Amphitheatre) and the Confederate Monument in Jackson Circle (at upper right). The Spanish-American War Memorial is shown on the upper left side of the photograph.

These Dead Shall Not Have Died In Vain." On the two piers supporting the arch above the stage are inscribed the names of fourteen Army commanders and fourteen Navy commanders, all from the period prior to World War I when the Amphitheatre was built. The names of all the men are listed chronologically from the War of Independence through the Spanish-American War. Each of the piers is filled to capacity precluding the addition of any more recent names. The names of these twenty-eight military leaders, of whom three are buried at Arlington, were approved by the Arlington Memorial Commission. Around the exterior wall above the colonnade are inscribed the names of forty-four major battles from the War of Independence, the War of 1812, the Mexican War, the Civil War, and the Spanish-American War.

The Memorial Amphitheatre now serves a variety of important functions. Many memorial services are held here annually, particularly on Memorial Day and Veterans' Day. The Amphitheatre has been used for funeral services on nine separate occasions. Three of those occasions were to bury the Unknowns who now rest on the East plaza of the Amphitheatre. The other six services held in the Amphitheatre were for Sculptor **Moses Ezekiel** who created the Confederate Monument, March 30, 1921; Colonel **Charles Young** (Sec. 3, Lot 1730, Grid RS–16/17), June 1, 1923, the first black graduate of the U.S. Military Academy; **Ignace Jan Paderewski**, July 5, 1941, the Polish statesman; General of the Armies **John J. Pershing**, July 19, 1948; Secretary of Defense **James V. Forrestal**, May 25, 1949; and General **Henry "Hap" Arnold**, First Air Force Chief of Staff, January 18, 1950.

In the lower level of the Amphitheatre is a vaulted chapel which is used for various religious functions. Among the services held here was the funeral for five U.S. airmen shot down over Yugoslavia in September 1946 and a service for General **Jonathan Mayhew Wainwright**.

Forming part of the east entrance to the Amphitheatre is a large hall, presently used as a Memorial Display Room. On the first floor of this area are the decorations, commendations, plaques, and other memorabilia associated with the four Unknowns buried on the plaza directly east of the Memorial Amphitheatre. Included are the flags which have draped the caskets of each of those servicemen, the Medal of Honor which each has been awarded, and the numerous American and foreign awards presented on their behalf. Together with these many awards is a pictorial history of the Unknowns' interment ceremonies.

On the second floor of the pavilion is the Medal of Honor Room, designed and used solely to display and honor the names of all servicemen who have been awarded the Medal of Honor, the highest of military decorations. Also located in the Amphitheatre is a carillon presented on October 25, 1949 by AMVETS to the People of the United States in memory of those who died during World War II. The carillon was rededicated during a ceremony on April 2, 1978.

On March 15, 1969, in honor of the Fiftieth Anniversary of the American Legion, President Richard Nixon dedicated the lighting system for the Tomb of the Unknowns which was provided by the American Legion and the American Legion Auxiliary. A plaque honoring the occasion is located in the Amphitheatre.

MEMORIAL ENTRANCE TO ARLINGTON NATIONAL CEMETERY

The entrance to Arlington National Cemetery extends across the Potomac River to near the Lincoln Memorial at the eastern edge of the Memorial Bridge. The Memorial Bridge, Memorial Drive (the parkway which leads into Arlington Cemetery), and the magnificent entrance to the cemetery were designed as a single project and were dedicated together on January 16, 1932 by President Herbert Hoover.

The Memorial Bridge was intended as a symbolic link, binding the North and the South together into one great Union. The theme of national unity continued as Architects McKim, Meade, & White designed the bridge to extend along an axis joining two great symbols of our nation: the Lincoln Memorial and the Robert E. Lee Memorial at Arlington House.

Connecting the bridge to the cemetery gates is a parkway known as Memorial Drive. Along this parkway is the rotary intersection with the George Washington Memorial Parkway, which leads to the first President's home at Mt. Vernon. At night, as visitors approach Arlington along Memorial Drive, the eternal flame which marks President **John Kennedy's** grave is visible on the hillside. Also located along Memorial Drive are several memorials and monuments not formally part of Arlington Cemetery. These include the Seabees Memorial, The United Spanish War Veterans Memorial (The Hiker), the monument to Admiral Richard Byrd, and the 101st Airborne Division Memorial. Near the Seabees Memorial is the Arlington Cemetery Metro subway stop. Memorial Drive ends in a sculpted court that has been partially excavated from the steep hillside below Arlington House.

At the western end of the court is a semicircular retaining wall which rises thirty feet and is 226 feet in diameter. In the center of this wall is a large semicircular niche which measures twenty feet across and thirty feet high. In the center of the niche is a bas-relief of the Great Seal of the United States. On either side of the Great Seal are seals of the Department of the Army and the Department of the Navy, with the Army on the south side and the Navy on the north.

From the court, roads lead both north and south through a pair of large ornate wrought iron gates in each direction. The set of gates on the north is called Schley Gate after Admiral **Winfield Scott Schley**. The set on the south side is called Roosevelt Gate in honor of President Theodore Roosevelt. In the center of each gate is mounted a gold wreath, thirty inches in diameter. Set within each wreath is a shield with the seal of one of the military services. On the Roosevelt Gate are the seals for the U.S. Marine Corps and the U.S. Army. Mounted on the Schley Gate are the U.S. Navy and U.S. Coast Guard seals. When the gates were installed, the United States Air Force was still a branch of the Army and so its own seal does not appear.

The Memorial Bridge, Memorial Drive, the memorials and monuments which line that drive, the Memorial Entrance, and The Robert E. Lee Memorial (Arlington House) all fall within the jurisdiction of the National Park Service, U.S. Department of the Interior.

MEMORIAL SECTIONS

Sections 2, 3 and 13

In Arlington Cemetery there are eleven separate Memorial Sections where the tombstones bear the special phrase, "In the Memory of. . . ." This phrase is not found on the standard regulation headstone. These stones mark the cenotaphs, or empty graves, of those service personnel whose bodies could not be recovered but whose deaths have been certified by the United States Department of Defense. These cenotaphs memorialize more than 1,200 dead from World War II, Korea and Vietnam in Arlington. These are not graves of unknowns, but rather of persons whose identities are established and whose remains cannot be located. In the Memorial Sections the headstones are placed more closely together and are usually located on steeper terrain that would prohibit the burying of caskets.

MEMORIAL TO THE SERVICEMEN KILLED IN BEIRUT, 1983

Sec. 59, Grid EE–26

In the summer of 1983 the United States agreed to take part in an effort to restore peace to Lebanon, a country shaken by civil war. Together with French and Italian troops, American forces were deployed near the International Airport in Beirut. Both Marines and Sailors were stationed in a temporary military compound.

Early on the morning of October 23, 1983, in a suicidal assault, a terrorist crashed a munitions-laden truck through the security gate of the compound and into the barracks where hundreds of American servicemen lay sleeping. The resulting explosion hurled debris hundreds of yards in every direction. When at last the rubble could be cleared and an accounting was made of missing Americans, one hundred sixty-one U.S. servicemen lay dead. These men, dedicated to keeping the peace, had no chance to defend themselves. The bodies of the servicemen were returned to the United States, accompanied by military honor guards.

Twenty-two of these men are now buried at Arlington National Cemetery in Section 59. On October 23, 1984 a ceremony was held to honor those 161 servicemen by the organization called "No Greater Love." In memory of these men, a Cedar of Lebanon tree was planted and a monument dedicated. Entitled "Let Peace Take Root," the monument proclaims that this cedar tree was placed as a living memory of those men who died in Beirut.

The monument also is dedicated to all victims of terrorism throughout the world. One such victim was Seaman **Robert Stethem**, who was serving in the United States Navy at the time this tree was planted. **Stethem**, another victim of terrorism, is now buried with these other victims. On June 15, 1985 **Stethem** was murdered by extremists when they discovered he was an American military serviceman traveling on the civilian airline flight they had hijacked.

MEMORIAL TO THE SERVICEMEN WHO DIED DURING THE ATTEMPT TO RESCUE AMERICAN HOSTAGES HELD IN IRAN, 1980

Sec. 46, Grid OP–23/24

The Fall of 1979 was a turbulent period in Iran. The Shah had been deposed by Islamic fundamentalists under the Ayatollah Khomeini, and although diplomatic relations still existed between the United States and Iran, these relations were very strained. On November 4, 1979 hundreds of Iranians seized the U.S. Embassy and took sixty-six Americans hostage. For days nothing was known of the hostages' condition until their captors finally released all female and black hostages. Later one other man was released for medical reasons, leaving fifty-three Americans captives of the Iranian Moslem fundamentalists.

By Spring of 1980 the situation had reached a virtual standstill, with all diplomatic channels apparently exhausted. In the absence of diplomatic options, President Jimmy Carter authorized a secret military operation on April 25, 1980 designed to rescue those remaining American hostages. The plan called for a rendezvous of helicopters and cargo planes at a remote desert site in Iran before attempting the actual rescue of the hostages. However, the mission was aborted when a freak accident caused two of the aircraft to collide. The ensuing explosion and fire claimed the lives of eight American service personnel. Their bodies could not be recovered before the surviving aircraft had to abandon the desert staging area. Shortly thereafter the eight bodies were returned to the United States, but the remaining fifty-three hostages were not freed until January 20, 1981, 444 days after they had been captured.

A monument dedicated to the memory of those gallant servicemen who died in the valiant effort to rescue the American hostages has been erected near the Memorial Amphitheatre at Arlington National Cemetery. The white stone marker bears a bronze plaque listing the names and ranks of the three Marines and the five Airmen. Three of those men are now buried at Arlington in a grave marked by a common headstone located about twenty-five feet adjacent to the group Memorial.

NETHERLANDS CARILLON

Following World War II, the people of the Netherlands wished to show their deep appreciation for the assistance provided by the United States both during and after the war. It was decided that a carillon, made in the Netherlands, would be presented to the people of the United States. A drive was undertaken to raise the funds. Contributions were received from Netherlanders young and old and from every walk of life.

After years of planning, on May 5, 1954, dedication ceremonies were held and, on behalf of her people, the Netherlands' beloved Queen Juliana presented the bell tower to the people of the United States. There are forty-nine bells with the smallest weighing forty-two pounds and the largest weighing over six tons. The unique bells were cast in three different Netherlands foundries.

The Netherlands Carillon is located on a beautifully landscaped site directly north of the Ord-Weitzel Gate of Arlington Cemetery, near the Iwo Jima Monument. During the warm weather months, the music of these famous bells can be heard throughout the cemetery during concerts which are performed at the Carillon on Saturday afternoons from 2:00 until 4:00.

NURSES MEMORIAL

Sec 21, Grid M–19/20

On the gentle sloping hillsides in Section 21 are buried hundreds of nurses who have served American troops from the time of the Spanish-American War until today. On a nearby knoll, rising above the simple headstones of these women, the figure of a nurse stands like a guardian angel keeping watch over her fellow medics. Frances Rich's sculpture captures the compassion, the gentleness, and the strength which are exemplified by the nurses of the United States Armed Forces.

In 1937 Army and Navy nurses began a drive to raise funds for a monument at Arlington National Cemetery dedicated to all nurses who had served in the United States Armed Forces. On May 4, 1937 permission was granted by Secretary of War Harry H. Wooding, to plan and erect the monument. On the afternoon of November 8, 1938, during a moving dedication ceremony, the eight-and-a-half foot marble statue was unveiled to the reverent applause of the scores of nurses assembled. Its simple inscription: Army and Navy Nurses.

On November 20, 1970 a rededication ceremony was held to extend it commemoration to include all nurses who had served since 1938, as well as to include all Air Force nurses.

OLD AMPHITHEATRE AND ROSTRUM

Section 26, Grid P–32

In 1868 the Old Amphitheatre and Rostrum (at left) provided a gathering place for memorial services at Arlington Cemetery. At right, The Old Amphitheatre during its restoration in 1985.

Near Arlington House, in a section of what was once the garden of Mary and Robert E. Lee, is the old Amphitheatre and Rostrum. Completed in 1868 in compliance with the order of General John A. Logan, it was dedicated as part of the first observance of Decoration Day (now Memorial Day) on May 30 of that year. The featured speaker on that occasion was General James

A. Garfield, later to become President of the United States.

The Amphitheatre is encircled by a colonnade which supports a latticed roof, once covered with thick vines. In the center of the Amphitheatre is a dais known as "the Rostrum," made of white marble in a classic design and inscribed with the phrase, *"E pluribus unum"* ("Out of many, one"). The Old Amphitheatre held 1500 seats and served as the principal area of assembly before the current Memorial Amphitheatre was completed in 1921. Among the great speakers who graced its podium was **William Jennings Bryan**.

101st ARMY AIRBORNE DIVISION MEMORIAL

Memorial Drive, Grid CC–38

This memorial commemorates the men of the 101st Airborne Division, popularly known as the "Screaming Eagles." A large bronze eagle with its wings uplifted proudly symbolizes the 101st which valiantly served this nation during World War II, the Vietnam War, and which continues to serve today. The campaigns the 101st participated in during World War II and Vietnam are listed on its gray granite base, which is emblazoned on all sides with the Division's insignia.

Also inscribed on the base is the often-quoted phrase of Major General William C. Lee who predicted on August 19, 1942 that the 101st "has no history but has a rendezvous with destiny."

Behind the statue, architect Harold J. Schaller and sculptor Bernhard Zukerman placed a low semicircular wall of granite on which the various areas of action of the Division are noted.

This monument was the scene of memorial services for the 101st following the death of the 248 members of the Screaming Eagles who were killed when their transport plane crashed in Gander, Newfoundland in December 1985.

THE ROADS AND WALKWAYS OF ARLINGTON NATIONAL CEMETERY

Within the confines of Arlington National Cemetery there are forty-five roads and walkways stretching more than fifteen miles. These arteries are named in honor of well-known American military figures, each of whom is noted below. Although not all of these famous Americans are buried at Arlington, the names of those whose graves are here appear in bold.

Arnold Drive.
World War II General of the Air Force **Henry ("Hap") Arnold**.
Capron Drive.
Named in honor of several family members.
Clayton Drive.
Civil War Brigadier General **Powell Clayton**.
Crook Walk.
Civil War Major General **George Crook**.
Custis Walk.
Arlington estate founder **George Washington Parke Custis**.
Dewey Drive.
Spanish-American War Admiral George Dewey.
Doubleday Walk.
Civil War Major General **Abner Doubleday**.
Eisenhower Drive.
General of the Army and President Dwight David Eisenhower.
Farragut Drive.
Civil War Admiral David Glasgow Farragut.

Garfield Drive.
   Civil War Brigadier General and President James Abram
   Garfield.
Grant Drive.
   Civil War General and President Ulysses S. Grant.
Halsey Drive.
   World War II Fleet Admiral **William "Bull" Halsey**.
Hobson Drive.
   Spanish-American War Rear Admiral Richmond P. Hobson.
Humphreys Drive.
   Civil War General Andres A. Humphreys.
Jackson Circle.
   Confederate Civil War General Thomas "Stonewall" Jackson.
Jesup Drive.
   Major General Thomas S. Jesup, War of 1812.
King Drive.
   World War II Fleet Admiral Ernest J. King.
Lawton Drive.
   Civil War Major General Henry W. Lawton.
Leahy Drive.
   World War II Flcct Admiral **William D. Leahy**.
Lee Drive.
   Confederate Civil War General Robert E. Lee.
L'Enfant Drive.
   Revolutionary War Captain **Pierre Charles L'Enfant**.
Lincoln Drive.
   President Abraham Lincoln.
MacArthur Circle.
   Lieutenant General **Arthur MacArthur**.
MacArthur Drive.
   World War II General of the Army Douglas MacArthur.
Marshall Drive.
   World War II General of the Army **George C.Marshall**.
McClellan Drive.
   Civil War Major General George B. McClellan.
McKinley Drive.
   Civil War Major and President William McKinley.
McPherson Drive.
   Civil War Major General James McPherson.

Meigs Drive.

Quartermaster Major General **Montgomery Meigs**.

Memorial Drive.

For all Americans who have served in the Armed Forces of the United States.

Miles Drive.

Civil War Lieutenant General **Nelson A. Miles**.

Nimitz Drive.

World War II Fleet Admiral Chester Nimitz.

Mitchell Drive.

Army Air Corps Major General William Mitchell.

Ord-Weitzel Drive.

Civil War Major Generals **Edward O. C. Ord** and Godfrey Weitzel.

Patton Drive.

World War II General George S. Patton, Jr.

Pershing Drive.

General of the Armies **John J. Pershing**.

Porter Drive.

Civil War Admiral **David Dixon Porter**.

Roosevelt Drive.

Rough Rider Colonel and President Theodore Roosevelt.

Schley Drive.

Spanish-American War Rear Admiral **Winfield Scott Schley**.

Sheridan Drive.

Civil War General **Philip Henry Sheridan**.

Sherman Drive.

Civil War General William Tecumseh Sherman.

Sigsbee Drive.

Spanish-American War Rear Admiral **Charles Dwight Sigsbee**.

Weeks Drive.

U.S. Secretary of War **John Wingate Weeks**.

Wilson Drive.

President Thomas Woodrow Wilson.

York Drive.

Sergeant Alvin C. York, World War I hero.

ROUGH RIDERS MEMORIAL

Sec. 22, Grid KL–21

They became one of the best known cavalry units in American history, though few people remember their official title, the First U.S. Volunteer Cavalry. But mention the name "Rough Riders" and visions come to mind of the charge up San Juan Hill, led by **Leonard Wood** and Teddy Roosevelt. The Rough Riders served with distinction during the Spanish-American War. This monument was erected to their memory by the members and friends of the regiment in 1906.

It is a large, dark-grey granite stone that displays the insignia of the First U.S. Volunteer Cavalry on its west face. It also lists the battles in which the Rough Riders took part-Las Guasimas, San Juan, and Santiago. The names of all the officers and enlisted men of the First Cavalry who lost their lives during the Spanish-American War are engraved on the imposing granite stone.

SEABEES MEMORIAL

Memorial Drive, Grid KK–40/41

When the United States was suddenly and dramatically pulled into World War II following the Japanese attack on Pearl Harbor in December 1941, there was an acute shortage of military bases to support American combat forces deployed in Europe and the Pacific. To alleviate the shortage, the United States Navy established an engineering and construction force known as the U.S. Naval Construction Battalion, or C.B. Soon its members were universally known by the nickname derived from those initials, the Seabees.

Along Memorial Drive near the Arlington Cemetery Metro stop is a memorial dedicated to the men who have served as Seabees. A larger-than-life figure dominates the monument depicting the momentous contributions made by the Construction Battalion. The image is that of a Seabee who, in the midst of a construction project, stops to make friends with a young child. Below the figures are the words, "With Compassion for Others We Build — We Fight for Peace With Freedom."

On a semicircular bronze bas-relief, sculptor Felix de Weldon (also sculptor of the Iwo Jima monument) depicted scenes of Seabees at work in various construction trades. Prominently displayed is the Seabee slogan "Can Do." This graphic memorial was dedicated on May 27, 1974.

SPANISH-AMERICAN WAR MEMORIAL

Sec. 22, Grid N–21

When the United States declared war on Spain in 1898, it was the first major conflict fought by our country since the Civil War. Many Civil War veterans, both Union and Confederate, volunteered to fight. President William McKinley realized that many of the enduring wounds between the North and the South could be healed by uniting the country behind a common enemy, so he offered commissions to former Confederate officers in the United States Armed Forces. Many of these veterans accepted as the country joined forces against the Spanish.

Following the war, the National Society of the Colonial Dames of America petitioned the Quartermaster General of the Army to erect a monument within Arlington National Cemetery. It was to be the first memorial to all American veterans who fought side by side in combat since the Civil War. The petition gained quick approval and on May 21, 1902 the Spanish-American War's most famous veteran – President Theodore Roosevelt – dedicated the monument.

The monument is a corinthian column of Barre granite standing nearly fifty feet tall. Atop the column is a sphere of Quincy granite on which a bronze eagle is mounted. On the tablet attached to the rear base of the memorial is an inscription honoring the soldiers and sailors of the United States who gave their lives for their country in the war with Spain.

In 1964 the Colonial Dames desired to honor those Americans

who lost their lives in the wars fought since the Spanish-American War. Accordingly, a rededication of the monument was held and a second bronze tablet was unveiled. Its special inscription reads:

TO THE GLORY OF GOD AND
IN GRATEFUL REMEMBRANCE
OF THE MEN AND WOMEN OF
THE ARMED FORCES WHO IN
THIS CENTURY GAVE THEIR
LIVES FOR OUR COUNTRY
THAT FREEDOM MIGHT LIVE

THIS TABLET IS DEDICATED BY THE
NATIONAL SOCIETY OF THE COLONIAL DAMES
OF AMERICA
OCTOBER 11, 1964

Behind the memorial are four guns mounted on concrete stands. The two inner guns were captured from the Spanish forces during that war; they are flanked by two American Naval guns.

SPANISH-AMERICAN WAR NURSES MEMORIAL

Sec. 21, Grid L–20

The Spanish-American War was the first war involving the United States in which nurses were organized and assigned as a special, quasi-military unit. During that war many nurses lost their lives. Many of those who served are now buried in Section 21 of Arlington National Cemetery.

The Society of Spanish-American War Nurses has erected a memorial to those brave nurses who died during that war. The Maltese cross, which serves as the insignia of the Society, rests atop a large granite megalith dedicated to the memory of their "brave comrades."

TOMB OF THE UNKNOWNS

World War I   World War II
Korean War   Vietnam War

Grid ST–22/23

Within the walls of Arlington National Cemetery can be found the tomb of an unknown soldier of every war in American history, except the American Revolution. The official Tomb of the

Unknown of the Revolutionary War is located in the burial grounds of the Presbyterian Meeting House in Alexandria, Virginia. Described below are the four Unknowns who are buried at the Tomb of the Unknowns on the East Plaza of the Memorial Amphitheatre, and the story of how they came to rest there.

World War I

On November 11, 1918 an armistice was declared, ending World War I. It was to be the war to end all wars. So pandemic were its effects that only when the fighting had finally stopped could Americans pause to remember the thousands of men and women who had given their lives in that global struggle. Throughout the country, local memorial services were held to commemorate those who had died and to honor those who had re-

The Tomb of the Unknowns on the East Plaza of the Memorial Amphitheatre as seen from Roosevelt Drive.

turned. Yet there were hundreds of Americans who did not return because their remains could not be identified in spite of the employment of every possible means to determine their identities. The bodies of more than 1,600 Americans were interred in France where they lost their lives. They are buried in four American cemeteries created for them.

Still reeling from the effects of the greatest war the world had ever known, many Americans felt that something special needed to be done to remember not the war, but rather what the war had cost our nation. Finally, in response to public sentiment, Congress followed the example of our allies and approved a resolution providing for the burial of an unidentified American soldier at Arlington National Cemetery. On March 4, 1921, the last day of his presidency, Woodrow Wilson signed the bill and an elaborate procedure began for choosing that honored unknown soldier.

The Unknown was to be symbolic of all persons who had given their lives during that war. Every American could pay homage to this fallen soldier, believing him to be the son, husband, brother, or friend who did not come home. To achieve this general feeling, it was imperative that there be no means to discover the soldier's actual identity. Even revelation of the name of the cemetery from which he was chosen for reinterment might compromise the secrecy surrounding the unknown soldier's selection. So one candidate-unknown was chosen from each of the four American cemeteries in France. On October 22, 1921 each of the four bodies were exhumed and transported under honor guard to the City Hall at Chalons-sur-Marne, France for final random selection. During that night the honor guard shifted the positions of the four identical caskets so that no one — not even the Graves Registration detail — could differentiate between them. As a last guarantor of secrecy, all burial records of these four servicemen were destroyed. On October 24, Army Sergeant **Edward F. Younger** of Chicago, who had been wounded in combat and highly decorated for valor, was given the honor of selecting the Unknown Soldier of World War I by placing a spray of white roses on one of the caskets. That spray of white roses accompanied the Unknown to Arlington and these flowers are buried with him. Sergeant **Younger** also is buried at Arlington National Cemetery (Sec. 18, Lot 1918–B, Grid LM–12/13).

The three remaining unknown soldiers were reinterred in the Meuse-Argonne Cemetery in France while the chosen Unknown began his journey home, symbolic of those who could not make that journey. The Unknown was placed in a special, American-made casket which bears the inscription, "An unknown soldier who gave his life in the Great War." The cortege containing the Unknown Soldier and his honor guard traveled from Chalons through Paris on its way to Le Havre. There the Unknown was placed on the *Olympia*, which had been Admiral Dewey's flagship during the Spanish-American War.

On its way to Washington the *Olympia* received full salutes and honors from every vessel it encountered on the high seas. Finally, on November 9, 1921, it docked at Washington, D.C. where

the Unknown was greeted by his former commander, General of
the Armies **John J. Pershing**. **Pershing** led the procession to the
United States Capitol, where the Unknown was to lie in state until Armistice Day, November 11. Nearly 100,000 mourners paid
their respects on November 10, the single intervening day; many
more were turned away when the guards were ordered to close
the doors at midnight.

The next day, November 11, 1921, President Warren G. Harding led the nation in solemn services held at Arlington in the new
Memorial Amphitheatre. Following his remarks, the President
placed the Congressional Medal of Honor and the Distinguished
Service Cross on the casket. Also present were representatives
of America's allies in World War I to pay tribute and to award
the Unknown their highest honors—the Victoria Cross of the British
Empire, the Croix de Guerre of France, the Order of Leopold of
Belgium, the Gold Medal of Bravery of Italy, as well as the highest
honors of Romania, Poland, Cuba, and Czechoslovakia. All of

During a spectacular ceremony in the new Memorial Amphitheatre in 1921, President
Warren G. Harding awards the Congressional Medal of Honor to the Unknown Soldier
of World War I.

these military decorations are now housed at Arlington in the Trophy Room adjacent to the Tomb of the Unknowns. Following these presentations, the remains were carried to the gravesite on the terrace just east of the Amphitheatre. At the bottom of that grave was placed a two-inch layer of soil from the battlefields of France.

Just before the remains were buried forever, a final honor was bestowed upon the fallen soldier by Native Americans. The seventy-four-year-old chief of the Crow Nation, Plenty Coups, stepped forward. In his native tongue, he offered a stirring prayer for all fallen soldiers. "I hope that the Great Spirit will grant that these noble warriors have not given up their lives in vain and that there will be peace to all men hereafter." With that, he placed upon the grave his coup stick and ancient headdress which had been with his tribe for generations. This was the highest tribute of his proud people. The headdress and coup stick from the Crow Nation are also kept in the Trophy Room at Arlington.

Although America's first Unknown Soldier was laid to rest in November of 1921, it was not until 1926 that Congress authorized the completion of the monument. What resulted from that enactment was the magnificent sarcophagus which has been viewed by millions of visitors over the decades. Although simple in its design, the sarcophagus' dimensions are impressive. The large white marble monument, which weighs fifty tons, was quarried in Colorado and rough-hewn in Vermont. It is relieved at the corners by neo-classic pilasters, or columns, set onto the surface. Sculpted into the east side facing Washington are three figures which represent Peace, Victory and Valor. On the west face are inscribed the immortal words:

HERE RESTS IN
HONORED GLORY
AN AMERICAN
SOLDIER
KNOWN BUT TO GOD

Immediately after the interment of the World War I Unknown, Americans offered homage to the hero buried at Arlington, unparalleled in our nation's history. In addition to the thousands of visitors who poured into the cemetery, flowers, Christmas cards, birthday cards, and letters arrived all to the Unknown. Tragically, among the letters were inquiries from mothers and wives wondering if the Unknown was in fact their son or husband. Despite the extraordinary precautions taken against discovery of the Unknown's identity and the widespread publicity about those precautions, still the letters of inquiry came. Proffering clues of a birthmark or a gold tooth, they hoped against hope that this soldier was their lost loved one. It is the belief that this soldier might be any American unknown that adds a special dimension to this symbolic memorial. For this honored yet anonymous hero represents all the unknowns who died in brave service to our country during World War I.

World War II, The Korean War

The Great War, in which the Unknown had given his life, did not end all wars. On September 1, 1939 Germany invaded Poland and a second worldwide conflagration began. Virtually no corner of the world was unscarred. When World War II ended in 1945, formal plans were made to inter at Arlington an unknown from that war; the ceremony was to take place on Memorial Day 1951. Unfortunately, however, before the date of that official ceremony arrived, America became embroiled in hostilities again, this time in Korea. So the plans to inter a World War II Unknown at Arlington were postponed.

On August 3, 1956 President Dwight D. Eisenhower signed legislation to select and pay tribute to the Unknowns of both World War II and the Korean War. Again, following the same procedures used after World War I, great precautions were taken to insure the complete anonymity of these two unknowns.

The World War II candidate-unknowns were exhumed from cemeteries in Europe, Africa, Hawaii, and the Philippines. In two separate ceremonies in France and Hawaii, a candidate-unknown for the European Theatre and for the Pacific Theatre were chosen. The Korean Unknown was chosen from four sets of unidentified remains of those who fought in Korea and who were buried in the National Cemetery of the Pacific in Hawaii. Army Master Sergeant Ned Lyle was granted the privilege of selecting the Unknown.

The three unknowns were brought together aboard the *Canberra*, off the Virginia Capes. There, Hospitalman First Class William R. Carette, then the Navy's only active-duty enlisted Medal of Honor recipient, selected the Unknown of World War II. The candidate not chosen was given a full honors burial at sea, while the Unknowns from World War II and Korea sailed on to Washington, D.C., docking on May 27, 1958.

The next morning the two caskets were removed to the Rotunda of the United States Capitol where they lay in state for forty-eight hours while thousands of Americans filed past paying their final respects. On Memorial Day the Unknowns were taken from the Capitol to Arlington, just as the first Unknown had been taken thirty-seven years earlier. The ceremonies at Arlington were solemn and brief. President Eisenhower spoke only twenty-six words. "On behalf of a grateful people, I now present Medals of Honor to these two unknowns who gave their lives for the United States of America." As in 1921, representatives of governments from around the world presented their highest honors to America's fallen heroes. These military decorations can also be viewed in the Trophy Room. The Unknowns were then laid to rest on the terrace next to the Unknown of World War I.

The Vietnam Era

As a tribute to the members of the United States Armed Forces who served in Southeast Asia during the 1960s and 1970s, Secretary of Defense Caspar Weinberger announced on April 13, 1984 that an Unknown from the Vietnam Era would be interred at Arlington National Cemetery on Memorial Day 1984. The selection process took place at the National Cemetery in Hawaii on May 17, 1984. The Unknown arrived in Washington on May 25 and was taken to the United States Capitol where he lay in state. Again, thousands of Americans filed past the casket to pay their respects. During funeral and interment services at Arlington, President Ronald Reagan awarded the Congressional Medal of Honor to the Unknown on behalf of the American people.

The Tomb Guard

Although the Tomb of the Unknowns is guarded at present by members of the crack Third Infantry, this was not always the case. The first guard established for the Tomb was a civilian watchman in November of 1925. In 1926 a military guard was posted for the first time, but only during daylight hours when the cemetery gates were open to the public. In 1937 a twenty-four-hour military guard was established. Finally, in 1948 the guardianship of the Tomb was assumed by the Third United States Infantry, known as the Old Guard.

A member of the Third Infantry, known as the Old Guard, provides a continuous honor guard for the Tomb of the Unknowns. Engraved on the Tomb of the World War I Unknown are the immortal words: HERE RESTS IN HONORED GLORY AN AMERICAN SOLDIER KNOWN BUT TO GOD.

The Changing of the Guard

This simple but impressive ceremony takes place every half-hour from April 1 through September 30, and every hour on the hour from October 1 through March 31. At night the guard changes every two hours throughout all seasons of the year.

At his post, the sentinel crosses the walkway in exactly twenty-one steps. He turns to face the Tomb for twenty-one seconds, turns again, pausing an additional twenty-one seconds, then retraces his steps. The number "21" is symbolic of the highest salute afforded dignitaries in military and state ceremonies. The guard will speak or change his pattern only under exceptional circumstances, including the issuance of a warning to anyone who attempts to enter the restricted area around the Tomb.

The Old Guard, the U.S. Army's official ceremonial unit, is the oldest active infantry unit of the Army. Often referred to as the President's Own, the Old Guard is the Army honor guard and escort for the President. Its soldiers participate in more than 3,500 ceremonies annually at the White House, Pentagon, and numerous other national memorials. Headquartered in the adjacent Fort Myer Army installation, they also perform military funeral rites in Arlington and participate in state funerals.

Wreath Laying Ceremonies

President Ronald Reagan honors the American Unknowns of four wars by laying a wreath during Veteran's Day services at the Tomb of the Unknowns.

Throughout the year, more than two thousand wreath laying ceremonies take place at the Tomb of the Unknowns. As a gesture of respect to the United States and in honor of our gallant dead, groups from every quarter of our country and every walk of life come to Arlington to participate in this time-honored tradition. Since 1921 every American President has made the pilgrimage to the Tomb at least once, and countless foreign dignitaries representing every nation on earth have placed wreaths here.

TOMB OF THE UNKNOWN CIVIL WAR DEAD

Sec. 26, Grid QR–32/33

Near Arlington House, in what was once part of its famous rose garden, stands a monument dedicated to the unknown soldiers who died in the Civil War. The monument, dedicated in September 1866, stands atop a masonry vault containing the remains of 2,111 soldiers gathered from the fields of Bull Run and the route to the Rappahannock. The remains were found scattered across the battlefields or in trenches and brought here. This monument was the first memorial at Arlington to be dedicated to soldiers who had

In 1866 a monument (left) was erected in the former rose garden of Arlington House honoring the unknown dead of the Civil War. The original stone was later replaced by the monument on the right.

died in battle and who later could not be identified. Because in some instances only a few bones or a skull were recovered, it is assumed that the vault contains the remains of Confederate soldiers as well as Union troops.

Quartermaster General **Montgomery Meigs** ordered that these bodies be gathered and buried on this particular site knowing that the presence of graves here would prevent the Lee family from inhabiting their house again.

TOMB OF THE UNKNOWN DEAD OF THE WAR OF 1812

Sec. 1, Lot 299, Grid N–33/34

On this site rest fourteen soldiers from the War of 1812, identities unknown. Although they are now buried in this mass grave, they were not originally buried on this site. Their remains were only discovered in 1905 during excavation work near the old Washington Barracks (now the Washington Navy Yard). The reinterment to this site took place in that same year.

On April 8, 1976 the National Society of the United States Daughters of the War of 1812 dedicated the large granite monument that now marks the tomb. The memorial displays the relevant dates of the War of 1812 and declares that these unknown soldiers are "Symbolic of All Who Made the Supreme Sacrifice in That War."

UNITED STATES COAST GUARD MEMORIAL

Sec. 4, Grid XY–9/10

Two tragic episodes in United States Coast Guard history prompted the construction of this memorial, which sits atop a hill near the southern edge of the cemetery. On September 21, 1918 the cutter *Seneca*, was lost while attempting to salvage the British steamer, *Wellington*, which had been torpedoed in the Bay of Biscay. All officers and crew of the *Seneca* were lost.

Only five days later, on September 26, 1918, the cutter *Tampa,* was sunk by an enemy submarine in the Bristol Channel, and all on board that ship were lost as well. The names of these vessels and their crewmen, as well as of all Coast Guard personnel who lost their lives during the Great War, are inscribed on the sides of the monument. The United States Coast Guard Memorial at Arlington was dedicated on May 23, 1928.

The Coast Guard was formed as the successor to the Revenue Cutter Service and the Life Saving Service on June 28, 1915. By law, both the *Tampa* and the *Seneca* were ordered to operate as part of the Navy when the United States entered World War I on April 6, 1918.

In the monument's rock foundation and pyramid design, architect George Howe and sculptor Gaston Lachaise have captured the spirit of the Coast Guard's legendary steadfastness. A bronze sea gull poised with its wings uplifted alights below the Coast Guard motto *Semper Paratus* (Always Prepared). This bird further symbolizes the tireless vigil that the United States Coast Guard maintains over our nation's maritime territory.

Perhaps the most famous photograph of World War II was the one taken of the flag-raising on Iwo Jima Island by Joe Rosenthal (left). That photograph inspired the construction of the U.S. Marine Corps Memorial (right) located just north of Arlington National Cemetery.

UNITED STATES MARINE CORPS MEMORIAL

Iwo Jima Monument

Located just north of the Ord-Weitzel Gate of Arlington

The United States Marine Corps Memorial was established to honor the thousands of Marines who have given their lives in the defense of this great nation and in the pursuit of liberty around the world. Although the memorial depicts just one of the hundreds of battles in which Marines have taken part, it vividly illustrates the courage, determination, and skill with which the Marines have performed their duties for more than two centuries, since the Marine Corps' founding on November 10, 1775.

Chosen to represent the contribution of all Marines is the famous scene of the flag-raising on Mount Suribachi during the battle of Iwo Jima in World War II. This scene was first immortalized by a chance photograph taken by Associated Press photographer Joe Rosenthal on February 23, 1945 as the Marines planted the U.S. colors during the raging battle for control of the strategically situated island of Iwo Jima.

Although Iwo Jima was a small island (less than five miles long and two miles wide), it held military importance because of its two Japanese-built airfields. Just 660 miles from the mainland of Japan, it served as a base for Japanese fighters to attack American bombers on sorties to the major military-industrial centers of Japan. If wrested from enemy control, those airfields would prove invaluable as a staging area for the American aerial campaign. For these reasons, the decision was made that the Fourth and Fifth Marine Divisions would undertake an assault of the island.

Prior to the Marines' landing, Navy and Army Air Force planes subjected the island to "the longest and most intensive" bombing in the Pacific theatre during World War II. The island had been fortified by 642 blockhouses, pillboxes, and other gun positions, and it was the intent of this massive, seventy-four day bombing campaign to weaken the firm Japanese defense of the island. Unfortunately, bad weather nullified some of the effect of the bombing raids.

On February 19, 1945 American Marines scrambled from their carriers and waded through an ankle-deep sea of volcanic ash to establish a beachhead. After gaining a hold on the beaches, it was their goal to take Mount Suribachi, the 550-foot volcanic peak on the southern tip of the island. Although the beachhead was established against only minor resistance, the Japanese emerged from underground shelters to unleash extensive firepower once the initial barrage was over.

It was the Twenty-eighth Marines of the Fifth Marine Division who were ordered to take the hill which they had managed to isolate from the rest of the island by the end of the first day of fighting. For four days the battle raged, until finally on February 23, a forty-man American combat patrol reached the rim of the crater, secured a small U.S. flag (45 by 28 inches) to a length of iron pipe left behind by the Japanese and proudly raised the Stars and Stripes. The sight of the U.S. colors flying atop the summit inspired the thousands of Americans still below.

But this was not the historic flag-raising that Rosenthal captured on film. Once the original flag was raised on that summit, a larger flag (96 by 56 inches) was taken from one of the landing craft. Photographer Rosenthal immediately realized the purpose of this second flag and closely pursued its bearer. Sergeant **Michael Strank**, Corporal Harlan Block, Private Franklin Sousley, and Private **Ira Hayes** carried the colors up the hill. As they reached the summit, commanding officer Lieutenant Harold G. Schrier ordered that the second flag be raised and the first flag be lowered. Sergeant Strank found a second length of pipe and fastened the larger flag to it. Seeing that the four men were having trouble raising the flag on the rugged terrain, two men standing nearby, Pharmacist's Mate Second Class John H. Bradley and Private **Rene A. Gagnon**, came to their aid. As the six men struggled to raise the colors, Rosenthal snapped the picture which has been called the single most famous photograph ever taken, and for which he was awarded the coveted Pulitzer Prize.

Although the flag-raising inspired the forces trying to take the tiny island, it could not minimize the heavy casualties suffered by the Americans. Before the battle ended on March 25, more than a month after the capture of Mount Suribachi, 17,372 Marines had been wounded and 5,931 Marines had lost their lives in an effort to take an area only one-eighth the size of Washington, D.C.

Nevertheless, the photo sent American morale soaring. When President Franklin Roosevelt saw the photograph, he ordered that the identities of the six men be determined and that they be recalled to the United States. He realized that both the photograph and the men had become a boon to our national morale. The scene became the subject of a poster during the Seventh War Bond Loan drive, and a three-cent commemorative postage stamp was issued. The six men in the photo became instant celebrities. It was not long, however, before the world was to learn that only three of those brave men survived the battle for Iwo Jima. Sergeant **Michael Strank**, Corporal Harlan H. Block, and Private Franklin R. Sousley were among the nearly 6,000 men killed in later phases of the fighting for control of the island.

These six men, hailing from very diverse backgrounds, shared one brief, immortalized moment in their lives. Three of them (**Rene Gagnon, Ira Hayes**, and **Michael Strank**) are now buried in Arlington National Cemetery. Their lives are outlined in the profile section of this book. The remaining Marines are introduced below:

Harlan Henry Block was born in Yorktown, Texas on November 6, 1924. He had graduated from Weslaco High School in 1943 and was drafted on February 18, 1943. He qualified as a parachutist on May 22 and was promoted to First Class the same day. After taking part in the Bougainville campaign, his unit disbanded and Block joined the 28th Marines on March 1, 1944.

Promoted to Corporal on October 27, 1944, Block landed on Iwo Jima on February 19, 1945. He was killed on the island on March 1 of that same year while attacking Nishi Ridge. Originally buried on Iwo Jima, his body was returned for private burial at Weslaco, Texas.

John Henry Bradley is the only surviving member of the six men who planted the flag on Iwo Jima. Born in Antigo, Wisconsin on July 10, 1923, he graduated from Appleton (Wisconsin) High School in 1941. He enlisted in the Navy on January 13, 1943 and, following boot camp, was assigned to the Hospital Corps School. Promoted to Pharmacist's Mate Second Class, Bradley attended Field Medical School and was assigned to the Twenty-eighth Marines on April 15, 1944. He was with the Twenty-eighth when they landed on Iwo Jima, for his first and only military campaign. Bradley was wounded on March 12, 1945 and was medically discharged from the Marine Corps on November 13, 1945.

Franklin Runyon Sousley was a native of Flemingsburg, Kentucky where he was born on September 19, 1925. Following his graduation from high school, he moved to Dayton, Ohio where he entered the Marine Corps Reserve through the Selective Service System on January 5, 1944. After boot camp in San Diego, he was assigned to the Twenty-eighth Marines of the Fifth Marine Division as an automatic rifleman and was promoted to First Class on November 22, 1944. He landed on Iwo Jima on February 19, 1945 and was killed one month later on March 21 during fighting around Kitano Point. Private Sousley was initially buried on Iwo Jima, but was reinterred at Elizaville, Kentucky.

Joe Rosenthal's photo generated widespread encouragement for the American war effort in 1945. Yet its most lasting inspiration was the creation of the Marine Corps Memorial which now stands near Arlington National Cemetery. Shortly after the news photo was released, sculptor Felix de Weldon, then on duty with the Navy, constructed a scale model, followed by a life-size model of the historic scene on Iwo Jima. These models were used for the bond drive poster and the postage stamp. Moved by these reproductions of the Iwo Jima flag-raising, friends of the Marine Corps proposed a monument to the memory of all Marines, a monument which would include the stirring scene in heroic proportions.

Sculptor de Weldon, who later designed and created the Seabees Memorial and the Memorial to Admiral Richard Byrd (both located on Memorial Drive near the main entrance to Arlington), began his formidable task in 1945. Recognizing that a work of this magnitude would require the detailing of every aspect of the figures from facial expressions to clothing and equipment, one of his first projects was to elicit the help of the three survivors, all of whom agreed to assist him. Using these three live models, together with all available pictures and physical data of the other three Marines, de Weldon cast their faces first in clay and later in plaster. A steel frame resembling the bone structure of a human body was assembled to support the huge figures under construction. Initially, the figures were molded nude so that muscular strain would be evident after clothing was added. When the statue was finished in plaster, it was carefully disassembled and taken in 108 pieces to the Bedi-Rassy Art Foundry in Brooklyn, New York. There, for three years, the artisans cast the pieces in bronze.

In 1954 the finished bronze sections were trucked to, and reassembled on, a seven and one-half acre tract just north of Arlington National Cemetery. The one hundred-ton monument, which is the largest cast bronze figure in the world, was dedicated by President Dwight D. Eisenhower on November 10, 1954 to coincide with the 179th anniversary of the founding of the Marine Corps. The total cost of the monument was $850,000, underwritten privately by U.S. Marines, former Marines, Marine Corps Reservists, friends of the Marine Corps, and U.S. Navy personnel.

Starting at the bottom of the flagpole and working upward, the six men depicted are: Corp. Harlan H. Block, PFC **Rene Gagnon** (whose downturned head is near Block's left elbow on the opposite side of the pole), PM2/C John H. Bradley (facing forward behind Block), SGT **Michael Strank** (leaning over Gagnon's back), PFC Franklin Sousley (immediately behind Bradley) and PFC **Ira Hayes** (the rear figure whose outstretched hands are not quite touching the flagpole).

The figures of the six men stand thirty-two feet high; the flagpole they are planting is sixty feet long. The rocky base on which they stand rises approximately six feet above a ten foot base, making the entire structure nearly seventy-eight feet tall. To further illustrate the immensity of the monument, the M-1 rifle carried by **Ira Hayes** is sixteen feet in length, and the carbines are twelve feet long. The canteen, if filled, would hold thirty-two quarts of water. The interior of the statue is reinforced by extruded bronze supports which required that the statue be bolted and welded from the inside. The workmen entered the statue through a 'trap door' in a cartridge belt which is now welded shut. The concrete base is covered with blocks of polished Swedish black granite with the names and dates of every major Marine Corps engagement burnished into it. Also inscribed is the tribute by Fleet Admiral Chester W. Nimitz regarding the Marines on Iwo Jima, "Uncommon Valor Was a Common Virtue."

By a proclamation signed by President **John F. Kennedy** on June 12, 1961, the United States flag now flies twenty-four hours a day on the lighted monument. In the summer months the Marine Corps Drum and Bugle Corps and Marine troops conduct ceremonies on the adjacent parade grounds.

The monument and the parade grounds are part of the National Capital Parks, which are administered by the National Park Service, U.S. Department of the Interior.

USS MAINE MEMORIAL

Sec. 24, Grid MN–23/24

In the latter half of the 1890s, the United States resisted pressures to intercede on behalf of Cuba in its struggle for independence from Spain, but by 1898 the situation had grown dangerously unstable. In an effort to counter that growing instability, the U.S. Navy ordered the USS *Maine* to Havana Harbor, believing that the presence of an American battleship would promote peace but, if necessary, could be used in the evacuation of American citizens. On January 25, 1898 the battleship under the command of Captain **Charles Dwight Sigsbee** sailed into Havana Harbor.

At that time the *Maine* carried a crew of 355 men, including 26 officers, 290 sailors, and 39 Marines. All was quiet for the crew during the first three weeks, but that changed on the evening of February 15 when, without warning, a violent explosion ripped through the *Maine*. Officers and crew scrambled to evacuate the ship. Captain Sigbee abandoned the vessel only after all surviving crew members were safe aboard rescue boats. He was taken aboard the pleasure ship, *City of Washington*, where he reported the night's events by message to the Secretary of the Navy:

> *Maine* blown up in Havana Harbor at nine-forty tonight and destroyed. Many wounded and doubtless more killed or drowned. Wounded and others on board Spanish Man-of-War and Ward Line Steamer. Send Light House Tender from Key West for crew and a few pieces of equipment above water. No one has clothing other than that upon him. Public opinion should be suspended until further notice.

It was finally determined that two officers and 251 enlisted men were killed in the initial explosion. Seven more later died from their wounds. Of the 260 men who died, 66 were aboard the *Maine* buried beneath the sea. The remaining 194 servicemen were buried in Colon Cemetery in Havana.

The sinking of the *Maine*, coupled with other international events, brought the U.S. to the brink of war with Spain. The American press seized upon the incident, coining the popular slogan, "Remember the *Maine*, to hell with Spain!" Political pressure was exerted on Congress to recover the bodies of the American servicemen, and on March 30, 1898 Congress approved provisions for the disinterment of the victims and for their transfer to Arlington National Cemetery. On April 24, 1898 Spain declared war on the United States and on the following day the United States issued its declaration against Spain. Although the war with Spain lasted less than four months, it was not until December 28, 1899 that members of the *Maine*'s crew were disinterred and returned to the United States. President William McKinley and Admiral George Dewey presided over the burial of those men in Section 24 at Arlington.

For more than twelve years after its sinking, the mast of the once-mighty battleship was all that could be seen rising above the water of Havana Harbor. The 66 bodies of the *Maine*'s crew who had gone down with the ship in 1898 were still on board. Finally, on May 9, 1910, Congress authorized the raising of the *Maine* from the bottom of the harbor and "for the proper interment of the bodies therein in Arlington National Cemetery." In addition, Congress authorized the Secretary of War to remove the *Maine*'s mast and place it upon a proper foundation as a memorial in Arlington near the bodies of the crew members interred there.

It took nearly two years to raise the battleship. In March 1912 the 66 bodies were recovered and returned to the United States. Only one of those bodies could be identified and that sailor was returned to his home state for burial. On March 23, 1912 President **William Howard Taft** presided over the services as the 65 men were interred next to their comrades in Section 24 who had earlier been disinterred from Colon Cemetery in Havana. This brought the total number of victims of the *Maine* explosion buried

The mast of the USS *Maine* is all that can be seen in Havana Harbor following the explosion which sank the battleship in 1898 (at left). By an Act of Congress the mast was removed and placed in Arlington National Cemetery in 1912.

at Arlington to 229, of which 62 are known and 167 are unidentified.

After fourteen years on the bottom of Havana Harbor, all that was left of the *Maine* was a twisted, rusted shell. That shell was towed out to sea, and on March 16, 1912 the *Maine* was scuttled with full honors in water six hundred fathoms deep. A Navy Court of Inquiry was impanelled to investigate the sinking of the *Maine*, chaired by **William T. Sampson**. The court's report that the explosion was caused by a submarine mine did not dispel widespread public doubt.

On the seventeenth anniversary of the sinking of the *Maine*, February 15, 1915, the USS *Maine* Memorial was dedicated at Arlington just south of the area where its 229 crewmen are buried. The base of the monument represents a battleship turret, and through its center rises the original mast of the *Maine*, now towering above the Cemetery. Around the sides of the turret are inscribed the names of all those who lost their lives in the disaster. On the north side, a doorway leads into the turret and one half of the ship's bell is welded on its inner door. The inside of the turret is a burial vault which is thirty feet in diameter.

During World War II the burial vault inside the *Maine* Memorial was used to temporarily inter the remains of leaders of countries who were allies of the United States and who had died here while their native lands were occupied. In 1944 the President of the Philippines, Manuel Quezon y Molina, was interred in this vault when he died here in exile during the Japanese occupation of his country. Following the war, his body was returned to the Philippines for burial.

In 1941 **Ignace Paderewski**, the exiled President of Poland, died in New York City. President Franklin Roosevelt allowed his remains to be temporarily interred here "until Poland is free." The body of Ignace Paderewski is still interred within the memorial.

Near the *Maine* Memorial is a large anchor and two cannons. While the anchor is not the actual anchor from the *Maine*, it is similar to that anchor and was brought especially to Arlington from the Boston Navy Yard. The cannons are captured Spanish guns.

USS SERPENS MEMORIAL

Sec 34, Grid XY–17

During the night of January 29, 1945 an explosion rocked the United States Coast Guard Ammunition Ship, USS *Serpens*, as it sat off the coast of Laguna Beach, Guadalcanal in the Solomon Islands. The devastation was so great, the destruction so immediate that nothing could be done to save the lives of the 250 American servicemen on board. Among those killed were 199 U.S. Coast Guardsmen, 50 Army servicemen, and one U.S. Public Health Service official.

Four and one-half years later, on June 15, 1949, an elaborate reinterment service was held to give these valiant men their final resting place in Arlington National Cemetery. The extraordinary nature of the catastrophe that claimed their lives made identification of the individuals aboard the *Serpens* impossible. Therefore, their remains were placed in fifty-two caskets and buried in twenty-eight gravesites. Two other gravesites in the middle of the group were set aside for the monument on which all of their names are inscribed.

An octagon-shaped monument bearing the name and rank of each serviceman killed aboard the USS *Serpens* marks their collective grave near the intersection of Jesup and Grant Drives.

WAR CORRESPONDENTS MEMORIAL

Grid OP–23/24

On October 7, 1986 a tree was planted in memory of those "journalists who died while covering wars and conflicts for the American people." At the base of that tree stands a marble monument in the form of an open book whose pages proclaim, "One who finds a truth lights a torch."

This memorial, which honors those who went into combat armed only with their pens and notebooks, was erected by The National Press Club, the Overseas Press Club, Society of Professional Journalists, Sigma Delta Xi, and No Greater Love.

OTHER NOTABLE MONUMENTS AND MEMORIALS AT ARLINGTON

Battle of the Bulge Memorial, 385th Bomb Group (H), 8th Air Force, Sec. 46 (O-23)

Daughters of the Founders and Patriots of America Memorial, Sec. 35 (QR-21/22)

Korean War Veterans Memorial, erected by No Greater Love, Sec. 48 (Q-24/25)

Polar Bear Regiment, Common Grave for 339th Inf. Killed in Siberia (1918), Sec. 18 (LM-13/14)

Seafarers Memorial, Naval Order of the United States, Sec. 48 (RS-24/25)

USS Forrestal Memorial, Common Grave of Crew Killed off the Coast of Vietnam (1967) Sec. 46, (NO-23)

USS Liberty Memorial, Common Grave of Crew Killed off the Coast of Israel (1967) Sec. 34, (WX-12/13)

Vietnam Era Veterans/Indian Warriors Memorial, Indigenous People of America, Section 8 (BBCC-8/9)

Woodhull Flagpole, Memorial to Commander Maxwell Woodhull, U.S.N., (1813-1863), Sec. 35, (PQ-21)

ARLINGTON
A VISITOR'S GUIDE

Arlington National Cemetery performs two very diverse, yet vital functions. It is not only a revered national shrine, but also an active modern cemetery where thousands of burials are conducted annually while, at the same time, accommodating millions of visitors.

A LARGE ACTIVE CEMETERY

The United States maintains 114 national cemeteries, of which only Arlington and the cemetery at the Soldiers Home in Washington, D.C. are under the jurisdiction of the United States Army. The remaining cemeteries are administered by the Veterans Administration. Arlington is not the largest cemetery, though it does rank second behind Long Island National Cemetery in New York in the number of graves located within its walls.

Arlington National Cemetery occupies an area of 612 acres, which is approximately one-half of the original Arlington estate owned by **George Washington Parke Custis**. The remainder of the estate is now Fort Myer, a U.S. Army installation adjacent to Arlington and closely connected with the cemetery's operations. Originally Arlington House was included in the 200-

The view from Bryan Circle of that section of Arlington National Cemetery which was formerly the South Post of Fort Myer. The Washington Monument can be seen across the Potomac River.

acre tract designated as a cemetery by Secretary of War Edwin
M. Stanton in 1864. Today, however, Arlington House and its immediate environs are no longer part of Arlington Cemetery. Instead, they are administered as the Robert E. Lee Memorial by
the National Park Service. Between 1864 and 1981, numerous
parcels of land were annexed to the original Arlington Cemetery
200-acre tract until it has grown to 612 acres. It is unlikely that
any further expansion of the cemetery grounds will occur because
there are no undeveloped tracts of land adjacent to the cemetery.

Arlington National Cemetery has evolved over a period of
more than one hundred years from a simple potter's field to a major national shrine. With the addition of numerous tracts of land
at various times, the result has been a network of diverse gravesite
arrangements and a confusing mixture of numerical gravesite
designations which have become a modern superintendent's con-
undrum. For this reason, the sectional outline of the cemetery does
not, at times, appear to progress in any logical order. However,
to help minimize confusion when looking for a particular gravesite,
cemetery officials provide the section and lot number of any gravesite, and supply visitors with a coordinated map to pinpoint the
specific location. A specially-commissioned map utilizing the same
coordinates as the map made available at the cemetery appears
inside the back cover of this book.

Soldiers From Every War

Interred within Arlington's walls are veterans from every
American war, a fact which makes Arlington unique among national cemeteries. Although Arlington was not established until
1864, veterans from the American Revolution and the War of 1812
have been reinterred here. Among these honored dead are 4,725
unknown persons, most of whom died during the Civil War. In
addition, there are over forty foreign nationals interred within
Arlington's walls, including exiled Polish President **Ignace
Paderewski** and World War II German POW **Anton Hilberath**
(Sec.15C, Lot 347-1, GridH-25). Also at Arlington are gravesites
dedicated to the memories of those service personnel whose deaths
were officially verified but whose remains were never recovered.

Cemetery Flagpoles

There are two primary flagpoles located within Arlington. One stands majestically on the hill in front of Arlington House, while the other, the Woodhull Memorial Flagpole, is located on the south lawn of the Memorial Amphitheatre. On days when a burial service is taking place within the cemetery, both flags are lowered to half-staff one-half hour before the beginning of the first service and, in tribute to the persons being buried, they remain at half-staff until one-half hour after the final service.

Visiting Dignitaries

Among the nearly four million visitors who make the pilgrimage to Arlington each year are people from every corner of the globe. Thousands of international travelers join Americans as they come to Arlington to pay their respects at the Tomb of the Unknowns and to view the graves of many of our national heroes. These visitors include kings and queens, presidents and prime ministers, military

The Prince and Princess of Wales visit the Tomb of the Unknowns on Veteran's Day, 1985. Accompanying Prince Charles and Princess Diana are Major General John L. Ballantyne, Commanding General of the Military District of Washington (left) and the British Ambassador.

chiefs and diplomats who often go to the Tomb of the Unknowns to lay a wreath in honor of all who have served this nation.

The Amphitheatres

Many organizations utilize both the Old Amphitheatre and the larger Memorial Amphitheatre (see descriptions under Monuments and Memorials) for various patriotic and religious functions throughout the year. Ceremonies on Veteran's Day and Memorial Day traditionally draw thousands of visitors who come to hear addresses by the President or other high-ranking government officials.

BURIAL REGULATIONS

In March 1986 the 200,000th person was interred or inurned in Arlington National Cemetery. With an average of nearly fifteen burials per weekday, current estimates predict that the cemetery will be filled to capacity in approximately the year 2020. Nevertheless, burial at Arlington is no longer an option available to *all* current or former military personnel. Certain restrictions have been imposed and a special procedure must be followed to gain admission. To request an interment or inurnment at Arlington, the person making funeral arrangements should contact the Office of the Superintendent as soon as possible. Cemetery personnel will verify eligibility and notify the person making the request. Military honors and the selection and engraving of headstones will also be arranged at the time of the request for interment.

Ground Burials

Following the death of President **John F. Kennedy**, requests for interments at Arlington rose dramatically. Cemetery officials were forced to make the difficult decision to limit eligibility for burial at Arlington. While the range of persons eligible is still quite broad, interested parties are well-advised to consult the cemetery's formal regulations. An official copy of the eligibility requirements issued by Arlington Cemetery can be found in Appendix III of this book.

Family Gravesites

Normally only one gravesite will be issued to a family requiring the interment of family members at different levels in a single grave. Exceptions, however, are made in cases where one site cannot accommodate a large family.

Reserving Gravesites

Prior to 1962 eligible parties could reserve burial sites at Arlington; thousands of such "reservations" remain valid today. However, allocation of a gravesite is now made only when the actual need arises. If the spouse or eligible child of a primary eligible party dies first, space is assigned for the spouse or child, provided the primary party agrees in writing to be buried in the same site. The cemetery cannot normally allow the family to choose a particular burial site. With nearly fifteen burials per weekday, logistics require that spaces be allocated to accommodate concurrent burial services. However, the cemetery does try to accommodate family members who wish to be buried near relatives, if a space is available next to or near that relative.

Cremations and the Columbarium

In addition to ground burials, Arlington National Cemetery also provides a Columbarium for cremated remains. Dedicated on April 26, 1980 it is the only columbarium located in a national cemetery.

In 1980, the first section of the Columbarium was completed at Arlington, the only such facility in a national cemetery.

With planned space for 50,000 niches, the eligibility requirements for inurnment are considerably more liberal than for ground burial. An official copy of the Columbarium regulations can be found in Appendix III of this book.

Burial by Military Rank or Race

When Arlington was first established in 1864, burial was by race and rank reflecting the structure of the military at that time. Burial sections were divided between officers and enlisted men, and between white and black servicemen. Black soldiers, primarily members of the United States Colored Troops, were buried in Sections 23 and 27. Many of the tombstones in these sections bear the "U.S.C.T." designation. Black

A grave in Section 13 showing the United States Colored Troops (U.S.C.T.) designation.

civilians were buried in Section 27. Following the United States Armed Forces' elimination of segregated units in 1948, burials by race were also eliminated at Arlington.

Although Arlington began principally as a cemetery for unknowns and for soldiers from modest backgrounds, soon after the Civil War more and more officers began requesting burial at Arlington, increasing the prestige of the cemetery. As the honor of an Arlington burial increased, competition developed for securing the most prominent sites within the cemetery. This led to a *de facto* separation of officers from enlisted men. Concurrent with the change in regulations regarding headstones in 1947, all differentiation between separation of officers and enlisted men was eliminated.

Expenses

Certain services related to burial at Arlington are provided without expense to the party. There is no cost for the site itself and the cemetery personnel prepare the grave and place the regulation headstone. The cemetery also provides normal maintenance for the grave as part of its overall maintenance program. Additionally, in those cases where private funeral services have taken place outside Arlington and the body has been transported to the cemetery at private expense, burial arrangements are also provided at no cost. Other services and expenses may also be provided for persons who die while on active duty in the Armed Forces. Such benefits should be determined by the family at the time of death.

Gravesite Decorations

In an attempt to maintain the dignity of Arlington National Cemetery and to provide for the uniform regulation of gravesite decorations, certain restrictions have been adopted. While cut flowers are permitted on gravesites at any time, artificial tributes are only permitted between October 10 and April 15. Potted plants, however, are allowed as early as one week before Easter. Statues, lights, glass, or other objects are not permitted at any time, and no tribute may be wired or tied to a headstone.

Flags

All graves are decorated with small flags during the twenty-four hour period preceding Memorial Day. No other flags are permitted on the graves at any time.

HEADSTONE REGULATIONS

History

The establishment of a cemetery at Arlington in 1864 was necessitated by the tragic and wholesale loss of life in the Washington vicinity during the Civil War. Dozens of burials took place every day. As row after row of fallen soldiers were interred, only simple whitewashed wooden headboards marked their graves. Within a few short years, time and nature had taken their toll on those boards, causing their decay. Quartermaster

Seemingly endless rows of wooden headboards dot the landscape in Section 13 of Arlington National Cemetery in this vintage nineteenth century photograph.

Gen-eral **Montgomery Meigs**, realizing that continuous replacement at a cost of $1.23 per headboard was impractical, ordered the study of an alternative marker. He proposed markers made of cast iron and coated with zinc to prevent rusting and placed several such markers in the cemetery. However, these iron markers were rejected by other government officials in favor of more traditional stone markers. Finally, in 1873 the U.S. Congress voted to utilize the marble headstones which are still in use today. Only one of the original cast iron markers still exists. It marks the grave of Captain **Daniel Keys** (Sec. 13, Lot 13615, Grid G–29/30).

Private Headstones

It has always been the policy of the United States Government to provide a headstone for any person interred in a U.S. national cemetery. However, unlimited use of private monuments was also allowed, provided they were erected and maintained at private expense. That policy regarding use of private headstones

A Civil War soldier adorns the only remaining cast iron marker in Arlington Cemetery, located in Section 13.

was altered in 1947 when the Government's Fine Arts Commission adopted regulations regarding the size, placement, and maintenance of headstones to maintain and ensure the dignified character of Arlington National Cemetery. All sections of the cemetery which have been opened since that time display only the simple, white regulation headstone. Should a party desire a private monument, that decision must be made at the time of interment because such monuments can only be placed in one of the sections where they already exist. Likewise, the size and shape of the monument must also meet certain guidelines. An official copy of these guidelines can be found in Appendix III of this book.

Government-issue Headstones

The United States Government will supply a headstone for each gravesite at Arlington. The regulation stone is made of white marble, which measures thirteen inches wide, four inches thick, and forty-two inches tall. Twenty-four inches of the white marble headstone remain above ground.

The government will engrave certain information on the stone at no cost. If the person being buried is a military person, his or her name, dates of birth and death, rank, branch of service and any war service will be included on the stone. If desired, one of twenty-six different religious symbols will also be inscribed near the top of the stone.

Prior to 1980 the home state of the deceased military person, as well as major military decorations, was also engraved on the stone at no expense. Now, however, a request must be made to permit the inclusion of a military decoration on the stone and, once verified and space permitting, it can be added at private expense.

Only government regulation tombstones are allowed in sections opened after 1947 as shown here in Sections 38 and 43.

For the spouse or eligible dependent of the military person, the back of the headstone will include his or her name, dates of birth and death, and relationship to the primary party. These general rules are modified under certain circumstances, such as when there are more than two family members in a single gravesite.

Due to the high regard given to recipients of the Congressional Medal of Honor, the graves of these men and women are marked with headstones engraved in gold.

A glossary of all terms and abbreviations, including those used to describe military rank, military decorations, and religious symbols can be found in Appendix I of this book.

MILITARY HONORS AND BURIAL SERVICES

Any former or current member of the United States Armed Forces is entitled to certain honors at the time of burial, if desired. Such honors, however, are never required and are often omitted. The honors bestowed during a military burial are steeped in tradition and reflect the deep respect accorded a person who has served our nation.

History

Anyone who has ever witnessed a military funeral is struck by the precision and grandeur that even the simplest of these services evokes. The use of a caisson to transport the casket, the riderless horse, and the rifle salute are honors which find their origins in military history. The caisson is an ammunition wagon which has evolved from the sixteenth century when it was used to remove bodies from the battlefields. A riderless horse, with boots reversed in the stirrups and carrying a blackhandled sword

The remains of Shuttle Astronaut Michael J. Smith are borne on a horse-drawn caisson, one of the military honors granted to veterans buried at Arlington National Cemetery.

in a silver scabbard, signifies a fallen soldier who will never ride again. A three-shot volley fired over the grave is another ancient tradition used originally to signal opposing forces that the truce called to allow the recovery of fallen soldiers was ended and that the armies were prepared once again to do battle. Another custom is the playing of "Taps" by a lone bugler. While final musical tributes are ancient in their origins, the use of "Taps" began only during the Civil War, first as a "lights out" signal at the end of the day and then as a "good sleep" salute to fallen comrades.

Available Honors

At Arlington, four different types of burial services are available, each involving military honors provided by the branch of the military in which the deceased served.

1. **Full Honors**. Every member of the Armed Forces with a rank equivalent to warrant officer or above is entitled to the following honors:

> a color guard,
> an escort platoon (which varies in size commensurate to rank),
> a military band,
> a casket team,
> a firing party,
> a bugler,
> and a flag over the coffin.

In addition, a flag officer (general or admiral) is also entitled to a caparisoned or riderless horse and a cannon salute. Each branch of the service may also designate its own variations on these honors.

At any military service, a military chaplain will conduct the service if requested by the family.

2. Modified (or Simple) Honors. Any current or former member of the Armed Forces of any rank is entitled to the following honors:

> a casket team,
> a firing party,
> a bugler,
> and a flag over the coffin.

In addition, if the military personnel had been mounted during service, a caparisoned horse can also be provided. As always, each branch of the military service may provide special variations on these honors and a military chaplain will conduct the services, if requested.

3. Body Bearers. When the spouse or other dependent of a current or former member of the Armed Forces is buried at Arlington, the military branch in which the primary party served will provide a casket team for the services and, if desired, a military chaplain. In such a case, no other military honor would be provided because the deceased was never a member of the U.S. Armed Forces.

4. Combined Armed Forces Honors. These honors are provided on rare occasions when the deceased exercised command authority over more than one branch of the service. These combined honors are usually reserved for current or former Presidents of the United States (as Commander in Chief), Secretaries of Defense, Chairmen of the Joint Chiefs of Staff, or an unusual officer granted multiple command, usually in a combat situation. These honors include escort platoons from each branch of the service over which the officer exercised command. President **John F. Kennedy** was awarded such honors in 1963, as was General **Omar Bradley** at his funeral in 1981.

The Chapel at Fort Myer, Virginia adjoins Arlington Cemetery and is often used in conjunction with services at the cemetery.

An artist's rendering of the New Visitors Center at Arlington National Cemetery located just off Memorial Drive near the main gates of the cemetery.

ARLINGTON: A VISITOR'S GUIDE

A visit to Arlington National Cemetery is an important part of any visit to Washington, D.C., and every American is encouraged to view its many landmarks and monuments. But it is important to remember that while Arlington is a national public shrine, it is also a hallowed burial ground. Visitors are reminded to afford the cemetery the dignity and respect it deserves and to refrain from littering or disfiguring the grounds. Food and beverages are not permitted within the cemetery.

Visitors Center

Located just inside the main gate to Arlington is the Visitors Center. Here, visitors can obtain brochures and maps of the cemetery, as well as specific information about the location of particular gravesites.

Hours

Arlington National Cemetery is open every day of the year. The hours, however, vary between winter and summer:

April 1 through September 30   8:00 A.M. – 7:00 P.M.
October 1 through March 31   8:00 A.M – 5:00 P.M.

Driving

Visitors are not allowed to drive into the cemetery, and so must park their cars in one of the lots provided. If, however, persons wish to visit the grave of a relative or friend, a temporary pass allowing them to drive to a gravesite may be obtained at the Visitors Center. Permanent passes are also available for the next of kin of persons interred at Arlington. These may be obtained by writing to the Office of the Superintendent, Arlington National Cemetery, Arlington, Virginia 22211.

Metro Subway

Because of the large amount of vehicular traffic both around Washington and at Arlington, visitors are encouraged to utilize the Capital area's Metro subway system. The Metro stop for Arlington Cemetery is located approximately two hundred yards from the main entrance to the cemetery.

Tours

Normally, visiting the cemetery must be done on foot. However, a commercial tour bus operates within Arlington Cemetery and, for a fee, transports visitors between any of four stops: the Visitors Center, the grave of President **John F. Kennedy**, the Tomb of the Unknowns, and Arlington House (the Robert E. Lee Memorial).

The Arlington Ladies

A member of the Arlington Ladies personally represents the chief of staff of each branch of the United States Armed Forces at every funeral conducted at Arlington. Begun as a service for Air Force families in 1948 by **Gladys Vandenburg** – wife of Chief of Staff **Hoyt Vandenburg** – the Arlington Ladies now includes the United States Army and Navy. At graveside services, the Arlington Ladies presents the next of kin with a personal note of sympathy on behalf of the chief of staff and the deceased's branch of service. But it is on those occasions when no family member is able to attend the ceremonies that the Arlington Ladies provide their most important service. Absent family members take great solace in knowing that someone is always present at the interment of their loved one.

APPENDIX I
GLOSSARY OF TERMS, ABBREVIATIONS, AND SYMBOLS FOUND ON HEADSTONES

(Excluding abbreviations for military rank.)

GENERAL TERMS AND ABBREVIATIONS

A.F.C.   Air Force Cross.

A.M.   Air Medal.

A.N.C.   Army Nurse Corps.

ARCOM.   Army Commendation Medal.

B.S.M.   Bronze Star Medal.

CITIZEN   This term appears primarily on tombstones for persons buried during the Civil War in Section 27. The person buried here was a free person, regardless of race.

CIVILIAN   Any person buried with this designation was nonmilitary, regardless of whether the person was a free person or considered a slave.

C.S.A.	Confederate States of America. Indicates a Confederate soldier.
D.S.C.	Distinguished Service Cross — awarded to Army personnel.
D.F.C.	Distinguished Flying Cross.
D.S.M.	Distinguished Service Medal.
IN MEMORY OF...	Designates a cenotaph — an empty grave. There are no remains buried here. The marker was placed as a memorial. (See Memorial Sections)
G.S.	Gold Star (Navy, Marines, and Coast Guard).
L.M.	Legion of Merit.
Mex. Bor.	Mexican Border Campaign.
M.O.H.	Congressional Medal of Honor.
M.S.M.	Meritorious Service Medal.
N.C.	Navy Cross — awarded to Navy or Marine personnel.
O.L.C.	Oak Leaf Cluster (Army and Air Force).
P.H.	Purple Heart.
S.A.W.	Spanish-American War veteran.
S.S.	Silver Star.

UNKNOWN	The remains of the person buried here could not be positively identified.
U.S.A.A.C.	United States Army Air Corps.
U.S.C.T.	United States Colored Troops. A black soldier who served in the United States military during that period prior to 1948 when the U.S. Armed Forces were segregated.
USS MAINE	The person buried here was a member of the crew of the USS Maine at the time it was destroyed in 1898. (See USS Maine Memorial)
W.A.A.C.	Women's Army Auxiliary Corps.
W.A.C.	Women's Army Corps.

NON-RELIGIOUS SYMBOLS:

The Confederate States of America Symbol. It denotes that the person buried here was a member of the Confederate Army.

An engraved shield which covers the front face of a tombstone indicates that the person buried here was a member of the United States Armed Forces prior to and including the Spanish-American War.

RELIGIOUS SYMBOLS:

Any person buried at Arlington National Cemetery whose grave is marked with a regulation tombstone is entitled to have a religious affiliation symbol engraved on the top front face of his or her tombstone. Twenty-six such symbols are available:

Aaronic Order

Atheist

Bahai

Christian
(Latin Cross)

Christian Reformed
Church

Episcopal

Greek Orthodox

Hindu

Konko-Kyo Faith

Lutheran

Mormon – L.D.S.

Muslim

Native American
of North America

Presbyterian

Reorganized
Church-Latter Day
Saints

Russian Orthodox

Seicho-No-Ie

Serbian Orthodox

Star of David
(Jewish)

Sufism Reoriented

Tenrikyo

Unitarian

United Church of
Religious Science

United Methodist

Wheel of
Righteousness

World Messianity
(Izunome)

APPENDIX II
GUIDE TO AMERICAN
MILTARY RANK

On April 19, 1775 the first shots for American independence were fired at Lexington, Massachusetts. Since that time American miltary rank has continued to change and evolve. As visitors view the rank listed on headstones at Arlington, it is important to consider the era in which a person served in order to fully appreciate that person's military rank. For example, a person with the rank of Lieutenant General in 1985 would not have attained as high a position as a Lieutenant General in 1885 when it was the highest rank in the U.S. Army. Also, during the nineteenth century there was a system of promotions known as "breveting." A soldier would be temporarily advanced in rank because of special circumstances, such as when a commanding officer might be disabled in combat, allowing a subordinate to be brevetted to a higher rank to assume command. Since the promotion was only temporary, the soldier would revert to his original rank once the special situation ended. Many of the tombstones of persons who served during the nineteenth century depict brevet rank. In numerous instances persons who were brevetted to a higher rank during the Civil War, for example, reverted to their lower rank once the war ended. It would then take as long as thirty years to again achieve the high rank they enjoyed during the war. This led to great confusion and ultimately to the elimination of brevet ranks.

What follows is a general chart of American military rank for officers as it has evolved throughout our nation's history. It is important to remember that each branch of the United States Armed Forces has its own designation of rank and that the Air Force was part of the Army until 1947.

1776–1800

ARMY	NAVY	MARINES
Ensign	Midshipman	
Lieutenant	Sailing Master	Lieutenant
Captain	Lieutenant	Captain
Major	Lieut.Commanding	Major
Lieutenant Colonel	Master Commandant	
Colonel	Captain	
Brigadier General	Commodore	
Major General	Rear Admiral	
Lieutenant General	Vice Admiral	

1800–1850

ARMY	NAVY	MARINES
Coronet	Midshipman	
Second Lieutenant		Second Lieutenant
First Lieutenant	Master	First Lieutenant
Captain	Lieutenant	Captain
Major	Lieut. Commanding	Major
Lieutenant Colonel	Master Commandant	Lieutenant Colonel
Colonel	Captain	Colonel
Brigadier General	Commodore	
Major General	Rear Admiral	
Lieutenant General	Vice Admiral	

1850–1900

ARMY	NAVY	MARINES
Second Lieutenant	Ensign	Second Lieutenant
First Lieutenant	Lieut., Jr. Grade	First Lieutenant
Captain	Lieutenant	Captain
Major	Lieutenant Commander	Major
Lieutenant Colonel	Commander	Lieutenant Colonel
Colonel	Captain	Colonel
Brigadier General	Rear Admiral, lower	Brigadier General
Major General	Rear Admiral, upper	Major General
Lieutenant General	Vice Admiral	
General	Admiral	

1900–PRESENT

ARMY	NAVY	AIR FORCE	MARINES
Second Lieut.	Ensign	Second Lieut.	Second Lieut.
First Lieut.	Lieut., Jr. Gd	First Lieut.	First Lieut.
Captain	Lieutenant	Captain	Captain
Major	Lt. Commander	Major	Major
Lt. Colonel	Commander	Lt. Colonel	Lt. Colonel
Colonel	Captain	Colonel	Colonel
Brig. General	Commodore	Brig. General	Brig. General
Major General	Rear Admiral	Major General	Major General
Lt. General	Vice Admiral	Lt. General	Lt. General
General	Admiral	General	General
General of the Army	Fleet Admiral	General of the Air Force	

APPENDIX III
ARLINGTON BURIAL AND TOMBSTONE REGULATIONS

Arlington National Cemetery is under the jurisdiction of the United States Army. U.S. Army Regulation AR290–5 covers the administration of National Cemeteries. Chapters 2 and 5 of those regulations – as amended on September 1, 1980 – cover the rules regarding interments and headstones, respectively. Copied below are the official regulations as they pertain to Arlington National Cemetery.

CHAPTER 2
INTERMENTS AND DISINTERMENTS

2–1. Explanation of terms. For purposes of this regulation, the following apply:

★*a. Interment.* Either ground burial or the inurnment of cremated remains, except where the context of this chapter makes clear that only ground burial is referred to.

b. Armed Forces. The Army, Navy, Air Force, Marine Corps, Coast Guard, and their Reserve Components. Reserve Components of the Armed Forces are—

  (1) Army National Guard of the United States
  (2) Army Reserve
  (3) Naval Reserve
  (4) Marine Corps Reserve
  (5) Air National Guard of the United States
  (6) Air Force Reserve
  (7) Coast Guard Reserve

★*c. Active duty.* Full time duty in the active military service of the United States. This includes duty on the active list; full-time training duty; annual training duty; attendance (while in the active military service) at a school designated as a Service school by law or by the Secretary of the military department concerned; and service as a cadet at the United States Military, Air Force or Coast Guard Academy, or as a midshipman at the United States Naval Academy.

★*d. Unmarried adult dependent child.* A natural, step, or adopted son or daughter of the eligible service-connected parent who is (1) unmarried;

(2) permanently incapable of self-support because of physical or mental disability incurred before age 21; and (3) up to the time of death, dependent for support upon the service-connected parent or surviving parent (or on others if both parents are deceased) because of physical or mental condition.

e. Minor child. A natural, step, or adopted son or daughter of the eligible service-connected parent who is unmarried and less than 21 or who, after attaining age 21 and until completion of his or her education or training (but not after age 23), is pursuing a course of instruction at an approved institution.

★*f. Close relative.* Close relatives include the spouse, parents, adult brothers and sisters and adult natural, step or adopted children of a decedent. So far as requests for disinterment are concerned, the term also refers to the person who requested the original interment, if living.

g. President or former President of the United States. The President or former President of the United States who, in his capacity as Commander in Chief of the Armed Forces, is a "member or former member of the Armed Forces who served". . ." (within the meaning of 24 USC 281).

2–2. Authority for interments. The Act of 14 May 1948 (62 Stat. 234), as amended by the Act of 14 September 1959 (73 Stat. 547; 24 USC 281), and other laws specifically cited in this regulation authorize interment in Arlington and Soldiers'

Home National Cemeteries under such regulations as the Secretary of the Army may, with the approval of the Secretary of Defense, prescribe.

★2-3. **Special provisions.** *a.* All eligible persons will be assigned graves, without discrimination as to military rank, race, color, sex, religion, age or national origin.

★*b. Proof of eligibility.* Although the Army will make every reasonable effort to verify eligibility from Government records, the burden of proving eligibility lies with the party who requests interment. The Director, Casualty and Memorial Affairs or the Superintendent, Arlington National Cemetery, acting for the Director, will determine whether the submitted proof, documentary or otherwise, is sufficient to support a finding of eligibility.

c. No one will be buried in a memorial section. These sections are designated for the erection of memorial markers in memory of those individuals specified in paragraph 3-4.

★2-4. **Persons eligible for ground burial in Arlington National Cemetery.** *a.* Any active duty member of the Armed Forces.

★*b.* Any retired member of the Armed Forces. A retired member of the Armed Forces, in the context of this paragraph, is any retired member of the Army, Navy, Air Force, Marine Corps or Coast Guard, or any present or former member of a Reserve Component, who has been retired for disability or performed at least 20 years of active duty or active reserve service which qualifies him or her for retired pay either upon departure from active service, or at age 60.

c. Any former member of the Armed Forces separated for physical disability before 1 October 1949 who has served on active duty (other than for training) and who would have been eligible for retirement under the provisions of 10 USC 1201 had that statute been in effect on the date of separation.

d. Any former member of the Armed Forces whose last active duty (other than for training) terminated honorably and who has been awarded one of the following decorations:

(1) Medal of Honor

(2) Distinguished Service Cross (Air Force Cross or Navy Cross)

(3) Distinguished Service Medal

(4) Silver Star

(5) Purple Heart

e. Persons who have held any of the following positions, provided their last period of active duty (other than for training) as a member of the Armed Forces terminated honorably—

(1) An elective office of the United States Government

(2) Office of the Chief Justice of the United States or of an Associate Justice of the Supreme Court of the United States

(3) An office listed, at the time the person held the position, in 5 USC 5312 or 5 USC 5313

(4) The chief of a mission who was at any time during his tenure classified in class I under the provisions of 411 of the Act of 13 August 1946, 60 Stat. 1002 as amended (22 USC 866).

f. The spouse, widow or widower, minor child and, at the discretion of the Secretary of the Army,

unmarried adult dependent child of any of the persons listed in *a* through *e* above.

(1) The term "spouse" refers to a widow or widower of an eligible member, including the widow or widower of a member of the Armed Forces who was lost or buried at sea or officially determined to be permanently absent in a status of missing or missing in action. A surviving spouse who has remarried and whose remarriage is void, terminated by death, or dissolved by annulment or divorce by a court with basic authority to render such decrees regains eligibility for burial in Arlington National Cemetery unless it is determined that the decree of annulment or divorce was secured through fraud or collusion.

(2) An unmarried adult dependent child may be interred in the same grave in which the parent has been or will be interred, provided that the child was incapable of self-support up to the time of death because of physical or mental condition. At the time of death of an adult dependent child, a request for interment will be submitted to the Superintendent of Arlington National Cemetery. The request must be accompanied by a notarized statement from an individual who has direct knowledge of the marital status and degree of dependency of the deceased child; the name of that child's primarily eligible parent; and the military service upon which the burial is requested. A certificate from a physician who has attended the decedent as to the nature and duration of the physical and/or mental disability must also be submitted for approval to HQDA (DAAG-PED), WASH, DC 20314, before interment.

g. Widows or widowers of service members who are interred in Arlington National Cemetery as part of a group burial may be interred in the same cemetery but not in the same grave.

★*h.* The surviving spouse, minor child and, at the discretion of the Secretary of the Army, unmarried adult dependent child of any person already buried in Arlington.

i. The parents of a minor child or unmarried adult dependent child whose remains, based on the eligibility of a parent, are already buried in Arlington.

★*j.* An honorably discharged former member of the Armed Forces may be interred in the same grave as a close relative who is the primary eligible for interment in the gravesite, provided (a) the close relative is already interred; (b) the former member is without minor or unmarried adult dependent children; (c) the former member will not occupy space reserved for the spouse or minor or unmarried adult dependent child of the primary eligible; (d) the burial is sanctioned by all close relatives of the primary eligible; (e) the former member's spouse waives his or her entitlement, on the basis of the former member's service, to interment in Arlington; and (f) the cost of moving or recasketing/revaulting remains as a result of the burial will be borne by the party requesting the interment.

2-5. **Assignment of gravesites.** *a.* Under present policy of the Department of the Army, only one gravesite is authorized for burial of a service member and eligible family members. This policy applies to Arlington National Cemetery except when the Director, Casualty and Memorial Affairs, specifically determines this is not feasible.

b. Gravesites will not be reserved.

c. Reservations made in writing, before the one-gravesite-per-family policy was established, for gravesites adjoining those of next of kin previously interred, will remain in effect as long as the reservee remains eligible for burial in Arlington.

2–6. Persons eligible for inurnment of cremated remains in the Columbarium in Arlington National Cemetery. *a.* Any member of the Armed Forces who dies on active duty.

b. Any former member of the Armed Forces who served on active duty (other than for training) and whose last service terminated honorably.

c. Any member of a Reserve Component of the Armed Forces whose death occurs under honorable conditions while he is—

(1) On active duty for training or performing full-time service under Title 32, USC;

(2) Performing authorized travel to or from that duty or service;

(3) On authorized inactive duty training including training performed as a member of the Army National Guard or the Air National Guard (Section 502 of Title 32, USC); or

(4) Hospitalized or undergoing treatment at the expense of the United States for injury or disease incurred or contracted under honorable conditions while he is on that duty or service, performing that travel or inactive duty training, or undergoing that hospitalization or treatment at the expense of the United States.

d. Any member of the Reserve Officers' Training Corps of the Army, Navy or Air Force whose death occurs under honorable conditions while he is attending an authorized training camp or on an authorized practice cruise, performing authorized travel to or from that camp or cruise, or hospitalized or undergoing treatment at the expense of the United States for injury or disease incurred under honorable conditions while attending that camp or cruise, performing that travel, or undergoing that hospitalization or treatment at the expense of the United States.

e. Any citizen of the United States who, during any war in which the United States has been or may hereafter be engaged, served in the Armed Forces of any government allied with the United States during that war, whose last service terminated honorably by death or otherwise, and who was a citizen of the United States at the time of entry on such service and at the time of death.

f. Commissioned officers, United States Coast and Geodetic Survey (now National Oceanic and Atmospheric Administration), who die during and subsequent to the service specified in the following categories and whose last service terminated honorably are eligible for inurnment of their cremated remains in the Columbarium regardless of time of death—

(1) Commissioned officers assigned to areas of immediate military hazard described in the Act of 3 December 1942 (56 Stat. 1038; 33 USC 855a) as amended.

(2) Commissioned officers serving in the Philippine Islands on 7 December 1941.

(3) Commissioned officers actually transferred to the Department of the Army or the Department of the Navy under the provisions of the Act of 22 May 1917 (40 Stat. 87; 33 USC 855).

★*g.* Any commissioned officer of the United States Public Health Service who served on full-time duty after 29 July 1945. If the service falls within the meaning of active duty for training as defined in 38 USC 101(22), or inactive duty training as defined in 38 USC 101(23), death must have resulted from a disease or injury incurred or aggravated in line of duty. Also, any commissioned officer of the Regular or Reserve Corps of the Public Health Service who performed active service prior to 29 July 1945 in time of war; while on detail for duty with the Armed Forces; or while the service was part of the military forces of the United States pursuant to executive order of the President.

h. Spouses, minor children and adult dependent children as described in paragraph 2–3*f*; and the same categories of spouses and children of the persons listed in *a* through *g* above.

2–7. Selection of the Columbarium for inurnment. *a.* Those persons eligible for ground interment in Arlington National Cemetery under paragraph 2–4 above are also eligible for inurnment in the Columbarium. However, once the initial interment is made in a gravesite, each additional interment in Arlington of eligible members of the family unit must be made in that gravesite.

b. In the event the Columbarium is selected for inurnment of a family member, the cremated remains of all eligible surviving members must be inurned in that facility if disposition of remains is in Arlington.

2–8. Persons eligible for burial in Soldiers' Home National Cemetery. The Board of Commissioners of the US Soldiers' and Airmen's Home will prescribe rules governing burial in the Soldiers' Home National Cemetery.

2–9. Persons ineligible for interment in an Army national cemetery. *a.* Except as indicated in paragraph 2–4*j* above, a father, mother, brother, sister or in-law is not eligible for interment by reason of relationship to an eligible service person even though he or she is dependent upon the service member for support and/or is a member of the service member's household.

b. A person whose last separation from one of the Armed Forces was under other-than-honorable conditions is not eligible for interment even though he/she may have received veterans benefits, was treated at a Veterans' Administration hospital, or died in such a hospital.

c. A person who has volunteered for service with the Armed Forces but has not actually entered on active duty.

★*d.* A spouse who is divorced from a service-connected person or who, if widowed, is remarried at the time of his or her own death.

e. Dependents are not eligible for interment in Arlington National Cemetery unless the service-connected family member has been or will be interred in that cemetery. This does not apply to widows or widowers or members of the Armed Forces lost or buried at sea or officially determined to be permanently absent in a status of missing or missing in action.

★2–10. Disinterments. a. Interments in Army national cemeteries are considered permanent. Disinterment and removal of remains are permitted only for cogent reasons, and only with the prior approval of the Director, Casualty and Memorial Affairs, TAGCEN, Department of the Army, Washington, D.C. 20314. All close relatives of the decedent must consent to the disinterment in writing, or there must be a court order directing the disinterment.

b. Requests for disinterment must be submitted to the Director, Casualty and Memorial Affairs, and must include the following:

(1) A full statement of reasons for the proposed disinterment;

(2) Notarized statements by all close relatives of the decedent stating that they do not object to the proposed disinterment;

(3) A sworn statement by a person who knows that the persons giving statements comprise all of the decedent's close relatives.

c. In lieu of the documents required in b above, an order of a court of competent jurisdiction will be recognized. As this is a matter between family members, the Army or cemetery officials should not be made parties to any court action.

d. Any disinterment authorized under this paragraph must be accomplished without expense to the Government.

CHAPTER 5

HEADSTONES AND MARKERS

5–1. General. a. Authority. All graves in Army national cemeteries will be appropriately marked in accordance with 24 USC 279. Government headstones and markers are provided by the Veterans Administration in accordance with the provisions of the National Cemeteries Act of 1973. When requested by the next of kin, an appropriate memorial headstone or marker will be furnished and placed in the appropriate memorial section of the cemetery. Headstones will be of white marble, upright slab design.

b. Applications. Headstones and markers furnished by the Government for graves in Arlington and Soldiers' Home National Cemeteries, as well as Army post cemeteries, will be ordered from the Veterans Administration on DA Form 2122 (Record of Interment). Applications from next of kin are not required. However, VA Forms 20–1330 (Applications for Headstone or Marker) are required for memorial markers and must be submitted to the Veterans Administration.

c. Inscriptions. Inscriptions on Government headstones will be in accordance with policies and specifications of the Administrator of Veterans Affairs. The section designation and grave number will be incised on the reverse side, near the top of the upright headstone. The Director, Personal Affairs, has responsibility for policies and specifications for private monuments in Arlington and Soldiers' Home National Cemeteries. Instructions concerning the section designation and grave number on private monuments are in TM 10–287.

d. Replacement policy. (1) Headstones and markers will be replaced only if they are damaged, weathered, or otherwise unsightly; if they constitute a safety hazard; or if the inscriptions are illegible.

(2) All Government replacement headstones and the inscriptions on them will be identical with the original headstone as far as is practicable and desirable.

(3) If the Director, Personal Affairs, determines that a private monument is not maintained in a safe and serviceable condition, the next of kin will be given an opportunity to have necessary repairs made or to replace the monument. If the next of kin cannot be located or will not accept

responsibility for repairing or replacing the monument, the Department of the Army reserves the right to remove it from the cemetery and have it replaced with a standard Government headstone or marker.

5–2. Furnished by the Government. a. Multiple interments. When an additional interment is made in a grave, the stone will be replaced with a multiple-inscribed stone of the same type. Upright replacement stones will be inscribed on the face with the names of all decedents, together with other pertinent inscription data, if space permits. When space is insufficient to accommodate the inscriptions of all decedents, inscriptions for the service-connected decedent and his spouse will be placed on the face of the stone, if possible; and inscriptions for the additional interments will be cut on the reverse side.

b. Group burials. The design of headstones or markers erected for group interments will be prepared by the Personal Affairs Directorate.

c. Memorial markers. Memorial markers erected in cemetery sections established for this purpose will be of the standard design authorization for the cemetery. In addition to the authorized inscriptions, the words "In Memory Of" are mandatory.

5–3. Monuments and inscriptions at private expense. a. The erection of markers and monuments at private expense to mark graves in lieu of Government headstones and markers requires prior approval of the Director, Personal Affairs, and is permitted only in sections of Arlington National Cemetery in which private monuments and markers were authorized as of 1 January 1947. These monuments will be of simple design, dignified, and appropriate to a military cemetery. The name of the member(s) or the name of an organization, fraternity, or society responsible for the purchase and erection of the marker will not be permitted on the marker or anywhere else in the cemetery. Approval for the erection of a private monument will be given with the understanding that the purchaser will make provision for its future maintenance in the event repairs are necessary. The Department of the Army will not be liable for maintenance of or damage to the monument.

b. Where a monument has been erected to an

individual interred in Arlington National Cemetery and the next of kin desires to have inscribed on it the name and appropriate data pertaining to a deceased spouse, parent, son, daughter, brother, or sister whose remains have not been recovered and who would have been eligible in their own right for burial in Arlington, such inscriptions may be incised on the monument at no expense to the Government, with the prior written approval of the Director, Personal Affairs. The words "In Memoriam" or "In Memory Of" are mandatory elements of these inscriptions.

c. Except as may be authorized for marking group burials, ledger monuments of free-standing cross design, narrow shafts, mausoleums, or overground vaults are prohibited. Underground vaults may be placed at private expense, if desired, at the time of interment.

d. Specific instructions concerning private monuments and markers are in TM 10-287.

APPENDIX IV
UNITED STATES MILITARY
DECORATIONS AND MEDALS

Listed below—in order of importance—are the major military awards granted to American service personnel and which are listed on many headstones at Arlington National Cemetery.

Congressional Medal of Honor   Gallantry in action

Distinguished Service Cross   Exceptional heroism in combat

Navy Cross   " "

Air Force Cross   " "

Distinguished Service Medal   Exceptional meritorious service in a duty of great responsibility

Silver Star   Gallantry in action

Legion of Merit   Exceptionally meritorious service in peace or war

Distinguished Flying Cross   Heroism or extraordinary achievement in flight

Soldier's Medal   Heroism not involving conflict with the enemy

Navy and Marine Corps Medal	" "
Airman's Medal	" "
Coast Guard Medal	" "
Bronze Star	Heroic or meritorious achievement during military operations
Air Medal	Meritorious achievement in flight
Meritorious Service Medal	Meritorious service in war or peace
Purple Heart	Wounds or death in combat

If a person earned a decoration for the second time, a Gold Star (for the Navy, Marines, and Coast Guard) or an Oak Leaf Cluster (for the Army and Air Force) would be awarded to the recipient instead of an additional decoration.

Those recipients of an award or decoration which appears in **bold** print are eligible for burial at Arlington National Cemetery.

INDEX

GUIDE TO MAP

Many of America's greatest heroes are buried at Arlington. In order to see as many of their graves as possible, the map at right has been divided into ten shaded areas which have been designated "A" through "J". Most of the persons, monuments, and memorials mentioned in this book are located within one of the shaded areas — although not all of them are. Please check individual profiles and monument descriptions within the book for the exact grid locations. These shaded areas are meant to alert visitors of their close proximity to other graves.

A: Arnold, Hayes, Maas, Pershing

B: Apollo One Astronauts, Bennett (Coulter), Ingersoll, Kellogg, Miles, Powers, Ream (Hoxie), Reed, Rice, Rosecrans, Selfridge

C: Abrams, Delano, Dulles, Sampson, Warren, Wood, Nurses Memorial, Rough Riders Memorial, Spanish-American War Memorial, Spanish-American War Nurses Memorial

D: Murphy, Paderewski, Scobee, Canadian Cross, Living Memorials, Memorial Amphitheatre, Memorial to Servicemen Who Died in Iran, 1980, Tomb of the Unknowns, USS *Maine* Memorial, Woodhull Flagpole

E: Hershey, Louis, Marshall, Nicholson, Reynolds, Michael Smith, Walter Bedell Smith

F: Belknap, Davis, Devers, Doubleday, Greely, Hopkins, Lingan, McGee, Meigs, Newcomb, Powell, Rodgers, Wainwright, Nine of the eleven Revolutionary War veterans are buried in this area, War of 1812 Unknown Dead

G: Chennault, Clem, Crook, Halsey, Kearny, Leahy, L'Enfant, MacArthur, Porter, Randolph, Schley, Schofield, Sheridan, Sternberg, Joseph Wheeler, Wilkes, Wright, Old Amphitheatre, Civil War Unknown Dead

H: Douglas, Holmes, John Kennedy, Robert Kennedy, Rickover, Stewart, Weeks

I: Byrd, Dill, Donovan, James, Knox, McAdoo, Mitscher

J: Black, Bradley, Evers, Forrestal, Lincoln, Taft, Vandenberg, Earle Wheeler